Zondervan 2019

Church and Nonprofit

Tax & Financial Guide

For 2018 Tax Returns

2019
EDITION

Dan Busby

Vonna Laue

Michael Martin

John Van Drunen

ZONDERVAN

Zondervan 2019 Church and Nonprofit Tax and Financial Guide
Copyright © 2019 by ECFA (Evangelical Council for Financial Accountability)

This title is also available as a Zondervan eBook.

Requests for information should be addressed to:
Zondervan, *3900 Sparks Dr. SE, Grand Rapids, Michigan 49546*

This title is also available as a Zondervan eBook.

ISBN 978-0-310-58876-4

Publisher's note: This guide is published in recognition of the need for clarification of tax and other laws for churches and nonprofit organizations. Every effort has been made to publish a timely, accurate, and authoritative guide. The publisher, author, and reviewers do not assume any legal responsibility for the accuracy of the text or any other contents.

Readers are cautioned that this book is sold with the understanding that the publisher is not rendering legal, accounting, or other professional service. Organizations with specific tax problems should seek the professional advice of a tax accountant or lawyer.

References to IRS forms and tax rates are derived from preliminary proofs of 2018 forms or 2017 forms. Some adaptation for changes may be necessary. These materials should be used solely as a guide in filling out 2018 tax and information returns. To obtain the final forms, schedules, and tables for filing returns and forms, contact the IRS or a public library.

The term "nonprofit organization" covers a broad range of entities such as churches, colleges, universities, health care providers, business leagues, veterans groups, political parties, country clubs, and united-giving campaigns. The most common type of nonprofit is the charitable organization.

The "nonprofit organization" concept is basically a state law creation, but tax-exempt organizations are based primarily on federal law. The Internal Revenue Code does not use the word "nonprofit." The Code refers to nonprofits as "exempt organizations." Certain state statutes use the term "not-for-profit." A not-for-profit organization under state law may or may not be tax-exempt under federal law. In this book, the term "nonprofit" refers to nonprofit organizations that are exempt from federal income tax.

Printed in the United States of America
18 19 20 21 22 23 24 25 / DHV / 20 19 18 17 16 15 14 13 12 11 10 9 8 7 6 5 4 3 2 1

Contents

SPECIAL INDEX
FOR CHURCH TREASURERS
A guide within a guide

Policy Checklist

Ministry policies that are distinct from personnel or accounting policies are needed and useful in a church or ministry. Below is a checklist to assess the types of documentation that may be helpful in a particular ministry.

➤ Conflict of interest policy (page 9)

➤ Policy on suspected misconduct, dishonesty, fraud, and whistleblower protection (page 203)

➤ Document retention/destruction policy (pages 112–14)

➤ Gift acceptance policy (pages 167–71)

➤ Accountable reimbursement plan (page 67)

➤ Compensation approval policy

This policy should address the overall compensation philosophy of the organization. It should include how compensation is determined and approved for the senior leader as well as his or her staff. The policy should also address who will review compensation and how often.

➤ Cell phone usage policy

This type of policy should discuss specific details related to the taxability of cell phone benefits for those devices/plans owned by the organization as well as those devices/plans owned by the employee. A cell phone usage policy should also address the expectations for cell phone usage while driving.

➤ Intellectual property policy

Under the Copyright Act of 1976, any intellectual property created by an employee in performing his or her job is owned by the organization. Some ministries opt to treat this differently. If there are any works created such as music, drama, or books, it is important to work with an attorney and be certain all expectations are clearly communicated up front.

➤ Honoraria policy guidelines (page 203)

➤ Endowment policy

Organizations that have, or solicit, funds to be held in perpetuity should have this type of policy. It identifies the activities that could be supported through permanently restricted gifts, minimum balance requirements to fund an endowment, and how the funds will be invested and earnings expended.

➤ Investment policy

Any organization that has excess funds beyond the immediate cash operating needs should consider an investment policy. The policy can vary from basic to quite complex. However, there should be agreement stated through policy on the risk versus return expectations as well as whether funds will be managed internally or professionally. It should also include any specific investment criteria the board or related committee may deem important such as percentage ranges for investment categories or any restrictions on investing in certain industries.

➤ International activities policy

This policy should address matters related to oversight and compliance of foreign program activities. It will vary depending on whether the activities are conducted directly by the organization, an affiliate, a 501(c)(3) organization, a foreign organization, or national workers. The policy should address expectations for oversight as well as compliance with related laws and regulations.

➤ Benevolence policy (page 196)

➤ Joint venture policy

A joint venture is an agreement between two or more organizations to carry out an activity together. The policy should address items such as the purpose for the arrangement, financial involvement of all parties, and management responsibilities of each party.

➤ Giver privacy policy (page 165)

➤ Policy of issuing receipts to non-givers (page 164)

➤ Policy on personal use of ministry-owned vehicles (discussion in Chapter 3)

➤ Board ethics policy (page 204)

➤ Staff and volunteer ethics policy (page 205)

Additional sample policy wording is available through the ECFA Knowledge Center at www.ecfa.org.

Sample Board Resolutions, Checklists, Charts, and Procedures

Sample Charitable Contribution Letters and Forms

Caution: You may need to consult with a tax or legal professional before adapting these materials to the specific needs of your organization.

How You Can Keep Up with Changes Impacting Minister's Taxes and Finances

When each of the 28 annual editions of the *Zondervan Church and Nonprofit Tax & Financial Guide* has gone to press, as authors we have done our best to be sure the latest changes coming from Capitol Hill, the courts, and beyond are included in the book.

Still, the tax and finance changes keep coming at a relentless pace between book editions. In this era, major tax reform was passed in December 2017, with a major impact on 2018 and later years, and the constitutionality attack on the minister's housing exclusion continues—and that is just to name two issues.

So, how can you keep up with the developments between book editions? Let us suggest two important ways:

- Check the "In the News" link at www.ECFA.org/News for breaking news that affects ministers and churches.

- Join the ChurchExcel community at www.ECFA.church/ChurchExcel to receive FREE monthly digital updates, including podcasts, ebooks, and much more.

We are committed to simplify the most complex minister's tax and financial issues, freeing you to more clearly focus on fulfilling the Great Commission.

Dan Busby

Vonna Laue

Michael Martin

John Van Drunen

CHAPTER

1 Faithful Administration

In This Chapter

- Independent board
- Managing conflicts of interest
- Compensation review and approval
- Proper stewardship practices

Accountability—it's a word that engenders strong feelings. The obligation or willingness to accept the responsibility embodied in accountability is embraced by many, misunderstood by some, and feared by a few.

But how do we know whether people accept responsibility or, in other words, truly submit to accountability? Are we accountable to ourselves (self-accountability), or accountable to someone else in a verifiable way? Verifiable accountability and self-accountability differ greatly.

When someone says they are accountable to themselves, it reminds us of New Year's resolutions that are often broken within hours of the start of the new year. The landscape of Christ-centered churches and ministries is littered with examples of ministries that were accountable to themselves and now they no longer exist, or operate as only a fraction of what they were at one time.

Contrast self-accountability with verifiable accountability. The latter isn't just a sound concept; it is a theme that runs through the Scriptures. This is why our colleague, Dr. Gary Hoag, says, "God cares more about accountability than we do."

As an example of Jesus' keen interest in this topic, he tells the story about investing funds in Matthew 25:14–30. The crux of the parable is verifiable accountability.

Jesus set the verifiable accountability example when he sent out the disciples two-by-two (Mark 6), the 72 (Luke 10), and others together who were involved in the early church mission (Acts).

In 1 Corinthians 4:2, we read these words: *"Now it is required that those who have been given a trust must prove faithful."* Proving faithful requires verifiable accountability!

Biblical Basis for Accountability

1 Chronicles 9:27 – They would spend the night stationed around the house of God, because they had to guard it; and they had charge of the key for opening it each morning. (NIV)

Ezra 8:28–29 – I said to them, "You as well as these articles are consecrated to the LORD. The silver and gold are a freewill offering to the LORD, the God of your fathers. Guard them carefully until you weigh them out in the chambers of the house of the LORD in Jerusalem before the leading priests." (NIV)

Ezra 8:34 – Everything was accounted for by number and weight, and the entire weight was recorded at that time. (NIV)

Job 5:24 – "You will know that your tent is secure; you will take stock of your property and find nothing missing." (NIV)

Psalm 25:21 – May integrity and uprightness preserve me, for I wait for you. (NRSV)

May integrity and honesty protect me, for I put my hope in you. (NLT)

Let integrity and uprightness preserve me, for I wait for You. (NASB)

Psalm 106:3 – Blessed are they who maintain justice, who constantly do what is right. (NIV)

Proverbs 10:9 – Whoever walks in integrity walks securely. (NRSV)

People with integrity have firm footing. (NLT)

He who walks in integrity walks securely. (NASB)

Proverbs 11:1 – The LORD abhors dishonest scales, but accurate weights are his delight. (NIV)

Proverbs 11:3 – The integrity of the upright guides them, but the unfaithful are destroyed by their duplicity. (NIV)

Proverbs 15:22 – Plans fail for lack of counsel, but with many advisers they succeed. (NIV)

Proverbs 21:5 – The plans of the diligent lead to profit as surely as haste leads to poverty. (NIV)

Proverbs 21:20 – In the house of the wise are stores of choice food and oil, but a foolish man devours all he has. (NIV)

Proverbs 22:3 – A prudent man sees danger and takes refuge, but the simple keep going and suffer for it. (NIV)

Proverbs 27:23 – Be sure you know the condition of your flocks, give careful attention to your herds. (NIV)

Ecclesiastes 8:6 – For there is a proper time and procedure for every matter, though a man's misery weighs heavily upon him. (NIV)

Matthew 18:12 – "If a man owns a hundred sheep, and one of them wanders away, will he not leave the ninety-nine on the hills and go to look for the one that wandered off?" (NIV)

Matthew 21:13 – "It is written," he said to them, "'My house will be called a house of prayer,' but you are making it a 'den of robbers.'" (NIV)

Matthew 25:16 – "The man who had received the five talents went at once and put his money to work and gained five more." (NIV)

Matthew 25:21 – "His master replied, 'Well done, good and faithful servant! You have been faithful with a few things; I will put you in charge of many things. Come and share your master's happiness!'" (NIV)

Luke 1:3 – Therefore, since I myself have carefully investigated everything from the beginning, it seemed good also to me to write an orderly account for you. (NIV)

Luke 8:17 – "For there is nothing hidden that will not be disclosed, and nothing concealed that will not be known or brought out into the open." (NIV)

Luke 14:28–29 – "Suppose one of you wants to build a tower. Will he not first sit down and estimate the cost to see if he has enough money to complete it? For if he lays the foundation and is not able to finish it, everyone who sees it will ridicule him." (NIV)

Luke 16:2 – "So he called him in and asked him, 'What is this I hear about you? Give an account of your management, because you cannot be manager any longer.'" (NIV)

Luke 16:10 – "Whoever is faithful in a very little is faithful also in much." (NRSV)

"Unless you are faithful in small matters, you won't be faithful in large ones." (NLT)

"He who is faithful in a very little thing is faithful also in much." (NASB)

John 3:21 – "But whoever lives by the truth comes into the light, so that it may be seen plainly that what he has done has been done through God." (NIV)

Romans 13:1 – Everyone must submit himself to the governing authorities, for there is no authority except that which God has established. The authorities that exist have been established by God. (NIV)

Romans 13:5–6 – Therefore, it is necessary to submit to the authorities, not only because of possible punishment but also because of conscience. This is also why you pay taxes, for the authorities are God's servants, who give their full time to governing. (NIV)

1 Corinthians 4:2 – Now it is required that those who have been given a trust must prove faithful. (NIV)

1 Corinthians 14:33 – For God is not a God of disorder but of peace. (NIV)

1 Corinthians 14:40 – But everything should be done in a fitting and orderly way. (NIV)

2 Corinthians 8:19 – What is more, he was chosen by the churches to accompany us as we carry the offering, which we administer in order to honor the Lord. (NIV)

2 Corinthians 8:20–21 – We want to avoid any criticism of the way we administer this liberal gift. For we are taking pains to do what is right, not only in the eyes of the Lord but also in the eyes of men. (NIV)

2 Corinthians 8:21 – We intend to do what is right not only in the Lord's sight but also in the sight of others. (NRSV)

We are careful to be honorable before the Lord, but we also want everyone else to know we are honorable. (NLT)

We want to do what pleases the Lord and what people think is right. (CEV)

2 Corinthians 13:1 – Every matter must be established by the testimony of two or three witnesses. (NIV)

Galatians 6:9 – So let us not grow weary in doing what is right. (NRSV)

So let's not get tired of doing what is good. (NLT)

Let us not lose heart in doing good, for in due time we will reap if we do not grow weary. (NASB)

Ephesians 4:16 – From him the whole body, joined and held together by every supporting ligament, grows and builds itself up in love, as each part does its work. (NIV)

Colossians 2:5 – For though I am absent from you in body, I am present with you in spirit and delight to see how orderly you are and how firm your faith in Christ is. (NIV)

1 Thessalonians 5:21 – Test everything. Hold on to the good. (NIV)

1 Timothy 6:20 – Timothy, guard what has been entrusted to your care. (NIV)

1 Peter 4:10 – Each one should use whatever gift he has received to serve others, faithfully administering God's grace in its various forms. (NIV)

(CEV) – Contemporary English Version
(NASB) – New American Standard Bible
(NIV) – New International Version
(NLT) – New Living Translation
(NRSV) – New Revised Standard Version

As ministry grew exponentially, there is continued attentiveness to verifiable accountability in the Apostle Paul's letters. For example, Paul instructed those he mentored to follow in his steps. He urged leaders to exhibit character that was *"above reproach"* and *"blameless"* (1 Tim. 3:1–13; Titus 1:6–11).

When Christ-centered ministries do not demonstrate verifiable accountability, they risk doing what is right in their own eyes, as the Israelites did (Judges 17:6).

In his early years, David, king of Israel, sought the counsel of wise and godly men. When his authority grew, he began to operate as the supreme ruler of Israel instead of God's servant and then troubles mounted when he went down the road of self-accountability (2 Sam. 11).

Because people form impressions of ministry by looking at outward appearances, the pattern for accountability of Christ-centered ministries and its leaders lies in biblical accountability — in the spirit of truth and love, holding each other to high standards in our individual journeys of faith and ministry service.

"Strong patterns of verifiable accountability keep the 'wolves' at bay," says ECFA board chairman Michael Batts. He continues, "Sadly, there is an element of society that revels when bad things happen in churches and ministries. This element of society looks for 'cracks in the armor' of churches and ministries to try to ruin their reputation. Maintaining appropriate accountability greatly reduces the risk of such damage. Furthermore, when a high-profile financial scandal occurs in the church and ministry realm, it increases scrutiny by government regulators and increases the likelihood of additional burdensome legislation or regulation."

The Commission on Accountability and Policy for Religious Organizations, a national group of nonprofit leaders convened by ECFA at the request of U.S. Sen. Charles Grassley (R-Iowa), extensively addressed the accountability topic in its report. The Commission noted:

➤ Churches and ministries should verifiably demonstrate their commitment to proper oversight and accountability.

➤ The methods for achieving and verifiably demonstrating accountability may vary.

➤ Givers, volunteers, and other stakeholders of churches and ministries should take advantage of opportunities to inform themselves about the organization's affairs and its measures for ensuring proper oversight and accountability.

When one thinks of verifiable accountability, it is natural to focus on finance-related issues. But verifiable accountability starts with a ministry's governance—carried out by the ministry's top leader and its governing board.

How do churches and ministries measure up on the verifiable accountability index? Many are doing excellently in this arena—but in the words of Paul, we must *"do so more and more"* (1 Thess. 4:10). There will always be outliers, but it is necessary to do one's part to reduce the number in that category and demonstrate the endeavor to prepare stewards and the ministries they serve to give an account to God.

Here are a few faces of accountability:

1. **Growing number of exemplar churches and ministries.** Most of the larger, Christ-centered ministries in the U.S.—more than 2,300—are accredited by ECFA and committed to ECFA's rigorous standards, and 45 of the 100 largest churches in the U.S. are ECFA members. There is a growing desire for larger churches to achieve accreditation. This is a most encouraging sign.

2. **Using the services of independent CPAs.** One of the primary reasons more churches and ministries are not ECFA-accredited is that the organizations feel they are too small, or have not chosen to have their annual financial statements audited, reviewed, or compiled by an independent CPA. The CPA expense is viewed as a significant barrier for many.

   Still, many more churches and ministries should step up and engage CPA services for their financial statements because the gain of increased trust far outweighs the expense. Smaller organizations that are interested in ECFA membership may pursue having financial statements reviewed or compiled until a full audit is appropriate.

3. **Performing internal audits.** A handful of larger churches and ministries have staff dedicated to performing internal audits in addition to using external auditors. These organizations are at the top of the class.

   This leaves most of the 300,000–400,000 churches in the U.S. without any internal or external audit work and tens of thousands of ministries in the same category. Internal audit work is one of the most neglected steps churches and ministries can take to ensure verifiable accountability.

Trusted ministries welcome verifiable accountability. It is what Jesus taught the disciples, and it remains the model for fruitful ministry today. God is more interested in accountability than we are because he knows our hearts. Verifiable accountability starts and ends with a heart of accountability towards God!

Faithful administration is characterized by board decisions made in the best interest of the ministry (often requiring a majority of independent board members), avoidance of conflicts of interest, and proper compensation-setting practices with respect to the ministry's top leaders. These topics and more are discussed in this chapter.

Independent Board

The importance of an independent board cannot be overemphasized. A lack of independent board oversight can impact the accountability and effectiveness of the ministry. In contrast, an independent board will determine the ministry's mission, set long-range goals, provide fiduciary oversight, establish adequate board policies, and ensure consistent adherence to these policies.

To demonstrate board independence, a majority of the board should be other than employees or staff or those related by blood or marriage. Even when employee membership on the board is slightly less than a majority, the independence of the board may be jeopardized, especially if the majority of members in attendance at particular meetings are not independent. Employees often lack independence and objectivity in dealing with many board-level matters. While the ministry's top leader is sometimes a member of a ministry's board of directors, other staff members are generally not members of the board.

Does your board have robust discussions on key issues? Are the values and policies of the ministry clearly articulated? Are annual evaluations, based on predetermined goals, made of the ministry's leader? Does the board evaluate itself as rigorously as it evaluates the ministry's leader?

Key Issue

Boards should develop a cyclical pattern of self-evaluation. The purpose of self-assessment is to individually and collectively improve board performance. It can take a variety of formats, from soliciting feedback from individual board members about their contributions to the board's performance, to evaluating the effectiveness of time spent together as a board.

Boards should meet at least semiannually, and many boards meet more frequently. Each board should determine the appropriate number of meetings based on the nature of the ministry.

The actions of a ministry's board and its committees should be recorded in written minutes, including the signature of the secretary, on a contemporaneous basis (within a reasonable time period after the meeting is held). Ministries filing the Form 990 must document whether board minutes are contemporaneously maintained. The same is true for committees with the authority to act for the board.

The actions of a ministry's board often include the approval and revision of policies. These policies should be reflected in the board policy manual, with the manual updated as appropriate. *Good Governance for Nonprofits*, by Fredric L. Laughlin and Robert C. Andringa, is an excellent guide for preparing board policy manuals.

Managing Conflicts of Interest

The potential for a conflict of interest arises in situations in which a person is responsible for promoting one interest at the same time he or she is involved in a competing interest. If this person exercises the competing interest over the fiduciary interest, a conflict of interest has occurred.

Related-party transactions occur between two or more parties with interlinking relationships. These transactions should be disclosed to the governing board and evaluated to ensure they are made on a sound economic basis. The organization may decide to pursue any related-party transactions that are clearly advantageous to the organization.

Caution

Integrity requires that a board member or other insider disclose a potential conflict of interest to the board. The individual should refrain from voting on the transactions involving a related issue and not be present during the voting.

Undertake *significant* transactions with related parties only in the following situations:

➤ The organization's board approves the transaction as one that is in the best interest of the organization.

➤ Related parties are excluded from the discussion and approval of related-party transactions.

➤ Competitive bids or comparable valuations are considered.

➤ The audited financial statements of the organization fully disclose related-party transactions.

Even when all of the above precautions are observed with respect to a related-party transaction, the church or nonprofit organization may be at risk to criticism from givers,

---

Sample Conflict of Interest Disclosure Annual Reporting Statement

Certification

I have read and understand the Conflict of Interest Policy. I hereby declare and certify the following real or apparent conflict(s) of interest:

Disclosure Statement

_____

_____

_____

_____

_____

_____

(If necessary, attach additional documentation.)

I agree to promptly inform the board upon the occurrence of each event that could potentially result in my involvement in (or implication in) a conflict of interest.

_____	_____
Date	Signature
	_____
	Title

Sample Conflict of Interest Policy Statement

All directors, trustees, officers, agents, and key employees of this organization shall disclose all real or apparent conflicts of interest that they discover or that have been brought to their attention in connection with this organization's activities. "Disclosure" shall mean providing properly, to the appropriate person, a written description of the facts comprising the real or apparent conflicts of interest. An annual disclosure statement shall be circulated to trustees, officers, and certain identified agents and key employees to assist them in considering such disclosures, but disclosure is appropriate and required whenever conflicts of interest may occur. The written notices of disclosures shall be filed with the board chair or such other person designated to receive such notifications. At the meeting of the governing body, all disclosures of real or apparent conflicts of interest shall be noted for the record in the minutes.

An individual trustee, officer, agent, or employee who believes that he or she or an immediate member of his or her immediate family might have a real or apparent conflict of interest, in addition to filing a notice of disclosure, must abstain from:

(1) participating in discussions or deliberations with respect to the subject of the conflict (other than to present factual information or to answer questions)

(2) using his or her personal influence to affect deliberations

(3) making motions

(4) voting

(5) executing agreements

(6) taking similar actions on behalf of the organization where the conflict of interest might pertain by law, agreement, or otherwise

A person with a real or apparent conflict of interest will be excused from all discussions or deliberations with respect to the subject of the conflict.

A member of the governing body or a committee thereof, who, having disclosed a conflict of interest, nevertheless shall be counted in determining the existence of a quorum at any meeting in which the subject of the conflict is discussed. The minutes of the meeting shall reflect the individual's disclosure, the vote thereon, and the individual's abstention from participation and voting.

The board chair shall ensure that all directors, trustees, officers, agents, employees, and independent contractors of the organization are made aware of the organization's policy with respect to conflicts of interest.

the media, or other members of the public. This risk may be so significant that it overshadows all of the benefits of the transaction.

Example 1: An organization purchases insurance coverage through a firm owned by a board member. This is a related-party transaction. The transaction might be approved if the cost of the insurance is disclosed, the purchase is subject to proper approvals, the price is equal to or below the competition's, the purchase is in the best interests of the organization, and the related party is not present at the meeting when the decision is made.

> ### Warning
> Information concerning prospective and current board members may reveal potential conflicts that will disqualify the individual. If a conflict is sufficiently limited, the individual may simply need to abstain from voting on certain issues. If the conflict of interest is material, the election or reelection of the individual may be inappropriate.

Example 2: The CEO and several employees are members of the board. When the resolution on salary and fringe-benefit adjustments comes to the board, those affected by the resolution should not discuss and vote on the matter. The CEO and employees should also excuse themselves from the meeting to avoid even the appearance of a conflict of interest.

Example 3: A nonprofit board considers a significant investment through a brokerage firm in which a board member has a material ownership interest. This investment might be approved if it is in the best interest of the nonprofit organization, is consistent with its investment policies, and meets its conflicts of interest policy.

Compensation Review and Approval

An annual review of a church or nonprofit leader's compensation package is important, particularly when leadership compensation reaches more significant levels. Satisfying the following requirements creates a rebuttable presumption or "safe harbor" that the compensation for an organization's leader is reasonable:

➤ determine comparable pay for similar positions

➤ make compensation decisions in an independent setting (the individual whose compensation is being considered should be recused from the decision-making process), and

➤ document gross pay and fringe benefits

> ### Caution
> Reasonable salary and fringe benefits should be carefully documented, especially for the highest paid employees of an organization. The intermediate sanction regulations provide penalties for "excess benefit transactions." Examples of such transactions include unreasonable salaries or bonuses to key employees and excessive travel expenses or other perks.

The review should focus on all elements of pay, taxable and nontaxable, and an objective evaluation of responsibilities, goals reached, and available resources. A comparison with positions in other organizations may be helpful. National salary surveys may provide meaningful data.

With increased scrutiny of nonprofit salaries by the media, the government, and the public (see chapter 3), it is important that compensation amounts be accurately documented. Gross pay may include the following elements (some taxable and some tax-free or tax-deferred): cash salary, fair rental value of a house (including utilities, provided by the organization), cash housing or furnishings allowance, tax-deferred payments, value of the personal use of organization-owned aircraft or vehicle, value of noncash goods and services, and cash bonuses.

Proper Stewardship Practices

Communications with givers

All statements made by an organization in its stewardship appeals about the use of a gift must be honored. The giver's intent may be shaped by both the organization's communication of the appeal and by any giver instructions with the gift. Any note or correspondence accompanying the gift or conversations between the giver and donee representatives may indicate giver intent, restricting the use of the gift to the intended purpose. If a giver responds to a specific appeal, the assumption is made that the giver's intent is that the funds will be used as outlined in the appeal.

All aspects of a proposed charitable gift should be explained fully, fairly, and accurately to givers. Any limitations on the use of the gift should be clear and complete, both on the response form and in the appeal. These items should be included in the organization's communications to the giver:

➤ **The organization's proposed use of the gift.** Realistic expectations should be communicated regarding what the gift will do within the programs of the ministry.

➤ **Representations of fact.** Any descriptions of the financial condition of the organization or narratives about events must be current, complete, and accurate. References to past activities or events should be appropriately dated. There should be no material omissions, exaggerations of fact, use of misleading photographs, or any other communication tending to create a false impression or misunderstanding.

➤ **Valuation issues and procedures.** If an appraisal is required, the giver should fully understand the procedures and who is responsible to pay for the appraisal.

Key Issue

In deciding whether to support a particular ministry or program, those who donate to Christ-centered organizations rely on the information the ministry provides. Therefore, organizations have the responsibility to represent facts truthfully when communicating with givers.

➤ **Tax consequences and reporting requirements.** While tax considerations should not be the primary focus of a gift, the giver should clearly understand the current and future income, estate, and gift tax consequences, and reporting requirements of the proposed gift. A charitable gift should never be represented as a tax shelter.

➤ **Alternative arrangements for making the gift.** The giver should understand the current and deferred gift options that are available.

➤ **Financial and family implications.** In addition to the tax consequences, the overall financial implications of the proposed gift and the potential impact on family members should be carefully explained.

➤ **Possible conflicts of interest.** Disclose to the giver all relationships that might constitute, or appear to constitute, conflicts of interest. The disclosure should include how and by whom each party is compensated and any cost of managing the gift.

Handling gifts with restrictions by givers

Properly handling giver-restricted gifts is a challenge for many ministries. This is because giver-restricted gifts present a complex combination of accounting, tax, legal, ethical, and other issues.

A giver's written instructions accompanying a gift may provide the basis for a gift restriction. However, in general, a giver's restriction may be either expressed or implied from relevant facts and circumstances. In some instances, the restrictions on donations are driven by the nature of a ministry's appeal. For example, if the appeal describes a project, then any response to the appeal is restricted. In other cases, a giver approaches a ministry desiring to make a restricted gift. Only givers can restrict a gift. In an accounting sense, gift restrictions are either temporary or permanent.

Designations of unrestricted assets or net assets by an organization's governing board do not create restrictions. Designations may be reversed by the board because they do not result from a giver's contribution. For example, unrestricted assets or net assets do not become restricted merely because a board designates a portion of them to fund future expenditures for a new building.

In certain situations, givers have the power to unrestrict gifts. For example, a giver restricts a gift for a certain project. Later, the ministry asks the giver's permission to redirect the gift for another purpose (unrestricted or restricted) and the giver agrees. The gift is then reclassified from either temporarily or permanently restricted to unrestricted.

Reporting for incentives and premiums

Fundraising appeals may offer premiums or incentives in exchange for a contribution. If the value of the premiums or incentives is not insubstantial, the ministry generally must advise the giver of the fair market value of the premium or incentive and clarify that the value is not deductible for tax purposes either before or after the contribution is made (see pages 159–63 for more detailed information).

Transparency to givers and the public

Churches and other nonprofits should make appropriate disclosures about their governance, finances, programs, and activities. As a demonstration of transparency, a ministry should provide a copy of its current financial statements upon written request. Additionally, many nonprofit organizations are subject to the public disclosure rules requiring charities to provide copies of annual information returns (Form 990) and certain other documents when requested to do so.

Compensation of gift planners

Payment of finders' fees, commissions, or other fees on a percentage basis by a ministry to an outside gift planner or to an organization's own employees as a condition for delivery of a gift is not appropriate under ECFA Standards. Competency-based pay is acceptable when it is paid to employees responsible for an organization's general fundraising program and includes a modest component for achieving broad fundraising goals.

Every effort must be made to keep giver trust. Giver attitudes can be unalterably damaged in reaction to undue pressure and the awareness that a direct commission will be paid to a gift planner from his or her gift, thus compromising the trust on which the ministry relies.

Acting in the interest of givers

Every effort should be made to avoid accepting a gift from, or entering into a contract with, a prospective giver that would knowingly place a hardship on the giver or place the giver's future well-being in jeopardy.

Fundraisers should recognize that it is almost impossible to properly represent the full interests of the giver and the ministry simultaneously. When dealing with persons regarding commitments on major estate assets, gift planners should seek to guide and advise givers so that they may adequately consider the broad interests of the family and the various organizations they are currently supporting before they make a final decision. Givers should be encouraged to discuss the proposed gift with competent and independent attorneys, accountants, or other professional advisors.

Peer accountability to an oversight organization

ECFA is the only peer accountability organization serving Christ-centered churches and other nonprofits. Founded in 1979, ECFA accredits over 2,300 churches and nonprofit organizations that faithfully demonstrate compliance with established standards for financial accountability, fundraising, and board governance. Members include ministries, denominations, churches, educational institutions, and other tax-exempt 501(c)(3) organizations. Annual revenue of ECFA members exceeds $27 billion.

The ECFA seal is tangible evidence to givers that ECFA member organizations adhere to the highest standards of financial integrity and Christian ethics.

INTEGRITY*Points*

- **Setting the biblical tone for financial accountability at the top.** Biblical financial accountability starts with the organization's board and top leadership and permeates down through the staff. If the organization is a church, the accountability tone starts with the senior pastor or equivalent leader. If it is a parachurch organization, accountability starts with the president, CEO, executive director, or with the person in a similar leadership position.

- **The importance of an independent board.** A majority of independent board members (board members other than staff members or relatives of staff or board members) is vital to ensure the board's action is done without partiality, undue influence, or conflict of interest.

- **Accountability to givers rises with gift restrictions.** When a giver makes an unrestricted gift, the ministry has a general accountability for the funds. However, when a giver places a purpose or time restriction on a gift, the donee charity accepts the responsibility to expend the funds within the limitations of the giver's restrictions.

- **The importance of the work of an independent CPA and/or internal audits.** Churches and other nonprofit organizations of a significant size should annually utilize the services of an independent CPA (annual revenue of $500,000 to $1,000,000 is often considered an appropriate threshold to obtain these services). Large organizations should always have an annual audit. For smaller organizations, an annual review or compilation by an independent CPA may be sufficient. One of the most overlooked CPA services is an "agreed-upon procedures" engagement where the CPA only focuses on certain issues; e.g., bank reconciliations, payroll tax returns, expense reimbursements, or another area that is often troublesome for an organization.

- **Compensation-setting and related-party transactions.** Organizations should establish policies to ensure that compensation-setting and related-party transactions are handled with excellence and integrity. Appropriate policies should require board members without a conflict of interest to set compensation of top leaders and approve related-party transactions only after considering reliable comparability information and documenting the board's review and approval in writing.

2 Tax Exemption

In This Chapter

- Advantages and limitations of tax exemption
- Tax exemption for churches
- Starting a church or other nonprofit organization
- Unrelated business income

- Private benefit and private inurement
- Filing federal returns
- Postal regulations
- State taxes and fees
- Political activity

Tax exemption for churches and other nonprofits is based on the federal government's recognition that many of the vital contributions to our society's common good are made outside its own agencies in the voluntary or civil society sector. Exempting these organizations from taxes (and additionally, in many instances, providing that contributions to them can be tax-deductible) is a vital governmental means of acknowledging and protecting, instead of burdening and directing, their unique identities and diverse contributions.

This same characteristic, which exists to some degree in every free society, is acknowledged in biblical theology, which regards not only persons but also a variety of institutions—families, churches, and charities—to have their own independent callings from God to serve their neighbors, beyond the government's responsibility to do good as well as to curb evildoers.

With regard to the many religious organizations that are a large part of civil society, tax-exempt status additionally reflects the government's commitment to the establishment clause of the constitution. By according churches and other houses of worship automatic recognition of tax-exempt status, the government refrains from illegitimate control of, and intrusion into, the sphere of religion and its institutions, and instead safeguards the free exercise of religion.

To say that government must respect religious organizations including both churches and religious institutions whose freedom it must safeguard is not to say that no government regulation is appropriate. Yet, to be legitimate, such regulation must as far as possible leave the institutions free to chart their own courses and practices.

How can your church or other nonprofit organization obtain federal tax exemption?

➤ **Churches.** A church is tax-exempt under Section 501(c)(3) of the Internal Revenue Code simply by functioning as a church. While tax law does not define a church, the IRS has developed guidelines that it applies (see pages 17–18). While there is no requirement for a church to file with the IRS for recognition of its tax-exempt status, many larger churches do so to formally establish this status.

➤ **Other nonprofits.** A formal filing with the IRS (using a Form 1023 or 1023-EZ) is generally required for other nonprofits to determine if the organization is tax-exempt under federal law.

Can tax-exempt status be lost? Yes. Failure to annually file Form 990, if required, often triggers the loss of tax-exempt status. As discussed further in this chapter, participating or intervening in a political campaign or having significant unrelated business activities may also be problematic for an organization's tax-exempt status.

Acquiring and maintaining tax-exempt status is not only vital to churches and other nonprofits but is also very important to givers who desire a charitable tax deduction for donations made to these organizations.

Advantages and Limitations of Tax Exemption

Tax exemption is available to organizations that meet the requirements of the tax code and are approved by the IRS. This exemption provides relief from federal income tax. This income tax exemption may or may not extend to state and local income taxes. Even if an organization receives tax-exempt status, certain federal taxes may still be imposed. There may be tax due on unrelated business income, excessive compensation, certain "political" activities, and excessive legislative activities.

Tax exemption advantages

Besides the basic exemption from federal income taxes, an organization that is recognized as a charitable organization under the Internal Revenue Code enjoys several advantages:

➤ Its givers can be offered the benefit of a tax deduction for charitable contributions.

➤ It can benefit from using special standard nonprofit mail rates.

➤ It is in a favored position to seek funding from foundations and other philanthropic entities, many of which will not support organizations other than those recognized as tax-exempt organizations under 501(c)(3).

Remember

A tax-exempt organization usually means the entity is exempt, in whole or in part, from federal income taxes. The entity may still be subject to social security taxes and certain excise taxes. Nonprofit organizations may be subject to taxes at the state level on income, franchise, sales, use, tangible property, intangible property, and real property.

➤ It is eligible for government grants available only to entities exempt under 501(c)(3).

➤ It often qualifies for exemption not only from state and local income taxes but from property taxes (for property used directly for its exempt function) and certain sales and use taxes as well.

➤ It may qualify for exemption from the Federal Unemployment Tax Act in certain situations.

➤ Its employees may participate in 403(b) tax-sheltered annuities.

➤ It is an exclusive beneficiary of free radio and television public service announcements (PSAs) provided by local media outlets.

➤ If it is a church or a qualified church-controlled organization, it may exclude compensation to employees from the FICA social security base if it meets certain qualifications. The organization must be opposed on religious grounds to the payment of FICA social security taxes. The social security liability shifts to the employees of the electing organizations in the form of SECA social security tax.

Tax exemption limitations

Offsetting the advantages of tax-exempt status are some strict requirements:

➤ Organizations must comply with annual IRS reporting requirements.

➤ Organizations must be engaged "primarily" in qualified charitable or educational endeavors.

➤ There are limitations on the extent to which they may engage in substantial legislative activities or other political activities.

➤ Organizations may not engage in unrelated business activities or commercial activities to an impermissible extent.

➤ There is a prohibition against private inurement or private benefit.

➤ Upon dissolution, organizations' assets must be distributed for one or more exempt purposes.

Tax Exemption for Churches

Tax law and IRS regulations do not define "religious," but the courts have defined "religious" broadly. In part, because of constitutional concerns, some religious organizations are subject to less intrusive reporting and auditing requirements under federal tax law.

Remember

All churches are religious organizations, but not all religious organizations are churches. While many churches have steeples, the definition of a church for IRS purposes is much broader. The term "church" may include religious schools, publishers, television and radio broadcasters, rescue missions, religious orders, and other organizations.

The "religious" category includes churches, conventions of churches, associations of churches, church-run organizations (such as schools, hospitals, orphanages, nursing homes, publishing entities, broadcasting entities, and cemeteries), religious orders, apostolic groups, integrated auxiliaries of churches, missionary organizations, and Bible and tract societies. IRS regulations define religious worship as follows: "What constitutes conduct of religious worship or the ministration of sacerdotal functions depends on the interests and practices of a particular religious body constituting a church."

Although not stated in the tax law, the IRS generally applies the following 14 criteria to decide whether a religious organization can qualify as a "church":

➤ Distinct legal existence

➤ Recognized creed and form of worship

➤ Definite and distinct ecclesiastical government

➤ Formal code of doctrine and discipline

➤ Distinct religious history

➤ Membership not associated with any other church or denomination

➤ Organization of ordained ministers

➤ Established places of worship

➤ Literature of its own

➤ Ordained ministers selected after completing prescribed courses of studies

➤ Regular congregations

➤ Regular religious services

➤ Sunday schools for religious instruction of the young

➤ Schools for preparation of its ministers

Churches receive favored status in that they are not required to file either an application for recognition of exemption (Form 1023) or an annual report (Form 990) with the IRS. If applicable, a church is still subject to filing and disclosing an annual report on unrelated business income (Form 990-T) and Form 5578 for private schools as well as payroll tax, sales tax, and other forms. Individuals employed by churches qualify more easily for the special ministerial tax treatments, including a housing allowance.

Because of the highly restrictive requirements of the Church Audit Procedures Act, churches are subject to IRS inquiries or audits only when an appropriate high-level Treasury official makes a reasonable belief determination that a church may not qualify for tax-exempt status. These restrictive audit procedures have also recently been extended by the IRS to apply to tax-related employment matters.

Starting a Church or Other Nonprofit Organization

One of the first and most basic decisions when starting a church or nonprofit is to choose an organizational form. Many churches are unincorporated associations. However, many other churches incorporate for the purpose of limiting legal liability. Most other nonprofit organizations are corporations. While incorporation is usually desirable for churches and other nonprofit organizations, it is generally not mandatory.

Organizations using the corporate form need articles of incorporation and bylaws. An unincorporated organization will typically have similar documents, although the articles may be in the form of a constitution.

> **Key Issue**
>
> If a church or other nonprofit organization wishes to incorporate, it must file articles of incorporation with the appropriate state office. Some states also require the filing of trust documents.

Several planning questions should be asked. If the organization is formed for charitable purposes, is public charity status desired or is a private foundation acceptable? Are any business activities contemplated, and to what degree will the organization be incorporated? Is an attorney competent in nonprofit matters available to help with the preparation of the legal documents? What provisions will the bylaws contain? Who will serve on the board of directors? What name will be used for the organization?

The following materials may provide useful information when starting a church or other nonprofit organization:

irs.gov	Package 1023–Application for Recognition of Exemption with Instructions
irs.gov	Publication 557–Tax-Exempt Status for Your Organization
ECFA.org	*10 Essentials of Forming a Charitable Organization*
ECFA.church	*10 Essentials of Forming a Church*

Obtaining an employer identification number

All entities, whether exempt from tax or not, must obtain an employer identification number (EIN) by filing IRS Form SS-4. An EIN is required for a church even though churches are not required to file with the IRS for tax-exempt status. This number is not a tax-exempt number, but is simply the organization's unique identifier in the IRS's records, similar to an individual's social security number. An EIN will often be necessary before opening a bank account in the name of the organization.

> **Filing Tip**
>
> The filing for tax-exempt status by a parachurch ministry will determine whether the organization will be recognized as tax-exempt, whether it will be eligible to receive deductible charitable contributions (and sometimes to what extent), and whether the organization will be a public charity or a private foundation.

Form **SS-4**	**Application for Employer Identification Number**	OMB No. 1545-0003	
(Rev. January 2010)	(For use by employers, corporations, partnerships, trusts, estates, churches, government agencies, Indian tribal entities, certain individuals, and others.)	EIN	
Department of the Treasury Internal Revenue Service	▶ See separate instructions for each line.　▶ Keep a copy for your records.		

1	Legal name of entity (or individual) for whom the EIN is being requested		
	Lynn Haven Church		
2	Trade name of business (if different from name on line 1)	**3**	Executor, administrator, trustee, "care of" name
4a	Mailing address (room, apt., suite no. and street, or P.O. box)	**5a**	Street address (if different) (Do not enter a P.O. box.)
	PO Box 4382		**3801 North Florida Avenue**
4b	City, state, and ZIP code (if foreign, see instructions)	**5b**	City, state, and ZIP code (if foreign, see instructions)
	Miami, FL 33014		**Miami, FL 33133**
6	County and state where principal business is located		
	Dade County, FL		
7a	Name of responsible party	**7b**	SSN, ITIN, or EIN
	Mark Smith, Treasurer		**516-03-9091**

Type or print clearly.

8a	Is this application for a limited liability company (LLC) (or a foreign equivalent)? . . . . ☐ Yes ☒ No	**8b**	If 8a is "Yes," enter the number of LLC members . . . . ▶
8c	If 8a is "Yes," was the LLC organized in the United States? . . . . ☐ Yes ☐ No		

9a Type of entity (check only one box). **Caution.** If 8a is "Yes," see the instructions for the correct box to check.

☐ Sole proprietor (SSN) ____
☐ Partnership
☐ Corporation (enter form number to be filed) ▶ ____
☐ Personal service corporation
☒ Church or church-controlled organization
☐ Other nonprofit organization (specify) ▶ ____
☐ Other (specify) ▶ ____

☐ Estate (SSN of decedent) ____
☐ Plan administrator (TIN) ____
☐ Trust (TIN of grantor) ____
☐ National Guard　☐ State/local government
☐ Farmers' cooperative　☐ Federal government/military
☐ REMIC　☐ Indian tribal governments/enterprises
Group Exemption Number (GEN) if any ▶

9b	If a corporation, name the state or foreign country (if applicable) where incorporated	State	Foreign country	

10 Reason for applying (check only one box)

☒ Started new business (specify type) ▶ ____
　Church
☐ Hired employees (Check the box and see line 13.)
☐ Compliance with IRS withholding regulations
☐ Other (specify) ▶

☐ Banking purpose (specify purpose) ▶ ____
☐ Changed type of organization (specify new type) ▶ ____
☐ Purchased going business
☐ Created a trust (specify type) ▶ ____
☐ Created a pension plan (specify type) ▶ ____

11	Date business started or acquired (month, day, year). See instructions.　**2/01/18**	**12** Closing month of accounting year
13	Highest number of employees expected in the next 12 months (enter -0- if none).　If no employees expected, skip line 14.	**14** If you expect your employment tax liability to be $1,000 or less in a full calendar year **and** want to file Form 944 annually instead of Forms 941 quarterly, check here. (Your employment tax liability generally will be $1,000 or less if you expect to pay $4,000 or less in total wages.) If you do not check this box, you must file Form 941 for every quarter. ☐

Agricultural	Household	Other **3**

15 First date wages or annuities were paid (month, day, year). **Note.** If applicant is a withholding agent, enter date income will first be paid to nonresident alien (month, day, year) . . . . ▶

16 Check **one** box that best describes the principal activity of your business.
☐ Health care & social assistance　☐ Wholesale-agent/broker
☐ Construction　☐ Rental & leasing　☐ Transportation & warehousing　☐ Accommodation & food service　☐ Wholesale-other　☐ Retail
☐ Real estate　☐ Manufacturing　☐ Finance & insurance　☒ Other (specify) **Religious Organization**

17 Indicate principal line of merchandise sold, specific construction work done, products produced, or services provided.

18 Has the applicant entity shown on line 1 ever applied for and received an EIN? ☐ Yes ☒ No
If "Yes," write previous EIN here ▶

Third Party Designee	Complete this section **only** if you want to authorize the named individual to receive the entity's EIN and answer questions about the completion of this form.	
	Designee's name	Designee's telephone number (include area code)　(　)
	Address and ZIP code	Designee's fax number (include area code)　(　)

Under penalties of perjury, I declare that I have examined this application, and to the best of my knowledge and belief, it is true, correct, and complete.

Name and title (type or print clearly) ▶	Applicant's telephone number (include area code)　(　)
Signature ▶ *Mark Smith*　Date ▶ **2/28/18**	Applicant's fax number (include area code)　(　)

For Privacy Act and Paperwork Reduction Act Notice, see separate instructions.　Cat. No. 16055N　Form **SS-4** (Rev. 1-2010)

When an organization is approved by the IRS for exemption from federal income tax (not required for churches), it will receive a "determination letter." This letter does not assign the organization a tax-exempt number.

If an organization is a "central organization" that holds a "group exemption letter," the IRS will assign that group a four-digit number, known as its group exemption number (GEN). This number must be supplied with the central organization's annual report to the IRS (updating its list of included subordinate organizations). The number is also inserted on Form 990 (if required) of the central organization and the subordinate organizations included in the group exemption.

When an organization applies for exemption from state or local income, sales, or property taxes, the state or local jurisdiction may provide a certificate or letter of exemption, which, in some jurisdictions, includes a serial number. This number is often called a "tax-exempt number." This number should not be confused with an EIN.

Application for recognition of tax-exempt status

Although a church is not required to apply to the IRS for tax-exempt status under Section 501(c)(3) of the Internal Revenue Code and is exempt from filing Form 990, it may be appropriate to apply for recognition in some situations:

Key Issue

Approval of tax-exempt status by the IRS is usually effective as of the date of formation of an organization. The effective date determines the date that contributions to the organization are deductible by givers. If an organization is required to alter its activities or substantially amend its charter to qualify, the effective date for tax-exempt purposes will be the date specified in the ruling or determination letter.

➤ National denominations typically file for group exemption to cover all local churches. A copy of the national body's IRS determination letter may be used by the local group to provide evidence of tax-exempt status.

Independent local churches that are not a part of a national denominational body often file for tax-exempt status to provide evidence of their status. The local congregation may wish to file for group exemption if it is a parent church of other local congregations or separately organized ministries.

➤ If a local congregation ordains, licenses, or commissions ministers, it may be helpful to apply for tax-exempt status. Ministers that are ordained by a local church may be required to provide evidence that the church is tax-exempt. This could be particularly true if the minister files Form 4361, applying for exemption from self-employment tax.

Organizations desiring recognition of tax-exempt status should submit Form 1023 or Form 1023-EZ (see pages 17–18 for churches filing for tax-exempt status). A streamlined Form 1023-EZ may generally be used by most ministries with gross receipts of $50,000 or less and assets of $250,000 or less.

The IRS must be notified that the organization is applying for recognition of exemption within 15 months from the end of the month in which it was organized. Applications made after this deadline will not be effective before the date on which the application for recognition of exemption is filed. If approved, the IRS will issue a determination letter describing the category of exemption granted.

Organizations that have applied and been approved for tax-exempt status are reflected on the IRS website in the "Tax-Exempt Organization Search" database.

Determination letter request

A user fee of $600 must accompany Form 1023 applications for recognition of tax-exempt status. There is a $275 user fee for organizations using the Form 1023-EZ. Group exemption letter fees are $2,000. Users should use www.Pay.gov to pay the appropriate fee for a determination letter request.

Granting tax exemption

Upon approval of the application for exemption, the IRS will provide a determination letter recognizing that the organizational and operational plans of the nonprofit entitle it to be classified as tax-exempt. The exempt status is usually effective as of the date of formation of the organization, if filing deadlines are met.

Group exemption

An affiliated group of organizations under the common control of a central organization can obtain a group exemption letter. Churches that are part of a denomination are not required to file a separate application for exemption if they are covered by the group letter.

The central organization is required to report annually its exempt subordinate organizations to the IRS. (The IRS does not provide a particular form for this reporting.) The central organization is responsible to evaluate the tax status of its subordinate groups.

Unrelated Business Income

Most churches and nonprofits are supported primarily from either contributions or revenue from activities directly related to their exempt purposes. Sales of religious books, tuition at schools, and campers' fees are examples of exempt purpose revenue. On the other hand, income from activities not directly related to fulfilling an organization's exempt purposes may be subject to the tax on unrelated business income (UBI).

All income of tax-exempt organizations is presumed to be exempt from federal income tax unless the income is generated by an activity that is:

➤ not substantially related to the organization's exempt purpose or function

➤ a trade or business

➤ regularly carried on

UBI is permitted for tax-exempt organizations. However, these organizations may have to pay tax on income derived from activities unrelated to their exempt purpose. UBI must not comprise a substantial part of the organization's operation. There is no specific percentage limitation on how much UBI is "substantial." However, organizations with 50% or more of their activities classified as unrelated have faced revocation of their tax-exempt status.

Filing Tip

Although churches are exempt from filing Form 990 with the IRS, they are still subject to tax on their unrelated business income. Tax law allows churches and other nonprofit organizations to conduct profit-making activities, but that profit is taxed if the income is from an unrelated business activity and none of the exceptions to the tax apply.

Form 990-T must be completed annually to report the source(s) of UBI and related expenses and to compute any tax. UBI amounts are also reportable on Form 990 (if the filing of Form 990 is required). Organizations required to file a Form 990-T will generally also be required to make a state filing related to the UBI. The Form 990-T is subject to the public disclosure rules, as well (see page 33).

Although exempt from filing Form 990, churches must file Form 990-T if they have $1,000 or more of gross UBI in a year. There is a specific deduction of $1,000 in computing unrelated business taxable income. This specific deduction applies to a religious order or a convention or association of churches with respect to each individual church, district, or other local unit.

Unrelated business income consequences

Some church and nonprofit leaders are paranoid about UBI to the point that they feel it must be avoided altogether. Some people equate UBI with the automatic loss of exempt status. A more balanced view is to understand the purpose of UBI and to minimize the UBI tax through proper planning.

The most common adverse result of having UBI is that all or part of it may be taxed. A less frequent, but still possible, result is that the organization will lose its tax exemption. It is possible that the IRS will deny or revoke the tax-exempt status of an organization when it regularly derives over one-half of its annual revenue from unrelated activities.

Congress has recognized that some nonprofits may need to engage in unrelated business activities to survive. For example, a nonprofit with unused office space might rent the space to another organization. Also, nonprofits are expected to invest surplus funds to supplement the primary sources of the organization's income.

Sample Unrelated Business Income Checklist

Determination of whether an activity produces unrelated business taxable income can be made by answering the questions below:

➤ *Is the activity regularly carried on?*

A specific business activity is regularly carried on if it is conducted with a frequency, continuity, and manner of pursuit comparable to the conduct of the same or similar activity by a taxable organization. An activity is regularly carried on if it is conducted:

- intermittently the year round, or
- during a significant portion of the season for a seasonal type of business

However, an activity is not regularly carried on if it is conducted:

- on a very infrequent basis (once or twice a year)
- for only a short period of the year, or
- without competitive or promotional efforts

➤ *Is the activity substantially related to the exempt purposes of the nonprofit?*

To be substantially related, the business activity must contribute importantly to the accomplishment of a purpose for which the nonprofit was granted tax exemption, other than the mere production of income to support such purpose.

➤ *Is the activity conducted with volunteer services?*

Any business activity in which substantially all (85% or more) of the work is performed by volunteers is specifically exempted from unrelated business income tax.

➤ *Is the activity primarily for the convenience of clients, patients, faculty, staff, students, or visitors?*

So-called "convenience" activities are exempt regardless of their nature. Examples are parking lots, food service, bookstores, laundry, telephone service, and vending machines.

➤ *Is the income from the rental of real property?*

Rental income is generally tax-exempt if it does not relate to debt-financed property. But if significant services such as setup, cleaning, and laundry service are also provided, then the income is usually taxable.

➤ *Is the income derived from debt-financed property?*

Examples of income from debt-financed property are dividends, interest, rents, etc., earned from stocks, bonds, and rental property that have been purchased with borrowed money.

A trade or business regularly carried on

A trade or business means any activity regularly carried on which produces income from the sale of goods or services and where there is a reasonable expectation of a profit. To decide whether a trade or business is regularly carried on, the IRS considers whether taxable organizations would carry on a business with the same frequency and continuity. Intermittent activities may escape the "regularly carried on" definition.

Example 1: If a church sells sandwiches at a local community event for only two weeks, the IRS would not treat this as the regular conduct of a trade or business.

Example 2: A one-time sale of property is not an activity that is regularly carried on and therefore does not generate unrelated business income unless the property was used in an unrelated business activity or was debt-financed.

Example 3: A church is located in the downtown section of a city. Each Saturday, the church parking lot is operated commercially to accommodate shoppers. Even though the business activity is carried on for only one day each week on a year-round basis, this constitutes the conduct of a trade or business. It is subject to the unrelated business income tax.

Substantially related

According to the IRS regulations, a trade or business must "contribute importantly to the accomplishment of the exempt purposes of an organization" if it is to be considered "substantially related." Even if all the profits from a business go to support the work of the nonprofit, the profits may still be taxed.

Example: If a church operates a restaurant and devotes all the proceeds to mission work, the church will not escape taxation on the restaurant's income.

Examples of types of income that may be "related" are:

➤ the sale of products made by handicapped individuals as a part of their rehabilitation

➤ the sale of homes constructed by students enrolled in a vocational training course

➤ a retail grocery store operated to provide emotional therapy for disturbed adolescents

Tours conducted by nonprofits usually create UBI. Tours may be exempt from UBI only if they are strongly educationally oriented, with reports, daily lectures, and so on. Tours with substantial recreational or social purposes are not exempt.

The definition of "unrelated trade or business" does not include:

➤ activities in which unpaid volunteers do most of the work for an organization

➤ activities provided primarily for the convenience of the organization's members

Form **990-T**	**Exempt Organization Business Income Tax Return** (and proxy tax under section 6033(e))		OMB No. 1545-0687
	For calendar year 2018 or other tax year beginning _____ , 2018, and ending _____ , 20 ____		**2018**
	▶ Go to *www.irs.gov/Form990T* for instructions and the latest information.		
Department of the Treasury Internal Revenue Service	▶ Do not enter SSN numbers on this form as it may be made public if your organization is a 501(c)(3).		Open to Public Inspection for 501(c)(3) Organizations Only

A ☐ Check box if address changed	Name of organization (☐ Check box if name changed and see instructions.) **Family Bible Church**	**D** Employer identification number (Employees' trust, see instructions.) **35-4427081**
B Exempt under section [X] 501(C)(3) ☐ 408(e) ☐ 220(e) ☐ 408A ☐ 530(a) ☐ 529(a)	Print or Type	Number, street, and room or suite no. If a P.O. box, see instructions. **400 North Sunset Avenue**	**E** Unrelated business activity code (See instructions.) **532000**
C Book value of all assets at end of year **2,342,700**	City or town, state or province, country, and ZIP or foreign postal code **Lemon Grove, CA 92045**	

F Group exemption number (See instructions.) ▶

G Check organization type ▶ [X] 501(c) corporation   ☐ 501(c) trust   ☐ 401(a) trust   ☐ Other trust

H Enter the number of the organization's unrelated trades or businesses. ▶ **1**   Describe the only (or first) unrelated trade or business here ▶ **Sales of unrelated merchandise** ____   If only one, complete Parts I–V. If more than one, describe the first in the blank space at the end of the previous sentence, complete Parts I and II, complete a Schedule M for each additional trade or business, then complete Parts III–V.

I During the tax year, was the corporation a subsidiary in an affiliated group or a parent-subsidiary controlled group? . . ▶ ☐ Yes [X] No
If "Yes," enter the name and identifying number of the parent corporation. ▶

J The books are in care of ▶ **Tom Jones**   Telephone number ▶ **506-321-145**

Part I — Unrelated Trade or Business Income

				(A) Income	(B) Expenses	(C) Net
1a	Gross receipts or sales					
b	Less returns and allowances	c Balance ▶	1c			
2	Cost of goods sold (Schedule A, line 7)		2			
3	Gross profit. Subtract line 2 from line 1c		3			
4a	Capital gain net income (attach Schedule D)		4a			
b	Net gain (loss) (Form 4797, Part II, line 17) (attach Form 4797)		4b			
c	Capital loss deduction for trusts		4c			
5	Income (loss) from a partnership or an S corporation (attach statement)		5			
6	Rent income (Schedule C)		6			
7	Unrelated debt-financed income (Schedule E) . . .		7	79,740	52,301	27,439
8	Interest, annuities, royalties, and rents from a controlled organization (Schedule F)		8			
9	Investment income of a section 501(c)(7), (9), or (17) organization (Schedule G)		9			
10	Exploited exempt activity income (Schedule I) . . .		10			
11	Advertising income (Schedule J)		11			
12	Other income (See instructions; attach schedule)		12			
13	**Total.** Combine lines 3 through 12		13	79,740	52,301	27,439

Part II — Deductions Not Taken Elsewhere
(See instructions for limitations on deductions.) (Except for contributions, deductions must be directly connected with the unrelated business income.)

14	Compensation of officers, directors, and trustees (Schedule K)	14	
15	Salaries and wages	15	
16	Repairs and maintenance	16	
17	Bad debts	17	
18	Interest (attach schedule) (see instructions)	18	
19	Taxes and licenses	19	
20	Charitable contributions (See instructions for limitation rules)	20	
21	Depreciation (attach Form 4562)	21		
22	Less depreciation claimed on Schedule A and elsewhere on return . .	22a		22b	
23	Depletion	23	
24	Contributions to deferred compensation plans	24	
25	Employee benefit programs	25	
26	Excess exempt expenses (Schedule I)	26	
27	Excess readership costs (Schedule J)	27	
28	Other deductions (attach schedule)	28	
29	**Total deductions.** Add lines 14 through 28	29	
30	Unrelated business taxable income before net operating loss deduction. Subtract line 29 from line 13	30	27,439
31	Deduction for net operating loss arising in tax years beginning on or after January 1, 2018 (see instructions)	31	
32	Unrelated business taxable income. Subtract line 31 from line 30	32	27,439

For Paperwork Reduction Act Notice, see instructions.   Cat. No. 11291J   Form **990-T** (2018)

The specific deduction of $1,000 is included on page 2, line 37 of this form.

➤ activities involving the sale of merchandise mostly donated to the organization

Rental income

Nonprofits often rent facilities, equipment, and other assets for a fee, with the following UBI implications:

> **Remember**
>
> Nonprofits are normally not taxed on income they receive from renting or leasing real estate, even if the rental activity has nothing to do with their exempt purpose. If the property is financed by debt, however, a portion of the otherwise nontaxable income is typically taxed as debt-financed income.

➤ Renting to another nonprofit may be termed "related" if the rental expressly serves the landlord's exempt purposes.

➤ Rental of real estate is excluded from UBI unless the excludable property is acquired or improved with original indebtedness. Rental income from the property becomes UBI to the extent of the ratio of the "average acquisition indebtedness" during the year to the total purchase price. The nonprofit may deduct the same portion of the expenses directly connected with the production of the rental income. Depreciation is allowable using only the straight-line method.

Debt-financed income

To discourage exempt organizations from borrowing money to purchase passive income items, Congress imposed a tax on debt-financed income. Any property held to produce income is debt-financed property if at any time during the tax year there was acquisition indebtedness outstanding for the property.

Acquisition indebtedness is the outstanding amount of principal debt incurred by the organization to acquire or improve the property:

➤ before the property was acquired or improved, if the debt was incurred because of the acquisition or improvement of the property, or

➤ after the property was acquired or improved, if the debt was incurred because of the acquisition or improvement, and the organization could reasonably foresee the need to incur the debt at the time the property was acquired or improved.

There are exceptions to the debt-financed income rules, including:

➤ use of substantially all (85% or more) of any property for an organization's exempt purposes

➤ use of property by a related exempt organization to further its exempt purposes

➤ life income contracts, if the remainder interest is payable to an exempt charitable organization

➤ neighborhood land rule, if an organization acquires real property in its "neighborhood" (the neighborhood restriction does not apply to churches) mainly to use it for exempt purposes within 10 years (15 years for churches)

Tax reform impact on UBI

In December 2017, Congress passed comprehensive tax reform which included modifications of UBI, subject to guidance by the Department of Treasury. At the time of this book's publication the Department of Treasury had not issued final guidance regarding these changes and there have been multiple legislative proposals introduced to reverse these changes. Under 2017 tax reform, nonprofit organizations must compute UBI on each type of UBI independently (so that a loss from one type of UBI does not offset a gain of another) and certain fringe benefits must be treated as UBI. These fringe benefits include commuting benefits and qualified parking. For the latest updates on this please visit ECFA.org.

Activities that are not taxed

Income from the following sources is generally not considered UBI:

➤ **Passive income.** Income earned from most passive investment activities is not UBI unless the underlying property is subject to debt. Types of passive income include:

☐ dividends, interest, and annuities

☐ capital gains or losses from the sale, exchange, or other disposition of property

☐ rents from real property (some rent is UBI if the rental property was purchased or improved subject to a mortgage)

☐ royalties (however, oil and gas working interest income generally constitutes UBI)

➤ **Volunteers.** Any business where volunteers perform most of the work without compensation does not qualify as UBI. To the IRS, "substantially" means at least 85% of total work performed.

> **Example:** A used-clothing store operated by a nonprofit orphanage where volunteers do all the work in the store would likely be exempt.

> **Idea**
> The use of volunteers to conduct an activity is one of the best ways to avoid tax on what would otherwise be a taxable activity. Intermittent activities may also escape the tax. To decide whether a trade or business is regularly carried on, the IRS considers whether taxable organizations would carry on a business with the same frequency and continuity.

➤ **Convenience.** A cafeteria, bookstore, or residence operated for the convenience of patients, visitors, employees, or students is not a business. Stores, parking lots, and other facilities may be dually used (part related and part unrelated).

➤ **Donated goods.** The sale of merchandise, mostly received as gifts or contributions, does not qualify as UBI. A justification for this exemption is that contributions of property are merely being converted into cash.

➤ **Low-cost items.** Items (costing less than $10.90—2018 adjusted amount) distributed incidental to the solicitation of charitable contributions are not subject to UBI. The amounts received are not considered an exchange for the low-cost articles, and therefore they do not create UBI.

➤ **Mailing lists.** Mailing lists exchanged with or rented to another exempt organization are excluded from UBI, although the commercial sale of the lists will generally create UBI. The structuring of the agreement as a royalty arrangement may make the income exempt from UBI treatment.

Calculating the unrelated business income tax

Income tax rules applicable to businesses, such as depreciation method limitations and rates, apply to the UBI computation. Direct and indirect costs, after proration between related and unrelated activities, may be used to offset income. The first $1,000 of annual net unrelated income is exempt from taxation.

Unrelated business income summary

➤ Be aware of the types of activities that may create UBI in your organization.

➤ Maintain careful records of income and related expenses (both direct and indirect, including depreciation) for any activities that might be considered unrelated to the exempt purpose of your organization. These records should include allocations of salaries and fringe benefits based on time records or, at a minimum, time estimates.

➤ It may be wise to keep a separate set of records on potential unrelated activities. This separate set of records would need to be submitted to the IRS only upon audit.

➤ Be sure that board minutes, contracts, and other documents reflect the organization's view of relatedness of various activities to the exempt purpose of the entity.

➤ If the organization has over $1,000 of gross UBI in a given fiscal (tax) year, file Form 990-T.

Private Benefit and Private Inurement

Tax laws and regulations impose prohibitions on nonprofit organizations concerning private benefit and private inurement. Excise taxes are imposed on "excess benefit transactions" between "disqualified persons" and nonprofits. An excess benefit transaction occurs when an economic benefit is provided by an organization, directly or indirectly, to or for the use of a disqualified person, and the value of the economic benefit provided by the organization exceeds the value of the consideration received by the organization in return for providing the benefit. A disqualified person is any person in a position to exercise substantial influence over the affairs of the organization (often referred to as an "insider").

Private benefit

Nonprofit organizations must serve public, and not private, interests. The private benefit prohibition applies to anyone outside the intended charitable class. The law does allow some private benefit if it is incidental to the public benefits involved. It is acceptable if the benefit to the public cannot be achieved without necessarily benefiting private individuals.

> **Example:** The IRS revoked the exemption of a charity as having served the commercial purposes and private interests of a professional fundraiser when the fundraiser distributed only 3% of the amount collected to the nonprofit organization.

Private inurement

Private inurement is a subset of private benefit. This is an absolute prohibition that generally applies to a distinct class of private interests. These "insiders" may be founders, trustees or directors, officers, managers, or significant givers to the organization. Transactions involving these individuals are not necessarily prohibited, but they must be subject to reasonableness, documentation, and applicable reporting to the IRS.

Technically, private inurement is a transfer of resources from a tax-exempt organization to an individual insider that creates a financial benefit for the individual, solely because of that individual's close relationship with the organization and without regard to accomplishing the organization's exempt purposes. In other words, when an individual insider receives something from a nonprofit organization for nothing or even less than what it is worth, private inurement may have occurred. Excessive, and therefore unreasonable, compensation can also result in prohibited inurement. The IRS may ask the following questions to determine if private inurement exists:

Remember

The most common example of private inurement is excessive compensation. However, the following transactions between a charity and a private individual are other examples of possible private inurement: (1) sale, exchange, or leasing of property; (2) lending of money or other extension of credit; or (3) furnishing of goods, services, or facilities.

> ➤ Did the expenditure further an exempt purpose, and if so, how?

> ➤ Was the payment at fair market value, or did it represent reasonable compensation for goods and services?

> ➤ Does a low-interest or no-interest loan to an employee or director fall within a reasonable compensation package?

Compensation-Setting Check List

1. Name: _____Frank Basinger_____

2. Effective date of compensation: ____January 1, 2019_____

3. Effective period (one year, two years, etc.): _____one year_____

4. Types of appropriate comparable data relied upon in approving compensation package (check applicable boxes):

    ☒ Compensation paid by similarly situated organizations (taxable and tax-exempt)

    ☒ Availability of similar services in the geographical area

    ☒ Independent compensation surveys

5. Explain how comparable data relied upon was obtained: __From nationally published compensation surveys.__

6. Range of total compensation from comparability data: __$120,000 –140,000__

7. Annual compensation summary:

	Cash	Approved Compensation
•	Salary	$ 95,000
•	Bonus or contingent payment (estimate)	5,000
	Noncash	
•	Deferred compensation	10,000
•	Premiums paid on insurance coverage (life, health, disability, liability, etc.)	18,000
•	Automobile (value of personal use)	2,000
•	Foregone interest on below market loan(s)	
•	Other (excluding nontaxable benefits under IRC Sec. 132)	1,000
	Total compensation	$131,000

8. Members of authorized body present during discussion of compensation package and vote cast:

Present	In Favor	Opposed
7	7	0

9. Members of authorized body having a conflict of interest with respect to the compensation arrangement and how the conflict was handled (e.g., left room during discussions and votes):

Member	Action re: Conflict
William McIlvain	Absent from board meeting for discussion and vote
Hugh Temple	Absent from board meeting for discussion and vote

10. Date compensation package approved: ____November 10, 2018____

➤ On an overseas trip for the nonprofit, did the employee (and perhaps a spouse) stay an additional week for a personal vacation and charge the expenses to the organization?

Example 1: An organization lost its exemption when it engaged in numerous transactions with an insider, including the purchase of a 42-foot boat for the personal use of the insider. The insider also benefitted from several real estate transactions, including donations and sales of real property to the organization that were never reflected on its books.

Example 2: A church lost its tax exemption after it operated commercial businesses and paid substantial private expenses of its founders, including expenses for jewelry and clothing in excess of $30,000 per year. The church also purchased five luxury cars for the founders' personal use. None of these benefits were reported as personal income to the founders.

Example 3: A tax-exempt organization transfers an auto to an employee for $1,000. The transfer was not approved by the board and does not constitute a portion of a reasonable pay package. The fair market value of the auto is $10,000. The net difference of $9,000 is not reported to the IRS as compensation. Private inurement has occurred.

Example 4: Same facts as Example 3, except the transfer was approved by the board and properly constituted a portion of the reasonable pay package, and the $9,000 was added to the employee's Form W-2 as compensation. There is no private inurement.

A two-tiered system of penalty taxes is imposed on insiders who improperly benefit from excess benefit transactions and on organization managers who are involved in illegal transactions. Sanctions cannot be imposed on the organizations themselves.

A first-tier penalty tax equal to 25% of the amount of the excess benefit is followed by a tax of 200% if there is no correction of the excess benefit within a certain time period. Additionally, there is a 10% penalty on an organization's managers if they knowingly approve an excess benefit transaction.

Filing Federal Returns

Nearly all nonprofit organizations must file an annual return with the IRS (churches, religious orders, and certain foreign missionary organizations are exempt from filing Form 990). The basic filing requirements are as follows:

Form to Be Filed	Conditions
Form 990-N	Gross annual receipts normally $50,000 or less
Form 990	Gross annual receipts over $200,000 or total assets over $500,000

Form 990-EZ	Gross annual receipts less than $200,000 with total assets of less than $500,000
Form 990-T	Any organization exempt under Sec. 501(a) with $1,000 or more gross income from a regularly conducted unrelated trade or business
Form 1120	Any nonprofit corporation that is not tax-exempt
Form 5500	Pension, profit-sharing, medical benefit, cafeteria, and certain other plans must annually file one of several series 5500 Forms

Remember

Form 990 should generally use the same accounting method as the organization uses to keep its books. If the accrual method is used for the books or the audit, use the accrual method on Form 990.

Public inspection of information returns

IRS regulations require the public disclosure of certain documents:

➤ **Materials made available for public inspection.** Nonprofits, other than private foundations, must provide access to the application for tax exemption (Form 1023 or Form 1023-EZ) and any supporting documents filed by the organization in support of its application. These also include any letter or other documents issued by the IRS in connection with the application.

Nonprofits must also provide access to their three most recent information returns. This generally includes Forms 990, 990-T, and schedules and attachments filed with the IRS. There is not a requirement to disclose parts of the information returns that identify names and addresses of contributors to the organization.

➤ **Places and times for public inspection.** Specified documents must be made available without charge at the nonprofit's principal, regional, and district offices during normal business hours. An office is considered a regional or district office only if the aggregate hours per week worked by its paid employees (either full-time or part-time) are 120 or more.

➤ **Responding to requests.** If a person requests copies in person, the request generally must be fulfilled on the day of the request. In unusual circumstances, an organization will be permitted to furnish the copies on the next business day. When the request is made in writing, the organization must provide the requested copies within 30 days. If the organization requires advance payment for reasonable copying and mailing

Remember

The law requires certain disclosures of financial information. Further, a general attitude of transparency serves to deter improper diversions of funds and other misdeeds. It also provides a defense to critics and a witness to both believers and nonbelievers.

Form **990**	**Return of Organization Exempt From Income Tax**	OMB No. 1545-0047
	Under section 501(c), 527, or 4947(a)(1) of the Internal Revenue Code (except private foundations)	**2018**
	▶ Do not enter social security numbers on this form as it may be made public.	**Open to Public Inspection**
Department of the Treasury Internal Revenue Service	▶ Go to *www.irs.gov/Form990* for instructions and the latest information.	

A For the 2018 calendar year, or tax year beginning _____, 2018, and ending _____, 20___

B Check if applicable:	**C** Name of organization **Lifeline Ministries**	**D** Employer identification number
☐ Address change	Doing business as	35 - 7438041
☐ Name change	Number and street (or P.O. box if mail is not delivered to street address) Room/suite	**E** Telephone number
☐ Initial return	**1212 South Palo Verde**	**480-344-8174**
☐ Final return/terminated	City or town, state or province, country, and ZIP or foreign postal code	
☐ Amended return	**Phoenix, AZ 85035**	**G** Gross receipts $ **1,618,911**
☐ Application pending	**F** Name and address of principal officer:	

H(a) Is this a group return for subordinates? ☐ Yes ☒ No
H(b) Are all subordinates included? ☐ Yes ☐ No
If "No," attach a list. (see instructions)

I Tax-exempt status: ☒ 501(c)(3) ☐ 501(c) ( ) ◀ (insert no.) ☐ 4947(a)(1) or ☐ 527
J Website: ▶
H(c) Group exemption number ▶

K Form of organization: ☒ Corporation ☐ Trust ☐ Association ☐ Other ▶   **L** Year of formation: **1994**   **M** State of legal domicile: **AZ**

Part I Summary

1	Briefly describe the organization's mission or most significant activities: **Lifeline Ministries is an international child sponsoring program. It provides food, education, health care, and spiritual nurture to children in need in 22 countries.**		
2	Check this box ▶ ☐ if the organization discontinued its operations or disposed of more than 25% of its net assets.		
3	Number of voting members of the governing body (Part VI, line 1a)	**3**	11
4	Number of independent voting members of the governing body (Part VI, line 1b)	**4**	4
5	Total number of individuals employed in calendar year 2018 (Part V, line 2a)	**5**	12
6	Total number of volunteers (estimate if necessary)	**6**	30
7a	Total unrelated business revenue from Part VIII, column (C), line 12	**7a**	4,100
b	Net unrelated business taxable income from Form 990-T, line 38	**7b**	(1,875)

		Prior Year	Current Year
8	Contributions and grants (Part VIII, line 1h)	976,624	1,063,877
9	Program service revenue (Part VIII, line 2g)	433,801	489,863
10	Investment income (Part VIII, column (A), lines 3, 4, and 7d)	1,012	608
11	Other revenue (Part VIII, column (A), lines 5, 6d, 8c, 9c, 10c, and 11e)	9,480	10,343
12	Total revenue—add lines 8 through 11 (must equal Part VIII, column (A), line 12)	1,420,917	1,573,691
13	Grants and similar amounts paid (Part IX, column (A), lines 1–3)	10,000	15,000
14	Benefits paid to or for members (Part IX, column (A), line 4)		
15	Salaries, other compensation, employee benefits (Part IX, column (A), lines 5–10)	431,002	452,900
16a	Professional fundraising fees (Part IX, column (A), line 11e)		
b	Total fundraising expenses (Part IX, column (D), line 25) ▶ _____		
17	Other expenses (Part IX, column (A), lines 11a–11d, 11f–24e)	984,903	930,087
18	Total expenses. Add lines 13–17 (must equal Part IX, column (A), line 25)	1,425,905	1,397,987
19	Revenue less expenses. Subtract line 18 from line 12	5,012	175,704

		Beginning of Current Year	End of Year
20	Total assets (Part X, line 16)	1,625,043	2,043,015
21	Total liabilities (Part X, line 26)	1,610,412	1,852,680
22	Net assets or fund balances. Subtract line 21 from line 20	14,631	190,335

Part II Signature Block

Under penalties of perjury, I declare that I have examined this return, including accompanying schedules and statements, and to the best of my knowledge and belief, it is true, correct, and complete. Declaration of preparer (other than officer) is based on all information of which preparer has any knowledge.

Sign Here	▶ *Harold T. Baldwin* Signature of officer	5/15/19 Date
	▶ **Harold T. Baldwin, President** Type or print name and title	

Paid Preparer Use Only	Print/Type preparer's name	Preparer's signature	Date	Check ☐ if self-employed	PTIN
	Firm's name ▶			Firm's EIN ▶	
	Firm's address ▶			Phone no.	

May the IRS discuss this return with the preparer shown above? (see instructions) · · · · · · · · · · · ☐ Yes ☐ No

For Paperwork Reduction Act Notice, see the separate instructions.   Cat. No. 11282Y   Form **990** (2018)

Key Issues in Completing the Form 990
CORE FORM 990

Page 1, Parts I and II – Summary Governance and Financial Information. This page is the focal point for the entire Form 990 and the related schedules. All of the information in Part I is carried forward from other sections of the Form.

Readers of the Form 990 (the media, the giving public, researchers, and others) will generally start their review of an organization's Form 990 with this page. Therefore, a nonprofit should be sure the information on this page accurately reflects the organization's information.

- **The organization's mission or most significant activities.** Describing the organization's mission or most important activities in three-plus lines is highly challenging. The key is referencing other information in the Form 990 such as the exempt purpose achievements on page 2, which provides more space to expand on achievements.

- **Board independence.** By comparing the two lines which reflect the number of independent voting members and the number of total voting members, it will be apparent whether the nonprofit has achieved a majority of independent voting board members.

- **Unrelated business income.** The two lines which reflect gross and net unrelated business revenue tell a reader at a glance whether the nonprofit is required to file Form 990-T (required if gross unrelated business revenue is $1,000 or more) and if the unrelated activity produced a positive or negative financial result.

- **Revenue, expenses, and net assets.** A review of these lines will indicate whether a charity has received more revenue than expenses for the current and previous years, the amount paid to professional fundraisers and the total of fundraising expense, and total assets, total liabilities, and net assets for the current and previous years.

Page 2, Part III – Program Service Accomplishments. The key to completing this section is to maximize the potential of describing the organization's achievements for each of its three largest program services, as measured by total expenses incurred. Activities considered of comparable or greater importance, although smaller in terms of expenses incurred (such as activities conducted with volunteer labor), may be reported on Schedule O. A fundraising activity should not be reported as a program service accomplishment unless it is substantially related to the accomplishment of the organization's exempt purposes (other than by raising funds).

You may report the amount of any donated services, or use of materials, equipment, or facilities received or used in connection with a specific program service on the lines for the narrative description of the appropriate program service. However, do not include these amounts in revenue, expenses, or grants reported in lines 4a-4e.

Pages 3 and 4, Part IV – Checklist of Required Schedules. An organization is not required to answer Yes to questions on these pages and complete the schedule to which the question refers if the organization is not required to provide any information in the schedule. Therefore, a minimum dollar threshold for reporting information in a schedule may be relevant in determining whether the organization must answer Yes to a line on these pages.

A few of the questions on these two pages are particularly noted:

- Line 6 should be answered Yes if the organization maintains a giver-advised fund or accounts where givers had advisory privileges on the distribution or investment of amounts in such funds or accounts.

- Line 10 should be answered Yes even if the organization only has quasi-endowments (funds functioning as an endowment that are established by the organization itself, often referred to as board-designated, quasi-endowments).

- Line 14b should be answered Yes if the organization expended more than $10,000 (in aggregate) outside the United States during the year.

- Line 20 only applies to hospitals that were required to be licensed, certified, or similarly recognized by a state as a hospital. This definition excludes hospitals operated internationally.

- On Line 29, an organization is required to answer Yes if it received more than $25,000 during the year in value of donations, gifts, grants, or other contributions of property. Contributed services or the use of facilities is not includable on this line.

Pages 4 and 5, Part V – Activities That May Require Filing of Other Returns. This page is used to document whether the organization completed the appropriate form or complied with certain other tax requirements. It is effectively a checklist for the organization and the IRS.

Page 6, Part VI – Governance, Management, and Disclosure. Some of the most significant questions on this page include:

- **Independent board.** Line 1b asks for the number of voting members that are independent. A member of the governing body is considered independent only if all three of the following circumstances were applicable at all times during the organization's tax year:

  - The member was not compensated as an officer or other employee of the organization or of a related organization, except in certain situations under a vow of poverty.

  - The member did not receive total compensation or other payments exceeding $10,000 during the organization's tax year from the organization or from related organizations as an independent contractor, other than reimbursement of expenses under an accountable plan or reasonable compensation for services provided in the capacity as a member of the governing body.

  - Neither the member, nor any family member of the member, was involved in a transaction with the organization that is required to be reported in Schedule L, or in a transaction with a related organization of a type and amount that would be reportable on Schedule L if required to be filed by the related organization.

- **Changes in organizational documents.** Line 4 asks whether significant changes in organizational documents were made since the prior Form 990 was filed. The IRS anticipates the reporting of changes in great detail, including changes in:

  - the number of the governing body's voting members

  - the number, composition, qualifications, authority, or duties of the organization's officers or key employees

- the quorum, voting rights, or voting approval requirements of the governing body

- the policies and procedures contained within the organizing document or bylaws regarding compensation of officers, directors, trustees, or key employees, conflicts of interest, whistle-blowers, or document retention and destruction

- the composition or procedures contained within the organizing document or bylaws of an audit committee

- **Contemporaneous minutes.** Line 8 asks about the contemporaneous documentation of the meetings of the governing body and each committee with authority to act on behalf of the governing body. While many committees do not have the standing authority to act on behalf of the governing body, it is a best practice for all committees to keep contemporaneous documentation of meetings. This practice will serve an organization well, because boards occasionally delegate responsibility to a committee to act with respect to a certain issue.

- **Providing the Form 990 to the governing body.** Line 11a asks whether the Form 990 was provided to the governing board before it was filed, and requires each organization to describe the process (if any) used to review Form 990.

- **Conflicts of interest.** Lines 12a, b, and c delve into the conflict of interest topic. The questions relate to family and business relationships among officers, directors, and key employees; whether the organization has a written conflict of interest policy; whether the policy requires officers, directors, and key employees to disclose annually interests that could raise conflicts; and whether and how the organization regularly and consistently monitors and enforces compliance with the policy.

- **Whistle-blower policy.** Line 13 asks whether the organization has a written whistle-blower policy. Such a policy is important to prevent retaliation against employees who report suspected illegal activities. Retaliation could violate both federal and state law.

- **Document retention and destruction policy.** Line 14 asks whether an organization has a written document retention and destruction policy. This, too, is important because federal law prohibits the destruction of documents under certain circumstances, particularly if they are relevant to a pending investigation or lawsuit. Establishment and compliance with a written document retention and destruction policy minimizes the likelihood that documents will be destroyed in violation of law, and it may protect an organization from sanctions for destruction of documents in accordance with its policy.

- **Executive compensation.** Lines 15a and b ask for the description of the process the organization uses to approve compensation of the organization's CEO and other officers and key employees, and whether the organization is following the "safe harbor" procedure for approving compensation of "disqualified persons." This procedure includes approval by independent directors or committee members, review of comparable data, and contemporaneous substantiation of the deliberation and decision by the board or committee.

- **Joint venture policy.** Lines 16a and b ask whether organizations that participate in a joint venture have a written procedure ensuring evaluation of the joint venture in light of income tax exemption requirements.

- **Disclosure of documents.** Line 18 asks how the organization makes its Form 1023, Form 990, and Form 990-T available for public inspection. Line 19 asks whether, and if so how, articles of incorporation, bylaws, conflict of interest policy, and financial statements are made available to the public. The tax code does not require this second group of documents to be published by the organization. However, articles of incorporation and amendments are public record documents, and many nonprofits are required to file their articles of incorporation, bylaws, and audited financial statements with state offices that regulate charitable solicitations.

Pages 7 and 8, Part VII – Compensation of Disqualified Persons and Highest Paid Independent Contractors. Organizations are required to list the following officers, directors, trustees, and employees of the organization whose reportable compensation from the organization and related organizations exceeded the following thresholds:

- current officers, directors, and trustees (no minimum compensation threshold)

- current key employees (over $150,000 of reportable compensation)

- current five highest compensated employees other than officers, directors, trustees, or listed key employees (over $100,000 of reportable compensation)

- former officers, key employees, and highest compensated employees (over $100,000 of reportable compensation, with special rules for former highest compensated employees)

- former directors and trustees (over $10,000 of reportable compensation in the capacity as a former director or trustee)

Independent contractors that received more than $100,000 in compensation for services must be listed. The amount paid to the independent contractors must be shown in column (C) whether or not the amount was reported on Form 1099-MISC.

Page 9, Part VIII – Revenue Statement. A few of the key reporting requirements on this page include:

- Fundraising event contributions. This data must now be broken out on line 1c.

- Sales of assets other than inventory. Attachments are not required to reflect the detail of the sale of assets and the sale of securities.

Page 10, Part IX – Functional Expense Statement. There are a number of new expense categories included on the functional expense statement.

"Other expenses" (line 24) should include only expenses not required to be itemized in lines 1–23.

Page 12, Part XII – Financial Statements and Reporting. Key questions in this section include:

a. Financial statements compiled, reviewed, or audited by an independent accountant.

b. Audit committee. The form asks if there is an audit committee. It does not ask if the audit committee is composed of independent members.

OBSERVATIONS ON CERTAIN SCHEDULES

Schedule D – Supplemental Financial Statements. Schedule D requires detailed information on giver-advised funds and endowment funds, even including quasi-endowment funds.

Schedule F – Activities Outside the U.S. Specific reporting of foreign activity is limited to foreign bank accounts and offices located outside the country, where the organization is required to provide the country in which the account or office is located, and checking a box if foreign grants are included in the reported amounts.

The form requires information about foreign activities from organizations that conduct fundraising, grant making, trade or business, or exempt activities outside the United States, or have accounts, offices, employees, or other agents outside the country by region.

Schedule I – Grants and Other Assistance to Organizations, Governments, and Individuals in the U.S. All of the information relating to grants and other assistance to persons inside the U.S. is reported in this schedule. (Foreign grants are reported on the form's Schedule F.) There is a $5,000 per grant filing threshold.

Schedule J – Compensation. This Schedule asks more in-depth questions regarding highly compensated individuals than are asked on the core form. The questions are clearly designed to uncover potentially abusive compensation arrangements.

If the reporting organization is required to complete Schedule J, it must first answer questions, contained in Part I of the Schedule, regarding compensation of all of the individuals it listed on the core form.

Schedule M – Noncash Contributions. In order to collect information from organizations receiving significant amounts of noncash contributions, and specific types of such items, Schedule M collects aggregate annual information on the types of noncash property an organization receives.

Organizations that must file Schedule M are asked if they have a gift acceptance policy that requires the review of any "non-standard contributions." A "non-standard contribution" is a noncash gift that is not used in the organization's activities, for which there is no market in which the gift can be readily liquidated, and whose value is "highly speculative or difficult to ascertain."

Although the definition of a "non-standard contribution" is narrow, organizations should have gift acceptance policies that guide executives regarding the circumstances under which the organization will accept noncash gifts. This is particularly important with respect to gifts of real estate (which may hold environmental cleanup liabilities) and of securities and other business interests that are not publicly traded.

Schedule O – Supplemental Information to Form 990. This form provides an opportunity to explain the organization's operations or responses to various questions. It is a series of blank pages on which to continue explanation from other parts of the form and include information typically included as notes to the current form.

fees, it can provide copies within 30 days of the date it is paid, instead of the date of the request.

➤ **Fees for providing copies.** Reasonable fees may be charged by nonprofits for copying and mailing documents. The fees cannot exceed the amounts charged by the IRS (based on fees listed in the Freedom of Information Act)—currently, for noncommercial requesters, 10 cents per page for black-and-white pages, and 20 cents per page for color pages. Organizations are also allowed to charge actual postage costs incurred in providing the copies.

➤ **Documents widely available.** A nonprofit organization does not have to comply with requests for copies if it has made the appropriate materials widely available. This requirement is satisfied if the document is posted on the organization's web page on the internet or in another database of similar materials.

> **Filing Tip**
>
> As with all tax returns, nonprofits are required by law to provide complete and accurate information on these annual returns. The IRS makes all Forms 990 available through guidestar.org and electronically filed data via online exports.

Reporting substantial organizational changes

An organization's tax-exempt status remains in effect if there are no material changes in the organization's character, purposes, or methods of operation. Significant changes should be reported by letter to the IRS soon after the changes occur and reported on Form 990 if appropriate.

> **Example:** An organization received tax-exempt status for the operation of a religious radio ministry. Several years later, the organization decided to add a facility for homeless children. This change would likely be considered to be material and should be reported to the IRS.

Change in accounting methods

A nonprofit organization may adopt any reasonable method of accounting to keep its financial records that clearly reflects income. These methods include the cash receipts and disbursements method; the accrual method; or any other method (including a combination of methods) that clearly reflects income.

An organization that wishes to change from one method of accounting to another generally must secure the consent of the IRS to make that change. Consent must be obtained both for a general change of method and for any change of method with respect to one or more particular items. Thus, a nonprofit organization that generally uses the cash method, but uses the accrual method with respect to publications for which it maintains inventories, may change its method of accounting by adopting the accrual method for all purposes. But the organization must secure the IRS's consent to do so.

To obtain the consent of the IRS to change an accounting method, the organization should file IRS Form 3115, Application for Change in Accounting Method.

Change of fiscal years

Generally, an exempt organization may change its fiscal year simply by timely filing Form 990 with the appropriate Internal Revenue Service Center for the "short year." The return for the short year should indicate at the top of page 1 that a change of accounting period is being made. It should be filed no later than the 15th day of the fifth month following the close of the short year.

If neither Form 990 nor Form 990-T must be filed, the ministry is not required to notify the IRS of a change in the fiscal year, with one exception. The exception applies to exempt organizations that have changed their fiscal years within the previous ten calendar years. For this exception, Form 1128 must be filed with the IRS.

Other IRS forms commonly used

➤ **Form 5578.** Form 5578 (see pages 100–1) must be completed and furnished to the IRS to provide information regarding racial nondiscrimination policies of private schools, but only for those organizations not already required to file and report this information on Form 990, Schedule E. Form 5578 must be filed for schools operated by a church, including preschools.

➤ **Forms 8717 and 8718.** Nonprofits wishing IRS private letter rulings on employee plans or on exempt organization information must include the new Form 8717 or 8718, respectively, with the appropriate fees.

➤ **Form 8282.** If a nonprofit donee sells or otherwise disposes of gift property for which an appraisal summary is required on Form 8283 within three years after receipt of the property, it generally must file Form 8282 with the IRS. See chapter 7 for more information on these reporting rules.

➤ **Employee and nonemployee payments.** As an employer, a nonprofit organization must file federal and state forms concerning payment of compensation and the withholding of payroll taxes. Payments to nonemployees may require the filing of information returns. See chapters 5 and 6 for more coverage of these requirements.

Postal Regulations

Churches and other nonprofits may qualify to mail at special standard nonprofit mail rates (formerly called bulk third-class). The application (Form 3624) is available at the post office where you wish to deposit the mail (see page 43 for a sample of Form 3624). The following information must be provided (some items apply only if the organization is incorporated):

➤ description of the organization's primary purpose, which may be found in the articles of incorporation or bylaws

➤ evidence that the organization is nonprofit, such as a federal (and state) tax exemption determination letter

➤ materials showing how the organization actually operated in the previous 6 to 12 months, such as program literature, newsletters, bulletins, and any other promotional materials

The U.S. Postal Service offers rate incentives to nonprofit mailers that provide automation-compatible mail. Automated mail must be readable by an Optical Character Reader (OCR). Contact your local post office for more information.

State Taxes and Fees

Separate filings are often necessary to obtain exemption from state income tax. The requirements vary from state to state. In some states it is also possible to obtain exemption from licensing fees and sales, use, franchise, and property taxes.

A nonprofit organization may be required to report to one or more states regarding its exemption from, or compliance with, state income, sales, use, or property taxation. Many states accept a copy of Form 990 as adequate annual reporting for tax-exempt status purposes. Annual reporting to the state in which the organization is incorporated is normally required even if there is no requirement to file Form 990 with the IRS. Check with the offices of the secretary of state and attorney general to determine required filings.

Caution

Do not send a list of major contributors to the state unless it is specifically required. While this list is not open to public inspection with respect to the federal filing, it may not be confidential for state purposes.

Property taxes

Church property is generally exempt from property tax. Whether real estate of a nonprofit organization is exempt from property tax usually depends on its use and ownership and varies based on local law. Many states restrict the exemption of church property to property used for worship. It is also important to note that not all religious organizations are churches. Contact the office of the county tax assessor or collector to determine what property tax exemptions might be available.

Caution

An initial (and perhaps annual) registration of the property with the proper state authorities is generally necessary to record exempt property. The initial purchase of real estate with notification of state authorities is usually not sufficient to exempt property from tax.

UNITED STATES POSTAL SERVICE ®

Application to Mail at
Nonprofit USPS Marketing Mail Prices

Application Number:

Section A - Application *(Please read section B on page 2 before completion.)*

Part 1 *(For completion by applicant)*

- All information entered below must be legible so that our records will show the correct information about your organization.
- The complete name of the organization must be shown in item 1. The name shown must agree with the name that appears on all documents submitted to support this application.
- A complete address representing a physical location for the organization must be shown in item 2. If you receive mail through a Post Office™ box, show your street address first and use alternate address for the box.

- The applicant named in item 7 must be the individual submitting the application for the organization and must be a responsible official of the organization. Printers and mailing agents may not sign for the organization.
- No additional organization categories may be added in item 9. To be eligible for the Nonprofit USPS Marketing Mail prices, the organization must qualify as one of the types listed.
- The applicant must sign the application in item 15.
- The application must be submitted to the Post Office in item 14 and on the date shown in item 17.

No application fee is required. *(All information must be complete and typewritten or printed legibly.)*

1. Complete Name of Organization *(If voting registration official, include title)*
Chapel Hill Charity

2. Street Address of Organization *(Include apartment or suite number)*	3. City, State, ZIP+4® Code
300 South Hillcrest Avenue	**Athens, GA 45701**

4. Alternate Mailing Address	5. Alternate City, State, ZIP+4® Code

6. Telephone *(Include area code)*	7. Name of Applicant *(Must represent applying organization)*
614-832-9061	**Lewis Foster**

8. Email Address

9. Type of Organization *(Check only one)*

[X] (01) Religious	[ ] (03) Scientific	[ ] (05) Agricultural	[ ] (07) Veterans	[ ] (09) Qualified political committee *(Go to item 12)*
[ ] (02) Educational	[ ] (04) Philanthropic	[ ] (06) Labor	[ ] (08) Fraternal	[ ] (10) Voting registration official *(Go to item 12)*

Not all nonprofit organizations are eligible for the Nonprofit USPS Marketing Mail prices. Domestic Mail Manual® 703.1 lists certain organizations (such as business leagues, chambers of commerce, civic improvement associations, social and hobby clubs, governmental bodies, and others) that, although nonprofit, do not qualify for the Nonprofit USPS Marketing Mail prices.

10. Is this a for-profit organization or does any of the net income inure to the benefit of any private stockholder or individual?	[ ] Yes [X] No	12. Has this organization previously mailed at the Nonprofit USPS Marketing Mail prices? *(If 'Yes,' list the Post Office locations where mailings were most recently deposited at these prices and provide the nonprofit authorization number, if known.)*	[ ] Yes [X] No

11. Is this organization exempt from federal income tax? *(If 'Yes,' attach a copy of the exemption issued by the Internal Revenue Service (IRS) that shows the section of the IRS code under which the organization is exempt. **Required if exempt**. Do not submit State tax exemption information.)*	[X] Yes [ ] No

Has the IRS denied or revoked the organization's federal tax exempt status? *(If 'Yes,' attach a copy of the IRS ruling to this PS Form 3624.)* — [ ] Yes [X] No

From your IRS exemption letter, check off the box corresponding to the section under which the organization is exempt:

[X] 501(c)(3)	[ ] 501(c)(5)
[ ] 501(c)(8)	[ ] 501(c)(19)
[ ] Other 501(c) (___) *(See statement in item 9 above)*	

13. Has your organization had Nonprofit USPS Marketing Mail privileges denied or revoked? *(If 'Yes,' list the Post Office (city and state) where the application was denied or authorization was revoked and provide the nonprofit authorization number, if known.)*	[ ] Yes [X] No

14. Post Office (not a station or branch) where authorization requested and bulk mailings will be made *(City, state, ZIP Code™).*
Athens, GA 45701

I certify that the statements made by me are true and complete. I understand that anyone who furnishes false or misleading information on this form or who omits material information requested on the form may be subject to criminal sanctions (including fines and imprisonment) and/or civil sanctions (including multiple damages and civil penalties). I further understand that, if this application is approved, a postage refund for the difference between the regular USPS Marketing Mail and Nonprofit USPS Marketing Mail prices may be made for only mailings entered at regular USPS Marketing Mail prices at the Post Office identified above while this application is pending, provided that the conditions set forth in Domestic Mail Manual 703.1 and 703.1.9 are met.

15. Signature of Applicant *Lewis E. Foster*	16. Title **Manager**	17. Date **1/20/18**

Part 2 *(For completion by postmaster at originating office when application filed)*

1. Signature of Postmaster *(Or designated representative)*	2. Date Application Filed With Post Office *(Round stamp)*

PS Form **3624**, January 2017 *(Page 1 of 3)* PSN 7530-02-000-9014

PRIVACY NOTICE: See our privacy policy on www.usps.com

Church-owned parsonages may be exempt from real estate tax in certain jurisdictions. This is true though there may be several ministers on the staff of one church and therefore multiple parsonages. If the pastor owns the property instead of the church, the property is usually subject to property tax.

Church parking lots are usually exempt if properly recorded. It may be possible to obtain an exemption for vacant land. Property tax exemption of church camps and recreation facilities often comes under attack because of income that may be generated through their use. Property partially used for church use and partially leased to a third-party for-profit entity generally results in the proration of the tax exemption.

Sales taxes

There are presently five states (Alaska, Delaware, Montana, New Hampshire, and Oregon) without a state-wide sales tax law (some localities may have sales taxes). In some states, a nonprofit organization is exempt from sales tax as a purchaser of goods used in ministry. It is generally necessary to obtain recognition of sales tax exemption from the state revenue department. Some states will accept a federal tax exemption as sufficient for a state sales tax exemption.

Even if an organization is exempt from paying sales tax, purchases used for the private benefit of the organization's members or employees are not eligible for exemption.

When a nonprofit organization sells goods to others, a sales tax may or may not be applicable. There are some indications that states may begin a stricter enforcement of laws on the books that allow them to impose sales tax on sales by nonprofit organizations. Occasional dinners and sales of goods at local community events are typically exempt from sales tax.

Sales by a nonprofit within the state where the nonprofit is located are sometimes taxable. Sales to customers located outside of the state, or interstate sales, may not be subject to sales tax. A 2018 Supreme Court decision cleared the way for states to require organizations to collect state sales taxes on out-of-state online purchases. This is a developing area of the law and organizations should review their potential sales tax liabilities.

When a nonprofit organization operates a conference or convention outside of its home state, it is often possible to obtain sales tax exemption for purchases made within the state where the meeting is held. Sales of products at the convention would generally be covered under sales tax laws without an approved exemption.

Political Activity

Churches and other organizations exempt from federal income tax under section 501(c)(3) of the Internal Revenue Code are prohibited from participating or intervening, directly or indirectly, in any political campaign on behalf of or in opposition to any candidate for public office. Even activities that encourage people to vote for or against a particular candidate on the basis of nonpartisan criteria violate the political campaign prohibition law.

To avoid violating the political campaign provisions of the law:

➤ Do not use a rating program to evaluate candidates.

➤ Do not endorse a candidate, or a slate of candidates, directly or indirectly through a sermon, speech, newsletter, or sample ballot.

➤ Do not publish a candidate's statement.

➤ Do not publish the names of candidates who agree to adhere to certain practices.

➤ Do not publish candidate responses to a questionnaire that evidences a bias on certain issues. Classifying particular candidates as too conservative or too liberal is an improper rating system.

Warning

If a church or nonprofit organization (under Section 501(c)(3)) participates in even one political campaign activity (no matter how small the occasion), it can potentially lose its tax-exempt status. The organization must not be involved or participate in the campaign of the individual seeking public office.

➤ Do not publish responses to an unbiased questionnaire focused on a narrow range of issues.

➤ Do not raise funds for a candidate or provide support to a political party.

➤ Do not provide volunteers, mailing lists, publicity, or free use of facilities unless all parties and candidates in the community receive the same services.

➤ Do not pay campaign expenses for a candidate.

➤ Do not publish or distribute printed or oral statements about candidates.

➤ Do not display campaign literature on the organization's premises.

If the IRS finds that an organization has engaged in these activities, the organization could lose its exempt status. Also, the IRS may assess an excise tax on the amount of the funds spent on the activity.

Forums or debates at which all candidates are treated equally may be conducted to educate voters, or a mailing list may be rented to candidates on the same basis as it is made available to others. Organizations may engage in voter registration or get-out-the-vote activities. However, it is wise to avoid defining a target group by political or ideological criteria (e.g., encouraging individuals to vote who are "registered Republicans").

INTEGRITY*Points*

- **The church audit potential.** Very few churches are audited each year. The number of churches audited is low because approval of an appropriate high-level IRS official is required to open a church tax inquiry. This is the protection provided in the tax law in recognition of the legitimate separation of church and state.

  The danger is for churches that conduct their financial operations beyond the bounds of the law believing they will never be audited. Integrity requires compliance with the law even if the IRS never calls.

- **The danger of "excess benefit transactions."** Excess benefit transactions (as defined on pages 29–32) are often overlooked by churches and other charities. The "insider" involved in the transaction can be subjected to a penalty of up to 225%.

  An excess benefit transaction can be as simple as providing a taxable fringe benefit and not reflecting it as taxable income to a senior pastor, executive director, president, CEO, or other insider. It could be as easy as transferring equipment from a nonprofit organization to an insider at less than fair market value and failing to treat the amount as taxable income to the recipient.

- **The challenge of the Form 990.** Most charities other than churches must annually file Form 990.

  The staff of very few charities have the ability to accurately file the Form 990. At a minimum, a charity should have the Form 990 reviewed by their external CPA or attorney. Better yet is to have the Form 990 prepared by an external professional. After the Form 990 is filed with the IRS, it is soon posted (minus Schedule B) on the internet. So, an improperly prepared Form 990 soon becomes available for anyone in the world to see. A poorly prepared Form 990 reflects negatively on the charity.

3 Compensating Employees

In This Chapter

- Reasonable compensation
- Internships
- Housing and the housing allowance
- Deferred compensation

- Maximizing fringe benefits
- Nondiscrimination rules
- Paying employee expenses

The three primary challenges for churches and nonprofits in the area of compensating employees are:

➤ **Determining the appropriate level of compensation.** Compensating employees too little can create issues for employees covered by the Fair Labor Standards Act. On the other hand, compensating employees excessively may jeopardize an organization's tax-exempt status in limited situations. While no absolute limits have been placed on compensation amounts to church and nonprofit leaders, appropriate total compensation should be determined, taking into consideration reliable comparability data, as well as the employee's skills, talents, education, experience, performance, and knowledge.

➤ **Documenting and reporting compensation.** The approval of the compensation, including fringe benefits, of the ministry's top leader should be contemporaneously documented. The taxable portions of compensation and fringe benefits should be reported to the appropriate taxing authorities.

➤ **Maximizing the tax advantages of certain fringe benefits.** Compensation may be maximized by effectively structuring fringe benefits. The tax-free or tax-deferred features of certain fringe benefits can significantly increase an employee's take-home pay without expending additional ministry funds.

Reasonable Compensation

Employees of churches and nonprofit organizations may receive reasonable compensation for their services. Excessive compensation can result in private inurement and may jeopardize the tax-exempt status of the organization. Reasonable compensation is based on what would ordinarily be paid for like services by a like organization under similar circumstances.

The intermediate sanction regulations impose penalties when excessive compensation or benefits are received by certain key employees and other individuals. These penalties may be avoided if the compensation arrangement was approved by an independent body that (1) was composed entirely of individuals unrelated to and not subject to the control of the employee involved in the arrangement, (2) obtained and relied upon appropriate data as to comparability, and (3) adequately documented the basis for its determination.

Compensation of church and nonprofit leaders should be reviewed by the board or other governing body on an annual basis.

Internships

There are many factors to consider when offering an internship. If the individual receives no compensation and is completely treated as a volunteer, there are few regulations that must be followed. However, any compensation will likely result in the individual being treated as an employee and subject to regulations such as minimum wage and overtime requirements as well as various state compliance issues.

The Department of Labor does have a list of criteria in which an intern is receiving the benefit of the internship and the organization is not and therefore a stipend may be paid that does not meet the above discussed requirements. That information is found in *Fact Sheet #71: Internship Programs Under the Fair Labor Standards Act* on the Department of Labor website (dol.gov).

Housing and the Housing Allowance

Housing for nonministers

Housing provided to nonminister employees by a church or nonprofit organization for its convenience, as a condition of employment, and on its premises is:

➤ exempt from income tax and FICA tax withholding by the church, and

➤ excluded from wages reporting by the church and employee

If these criteria are not met, the fair rental value should be reported as compensation on Form W-2 and is subject to withholding and FICA taxation.

Housing for ministers

The 2019 edition of the *Zondervan Minister's Tax & Financial Guide* includes a thorough discussion of the availability of the housing allowance for ministers serving local churches. Ordained, commissioned, or licensed ministers not serving local churches may qualify as "ministers" for federal tax purposes in the situations described below.

➤ **Denominational service.** This category encompasses the administration of religious denominations and their integral agencies, including teaching or administration in parochial schools, colleges, or universities that are under the authority of a church or denomination.

The IRS uses the following criteria to determine if an institution is an integral agency of a church:

☐ Did the church incorporate the institution?

☐ Does the corporate name of the institution suggest a church relationship?

☐ Does the church continuously control, manage, and maintain the institution?

☐ If the institution were to dissolve, would the assets be turned over to the church?

☐ Are the trustees or directors of the institution appointed by, or must they be approved by, the church, and may they be removed by the church?

☐ Are annual reports of finances and general operations required to be made to the church?

☐ Does the church contribute to the support of the institution?

➤ **Assignment by a church.** Services performed by a minister for a parachurch organization based upon a substantive assignment or designation by a church may provide the basis for ministerial tax treatment. The housing allowance should be designated by the employing organization, not the assigning church.

The following characteristics must be present for an effective assignment:

☐ There must be a sufficient relationship between the minister and the assigning church to justify the assignment of the minister.

☐ There must be an adequate relationship between the assigning church and the parachurch organization to which the minister is assigned to justify the assignment.

To substantiate the relationship between the minister and the church, the church must determine "if there is sufficient authority, power, or legitimacy for the church to assign this particular minister." Such matters as being the ordaining church, providing ongoing supervision, having denominational affiliation, contributing significant financial support, or being the long-term "home church" would all appear to support this relationship.

Caution

Often, a denomination lists a minister as being assigned to a parachurch ministry, for example, in an annual directory, and the minister believes he or she has been assigned for tax purposes. But effective assignments are rare because of the substantive relationship and ongoing documentation of the assignment that are needed.

In addressing the relationship between the church and the parachurch organization, the church must answer the question of "why should the church assign a minister to this particular ministry?" Essentially, the assignment of the minister must accomplish the church's ministry purposes.

In considering an assignment, it is important to distinguish between the process of assigning and the documentation of the assignment. The process of assigning may include the church's theology, philosophy, and policy of operation—its way of doing ministry. The documentation of the assignment provides evidence that the church is doing ministry through the particular individual assigned. The following are keys to a proper assignment:

☐ A written policy describing the specific requirements for the relationship of the church both to the minister being assigned and to the parachurch organization to which the minister is assigned. This would include the church's theological and policy goals for the assignment.

☐ A formal review to confirm that the minister and the proposed ministry with a parachurch organization qualify.

☐ A written assignment coupled with guidelines for supervision of and reporting by the minister and the parachurch organization to the church (see page 75 for a sample board resolution).

☐ A periodic (at least annual) formal review of the minister's activities to confirm that the assignment continues to comply with the policy.

➤ **Other service.** If a minister is not engaged in service performed in the exercise of ministry of a local church or an integral agency of a church, or a church does not assign a minister's services, the definition of a qualifying minister becomes much narrower. Tax law and regulations provide little guidance for ministers in this category. However, Tax Court cases and IRS rulings suggest that an individual will qualify for the special tax treatments of a minister only if the individual's services for the employer substantially involve conducting religious worship or performing sacerdotal functions. This definition includes conducting Bible studies and spiritual counseling.

How much time constitutes substantial involvement in conducting worship or administering the sacraments? This is difficult to say. However, in two IRS letter rulings, the IRS determined that 5% of the

Caution

Many ministers are serving organizations other than local churches or integral agencies of churches and do not have an effective assignment by a church. The employer may be a rescue mission, a youth ministry, a Christian radio or TV station, or a missionary-sending organization. Qualifying for ministerial status is often based on the degree to which the individual is performing sacerdotal functions or conducting religious worship.

Sample Housing Allowance Resolutions

Parsonage Owned by or Rented by a Church

Whereas, The Internal Revenue Code permits a minister of the gospel to exclude from gross income "the rental value of a home furnished as part of compensation" or a church-designated allowance paid as a part of compensation to the extent that actual expenses are paid from the allowance to maintain a parsonage owned or rented by the church;

Whereas, Nelson Street Church compensates the senior minister for services in the exercise of ministry; and

Whereas, Nelson Street Church provides the senior minister with the rent-free use of a parsonage owned by (rented by) the church as a portion of the compensation for services rendered to the church in the exercise of ministry;

Resolved, That the compensation of the senior minister is $2,500 per month, of which $600 per month is a designated housing allowance; and

Resolved, That the designation of $600 per month as a housing allowance shall apply until otherwise provided.

Home Owned or Rented by a Minister

Whereas, The Internal Revenue Code permits a minister of the gospel to exclude from gross income a church-designated allowance paid as part of compensation to the extent used for actual expenses in owning or renting a home; and

Whereas, Nelson Street Church compensates the senior minister for services in the exercise of ministry;

Resolved, That the compensation of the senior minister is $3,500 per month, of which $1,250 per month is a designated housing allowance; and

Resolved, That the designation of $1,250 per month as a housing allowance shall apply until otherwise provided.

Evangelists

Whereas, The Internal Revenue Code permits a minister of the gospel to exclude from gross income a church-designated allowance paid as part of compensation to the extent used in owning or renting a permanent home; and

Whereas, Nelson Street Church compensates Rev. John Doe for services in the exercise of ministry as an evangelist;

Resolved, That the honorarium paid to Rev. Doe shall be $1,512, consisting of $312 in travel expenses (with documentation provided to the church), a $500 housing allowance, and a $700 honorarium.

minister's working hours was not sufficient to qualify for tax treatment as a minister.

Based on IRS rulings, it is clear that ministers serving as chaplains in government-owned-and-operated hospitals or in state prisons fall in a special category. They are employees for social security (FICA) purposes but qualify for the housing allowance.

➤ **Individuals not qualifying for ministerial tax treatment.** You do not qualify as a "minister" for federal income tax purposes if you are:

- ☐ a theological student who does not otherwise qualify as a minister

- ☐ an unordained, uncommissioned, or unlicensed individual not performing sacerdotal functions or conducting religious worship

- ☐ an ordained, commissioned, or licensed minister working as an administrator or on the faculty of a nonchurch-related college or seminary

- ☐ an ordained, commissioned, or licensed minister working as an executive of a nonreligious, nonchurch-related organization

- ☐ a civilian chaplain at a Veteran's Administration hospital (the tax treatment of ministers who are chaplains in the armed forces is the same as for other members of the armed forces)

- ☐ an ordained, licensed, or commissioned minister employed by a parachurch organization but do not perform sacerdotal functions or conduct religious worship

➤ **Applying the minister's housing allowance.** Qualified ministers receive preferred treatment for their housing. If a minister has a home provided as part of compensation, the minister pays no income tax on the rental value of the home. If a home is not provided but the minister receives a rental or housing allowance designated in the minister's salary, the minister pays no income tax on the allowance if it is used for housing expenses subject to certain limitations.

Every minister should have a portion of salary designated as a housing allowance. For a minister living in organization-owned housing, the housing allowance may be only a modest amount to cover incidental expenses such as maintenance, furnishings, and utilities. But a properly designated housing allowance may be worth thousands of dollars in tax savings for ministers living in their own homes or rented quarters.

Filing Tip

The designation of a housing allowance for a minister living in church-provided housing is often overlooked. While the largest housing allowance benefits go to ministers with mortgage payments on their own homes, a housing allowance is often also beneficial to a pastor living in church-provided housing.

The excludable housing allowance for ministers, which is part of a total compensation package that is determined to be reasonable pay for services performed, is subject to the lowest of these factors:

☐ **Amount prospectively and officially designated by the employer.** The allowance must be officially designated before payment by the organization. The designation should be evidenced in writing, preferably by resolution of the appropriate governing body, in an employment contract, or, at a minimum, in the church budget and payroll records.

If the only reference to the housing allowance is in the organization's budget, the budget should be formally approved by the top governing body. However, it is highly preferable for the governing board to use a specific resolution to authorize housing allowance designations.

☐ **Amount used from current ministerial income to provide the home.** Only actual housing-related expenses can be excluded from income.

☐ **The fair rental value of the home including utilities and furnishings.** The IRS has not provided any guidance to assist ministers in determining the fair rental value of the home. The value should be based on comparable rental values of other similar residences in the immediate community, comparably furnished.

Deferred Compensation

In addition to 403(b) and 401(k) plans, churches and nonprofit organizations have available all the qualified retirement plan options that are available to any for-profit. These must be operated according to their terms and are generally subject to the same nondiscrimination and coverage rules as plans in for-profit organizations.

Churches and nonprofit organizations may defer the compensation of executives, but the amount of the deferral is limited in nonprofit organizations by Internal Revenue Code Section 457. For the year 2018, the annual limitation was $18,500. Salary reduction contributions to a 403(b) or 401(k) plan, however, "count" against the annual limitation. For example, if an employee contributed $18,500 to a 403(b) plan, it would use up the entire $18,500 limitation.

Under Section 457(f) there is the ability to set aside deferred compensation without limitation if it is not "vested." The requirement is that it be subject to "significant risk of forfeiture." This is often established by requiring future years of service for it to vest. When vested, it becomes taxable income at that date.

Idea

Occasionally, churches and nonprofit organizations will set up a reserve to pay bonuses to employees at a later date. Such a reserve cannot be "designated" or "subject to an understanding" that it will be used for a specific employee. It avoids current taxation because the organization has not allocated it to specific employees nor paid it over.

Setting up the deferred compensation as a 457(f) arrangement requires a written agreement that meets the requirements. The agreement between the employee and employer to defer the income must be made before it is earned. Once it has been earned, it is too late for the employee to request its deferral.

Amounts that are deferred are often put into a "Rabbi Trust." A Rabbi Trust is established with an independent trustee, who invests the amounts that have been deferred. The assets may still be used to pay creditors of the organization (in a bankruptcy, for instance), but cannot be reclaimed by the corporation for its operations. Essentially, a Rabbi Trust protects the executive from the board's changing its mind and using the money somewhere else.

403(b) plans

Employees of churches and other nonprofit organizations may have a Section 403(b) salary reduction arrangement based on a written plan. These plans are also called tax-sheltered annuities (TSAs).

Both nonelective and elective employer contributions for a minister to a TSA are excludable for income and social security tax (SECA) purposes. Elective contributions for nonministers are subject to FICA. Some individuals choose to contribute additional amounts to their plans utilizing after-tax or "Roth" contributions. This is permissible but must be included in the organization's plan document.

See the 2019 edition of the *Zondervan Minister's Tax & Financial Guide* for additional information on TSA contribution limitations.

Typically, there is very little cost to establish and maintain a 403(b) plan. It is an important planning option to defer taxes and encourage individuals in a ministry to save for retirement. Employer contributions are not required and could be evaluated annually if the plan is written accordingly. This would allow flexibility from a budget perspective while not eliminating the benefit entirely.

401(k) plans

A church or nonprofit organization may offer a 401(k) plan to its employees. Under a 401(k) plan, an employee can elect to have the employer make tax-deferred contributions to the plan (up to $18,500 for 2018), of amounts that had been withheld from employee pay.

Maximizing Fringe Benefits

Employer-provided cell phones

As long as an employer has provided a cell phone to an employee primarily for noncompensatory business reasons, it is treated as a tax-free fringe benefit. Additionally, an employee's personal use will be treated as a *de minimis* fringe benefit. The net effect is that employer-provided cell phones are not taxable income to employees as long as the phone is provided primarily for noncompensatory purposes.

While the IRS certainly did not identify all business purposes, if cell phones are provided to promote the morale or goodwill of an employee, this is not a sufficient business purpose and the value would be treated as taxable compensation.

To assist in demonstrating the business purpose for employer-provided cell phones, employers may want to consider adding the business reason as part of an employee's job description, in a written cell phone policy, or as part of the employment handbook. Employers should generally avoid considering a cell phone as some type of employment perk or as recruitment incentive, as this may give the appearance of compensatory purposes.

Tip

Employers should avoid considering a cell phone as some type of employment perk.

Employers should also consider any security risks that may be caused with the loss of a mobile device such as a cell phone. Some phone systems offer additional location and remote data erasing features that can mitigate the risks associated with losing one of these devices. The accidental release of sensitive ministry information could pose serious risks to an organization or its employees.

Employer reimbursement for employee-owned cell phones

The IRS has issued separate internal guidance to its field staff to address situations where employers provide a reimbursement for employee-owned cell phones. In this guidance, the IRS indicates that a similar analysis should be used for reimbursements as if the employer had actually provided a cell phone to an employee. Thus, where employers have substantial business reasons other than providing compensation to employees, then it is possible that this does not result in taxable income to the employee.

In order to be eligible for the nontaxable treatment, the reimbursement must:

➤ be for business reasons other than providing compensation to employees

➤ not exceed actual expenses in maintaining the cell phone, and

➤ not substitute a portion of an employee's wages

Examples of substantial noncompensatory business reasons for requiring employees to maintain personal cell phones and reimbursing them for their use include, but are not limited to:

➤ employer needing to contact the employee at all times for work-related emergencies

➤ employer requiring that the employee be available at times outside of an employee's normal work schedule

It is not considered reasonable to reimburse an employee for international or satellite phone usage if all the employer's necessary contacts are in the local geographic area where the employee works or where reimbursements deviate significantly from normal use in the employer's work.

Employer-owned laptops or reimbursements

With the passage of tax reform, the treatment of employer-owned laptops or reimbursements now follow similar rules for cell phones as discussed above. As long as an employer has provided computer equipment (or reimbursements for the equipment) primarily for noncompensatory business reasons, it is treated as a tax-free fringe benefit.

Personal use of employer-provided vehicles

Vehicles provided by organizations to employees for business use are sometimes also used for personal purposes. The IRS (see IRS Publication 535) treats most types of personal use of an employer-provided vehicle as a noncash fringe benefit and generally requires the fair market value of such use be included in the employee's gross income (to the extent that the value is not reimbursed to the employer).

If the employee reimburses the employer for the full dollar value of the personal use, it will cost the employee more than if the employer includes the personal use value in the income of the employee.

> **Example:** The personal use value of an automobile provided to a lay employee is determined to be $100; if fully reimbursed, the employee would pay $100 to the employer. If there is no reimbursement, the employer includes the $100 in the employee's income, and the employee will be subject to payroll taxes on $100 of income. Assuming a federal income tax rate of 28% and a FICA rate of 7.65%, the total would be $35.65 compared with the $100 cash out-of-pocket chargeback.

➤ **Valuation of personal vehicle use.** There are three special valuation rules, in addition to a set of general valuation principles, which may be used under specific circumstances for valuing the personal use of an employer-provided vehicle. This value must be included in the employee's compensation if it is not reimbursed by the employee.

Under the general valuation rule, the value is based on what the cost would be to a person leasing from a third party the same or comparable vehicle on the same or comparable terms in the same geographic area. The special valuation rules, which are used by most employers, are:

☐ **Cents-per-mile valuation rule.** Generally, this rule may be used if the employer reasonably expects that the vehicle will be regularly used in the employer's trade or business, and if the vehicle is driven at least 10,000 miles a year and is primarily used by employees. This valuation rule is available only if the fair market value of the vehicle, as of the date the vehicle was first made available for personal use by employees, does not exceed a specified value set by the IRS. For 2018, this value is $15,600.

The value of the personal use of the vehicle is computed by multiplying the number of miles driven for personal purposes by the current IRS standard mileage rate (54.5 cents per mile for 2018). For this valuation rule, personal use is "any use of the vehicle other than use in your trade or business."

Idea

Start with a policy that requires a contemporaneous log, with the date and personal miles recorded for all ministry vehicles. The log is the basis for determining the personal vs. business use of the vehicle. Then the employer chooses a valuation rule to determine the value of the personal use for Form W-2 reporting. Simply paying for the gas during personal use does not satisfy these rules.

☐ **Commuting valuation rule.** This rule may be used to determine the value of personal use only where the following conditions are met:

- The vehicle is owned or leased by the employer and is provided to one or more employees for use in connection with the employer's trade or business and is used as such.

- The employer requires the employee to commute to and/or from work in the vehicle for bona fide noncompensatory business reasons. One example of a bona fide noncompensatory business reason is the availability of the vehicle to an employee who is on-call and must have access to the vehicle when at home.

- The employer has a written policy that prohibits employees from using the vehicle for personal purposes other than for commuting or *de minimis* personal use such as a stop for a personal errand on the way home from work.

- The employee required to use the vehicle for commuting is not a "control" employee of the employer. For churches and nonprofit organizations, a control employee for 2018 will generally be any board-appointed, confirmed, or elected officer whose pay is $110,000 or more, a director, or an employee whose pay is $220,000 or more.

The personal use of an employer-provided vehicle that meets the above conditions is valued at $1.50 per one-way commute, or $3.00 per day.

☐ **Annual lease valuation rule.** Under the annual lease valuation rule, the fair market value of a vehicle is determined by referring to an annual lease value table published by the IRS (see below). The annual lease value corresponding to this fair market value, multiplied by the personal use percentage, is the amount to be added to the employee's gross income. If the organization provides the fuel, 5.5 cents per mile must be added to the annual lease value. Amounts reimbursed by the employee are offset.

The fair market value of a vehicle owned by an employer is generally the employer's cost of purchasing the vehicle (including taxes and fees). The fair market value of a vehicle leased by an employer is generally either the manufacturer's suggested retail price less 8%, the manufacturer's invoice plus 4%, or the retail value as reported in a nationally recognized publication that regularly reports automobile retail values.

Again, if the three special valuation rules described above do not apply, the value of the personal use must be determined by using a set of general valuation principles. Under these principles, the value must be generally equal to the amount that the employee would have to pay in a normal business transaction to obtain the same or a comparable vehicle in the geographic area in which that vehicle is available for use.

Lease Value Table

Fair Market Value of Car			Annual Lease Value	Fair Market Value of Car			Annual Lease Value
$0	–	$999	$600	22,000	–	22,999	6,100
1,000	–	1,999	850	23,000	–	23,999	6,350
2,000	–	2,999	1,100	24,000	–	24,999	6,600
3,000	–	3,999	1,350	25,000	–	25,999	6,850
4,000	–	4,999	1,600	26,000	–	27,999	7,250
5,000	–	5,999	1,850	28,000	–	29,999	7,750
6,000	–	6,999	2,100	30,000	–	31,999	8,250
7,000	–	7,999	2,350	32,000	–	33,999	8,750
8,000	–	8,999	2,600	34,000	–	35,999	9,250
9,000	–	9,999	2,850	36,000	–	37,999	9,750
10,000	–	10,999	3,100	38,000	–	39,999	10,250
11,000	–	11,999	3,350	40,000	–	41,999	10,750
12,000	–	12,999	3,600	42,000	–	43,999	11,250
13,000	–	13,999	3,850	44,000	–	45,999	11,750
14,000	–	14,999	4,100	46,000	–	47,999	12,250
15,000	–	15,999	4,350	48,000	–	49,999	12,750
16,000	–	16,999	4,600	50,000	–	51,999	13,250
17,000	–	17,999	4,850	52,000	–	53,999	13,750
18,000	–	18,999	5,100	54,000	–	55,999	14,250
19,000	–	19,999	5,350	56,000	–	57,999	14,750
20,000	–	20,999	5,600	58,000	–	59,999	15,250
21,000	–	21,999	5,850				

Note: The annual lease value (calculated using the above table) is based on four-year terms. In other words, employers should refigure the annual lease value every four years that the vehicle is in service, based on the vehicle's fair market value at the beginning of each four-year cycle.

Employer-provided dependent care assistance plan

A church or nonprofit organization can provide employees with child care or disabled dependent care services to allow employees to work. The amount excludable from tax is limited to the smallest of the employee's earned income, the spouse's earned income, or $5,000 ($2,500 if married filing separately). The dependent care assistance must be provided under a separate written plan that does not favor highly compensated employees and that meets other qualifications.

Dependent care assistance payments are excluded from income if the payments cover expenses that would be deductible by the employee as child and dependent care expenses on Form 2441 if the expenses were not reimbursed. It may be necessary to file Form 2441, even though the dependent care assistance payments are excluded from income, to document the appropriateness of the payments.

Medical, Dental, and Vision Insurance

Insurance may be provided or made available for purchase by the employees for medical, dental, and vision coverage. Premiums paid by the employer for the employee, including dependents, are excluded from income for income tax purposes as well as Social Security and Medicare. A group plan should be established even if the employer will pay little or none of the premium to offer pre-tax benefits to the employees for amounts they are responsible to pay. Keep in mind it is no longer permissible to pay for an individual health care plan or reimburse employees for premiums they pay for such a policy. All benefits must be handled through a group plan. If an organization chooses to pay a stipend or allowance to cover any health-related costs, it is treated as additional compensation and included as taxable income on the employee's W-2 form.

Affordable Care Act

This Act continues to be controversial and changes are possible, so organizations are encouraged to monitor legislation closely to determine the applicability of any potential changes. Below are some of the key aspects of this Act to consider:

➤ **Individual mandate.** All U.S. citizens and legal residents who do not maintain "minimum essential" health insurance coverage are required to pay an annual penalty equaling the greater of (1) $695 per person ($347.50 per child under 18), up to a maximum of $2,085 per family, or (2) 2.5% of household income over the threshold amount of income required for income tax return filing, up to a maximum of the national premium for a Bronze plan. This mandate was repealed by Congress in tax reform beginning in 2019, but several states have begun incorporating a state-level mandate in the absence of the federal tax law requirement.

➤ **Employer mandate.** Large employers with 50 or more full-time equivalent employees working in the U.S., are subject to a penalty for failure to offer affordable, qualifying health insurance to employees if they (1) offer no health insurance coverage at all,

(2) offer coverage to fewer than 95% of full-time employees and their dependents, (3) offer coverage that is unaffordable, or (4) offer coverage that does not measure up to the standards of "minimum essential coverage." The penalty is based on the number of employees or for those offering coverage to at least 95% of full-time employees it is based on any employee who was not offered coverage and who obtained a premium tax credit from a government-run exchange.

To be considered "affordable," the employee's share of the insurance premium must be no more than 9.56% (for 2018) of that employee's annual household income. There are safe harbors available if the employee's household income is unknown.

➤ **Employer reporting.** Organizations are required to report the total costs of coverage paid by the employer and the employee on Form W-2 in Box 12 using code DD. In addition, forms 1094-B and 1095-B or 1094-C and 1095-C may be required.

More information on the calculations and details of this Act is available at www.irs.gov/affordable-care-act.

Disability insurance

Disability insurance may be provided for church and nonprofit organization employees. Coverage is usually limited to 60% to 75% of the annual salary of each individual. Social security and pension benefits are often offset against disability insurance benefits. Disability insurance premiums may be paid through a flexible benefit plan (FSA) to obtain income tax and social security tax (FICA) savings.

If the organization pays the disability insurance premiums, the premiums are excluded from the employee's income. If the organization pays the premiums (and the employee is the beneficiary) as part of the compensation package, any disability policy proceeds are fully taxable to the employee. This is based on who paid the premiums for the policy covering the year when the disability started.

Idea

The probability of disability greatly exceeds the probability of death during an individual's working years. Individual or group policies may be purchased. These plans may include a probationary period, which excludes preexisting sickness from immediate coverage, and an elimination period, which specifies the time after the start of a disability when benefits are not payable.

If the premiums are shared between the employer and the employee, then the benefits are taxable in the same proportion as the payment of the premiums.

Compensation-related loans

Some churches and nonprofit organizations make loans to employees. The loans are often restricted to the purchase of land or a residence or the construction of a residence. Before a loan is made, the organization should determine if the transaction is legal under state law. Such loans are prohibited in many states.

If an organization receives interest of $600 or more in a year relating to a loan secured by real estate, a Form 1098 must be provided to the payer (see page 95). For the interest to be deductible as an itemized deduction, an employee loan must be secured by the residence and properly recorded.

If an organization makes loans to employees at below-market rates, the organization may be required to report additional compensation to the employee. If the loan is below $10,000, there is no additional compensation to the borrower. For loans over $10,000, additional compensation is calculated equal to the foregone interest that would have been charged if the loan had been made at a market rate of interest. The market rate of interest is the "applicable federal rate" for loans of similar duration. The IRS publishes these rates monthly. The additional compensation must be reported on Form W-2, Box 1.

There are certain exceptions to the general rules on below-market loans. These exceptions relate to loans secured by a mortgage and employee relocation loans.

Social security tax reimbursement

Churches and nonprofit organizations often reimburse ministers for a portion or all of their self-employment tax (SECA) liability. Reimbursement also may be made to lay employees for all or a portion of the FICA tax that has been withheld from their pay. Any social security reimbursement must be reported as taxable income for both income and social security tax purposes. The FICA reimbursement to a lay employee is subject to income tax and FICA withholding.

Because of the deductibility of the self-employment tax in both the income tax and self-employment tax computations, a full reimbursement is effectively less than the gross 15.3% rate:

Marginal Tax Rate	Effective SECA Rate
0%	14.13%
12	13.28
22	12.58
24	12.43

For missionaries who are not eligible for the income tax deduction of one-half of the self-employment tax due to the foreign earned-income exclusion, the full reimbursement rate is effectively 14.13%.

Sabbaticals

Some churches and nonprofit organizations choose to provide their leaders a sabbatical either to focus on a project, such as writing a book, or as a respite for a certain number of years of service. This usually takes the form of an extended paid leave, which is taxable for income and social security tax purposes. A housing allowance would still be appropriate if they otherwise qualify. No other benefits would be impacted.

Property transfers

➤ **Unrestricted.** If an employer transfers property (for example, a car, residence, equipment, or other property) to an employee at no charge, this constitutes taxable income to the employee. The amount of income is generally the fair market value of the property transferred.

➤ **Restricted.** To recognize and reward good work, some churches or nonprofits transfer property to an employee subject to certain restrictions. The ultimate transfer may occur only if the employee lives up to the terms of the agreement. Once the terms are met, the property is transferred free and clear. Property that is subject to substantial risk of forfeiture and is nontransferable is substantially not vested. No tax liability will occur until title to the property is vested with the employee. This is a deferral of tax.

When restricted property becomes substantially vested, the employee must report the transfer as taxable income. The amount reported must be equal to the excess of the fair market value of the property at the time it becomes substantially vested, over the amount the employee pays for the property.

Example: A church transfers a house to the pastor subject to the completion of 20 years of service for the church. The pastor does not report any taxable income from the transfer until the 20th year. This situation will generally require advance tax planning since the pastor could have a substantial tax liability in the year of the transfer.

➤ **Property purchased from employer.** If the employer allows an employee to buy property at a price below its fair market value, the employer must include in income as extra wages the difference between the property's fair market value and the amount paid and liabilities assumed by the employee.

Moving expenses

Prior to the 2018 tax year, moving expenses that were paid or reimbursed by an employer to their employees could be treated as tax-free if certain requirements were met. If the expenses were not paid or reimbursed by the employer, they could be deductible by the employee.

After tax reform, these tax advantages for moving expenses are no longer available beginning in the 2018 tax year (and expiring in 2025 unless made permanent by Congress). This represents a major change for many church and ministry employers that previously could leverage this tax benefit when relocating a new employee.

Caution

A new provision in tax reform now makes employer-paid moving expenses taxable income to employees. These same expenses are also no longer deductible by employees. This represents a significant change in the law for church and ministry employers and their employees.

Gifts

The value of a turkey, ham, or other nominally valued item distributed to an employee on holidays need not be reported as income. However, a distribution of cash, a gift certificate, or a similar item of value readily convertible to cash must be included in the employee's income.

Gifts to certain nonemployees up to $25 per year may be tax-free. Gifts of an advertising nature that cost $4 or less given for use on the organization's premises are excluded from the $25 annual limit.

Workers' Compensation

Workers' compensation insurance coverage compensates workers for losses caused by work-related injuries. It also limits the potential liability of the organization for injury to the employee related to his or her job.

Workers' compensation benefits are generally required by law in all states to be provided by the employer. This may be done by insurance or many states allow for self-funded or group-funded plans within specific guidelines. A few states exempt churches from workers' compensation coverage, and several states exempt all nonprofit employers. Most states also consider ministers to be employees regardless of the income tax filing method used by the minister, and therefore they must be covered under the workers' compensation policy. Contact your state department of labor to find out how your state applies workers' compensation rules to churches and nonprofits.

Workers' compensation premiums are based on the payroll of the organization with a minimum premium charge to issue the policy. An audit is done later to determine the actual charge for the policy.

Most workers' compensation insurance is purchased through private insurance carriers. A few states provide the coverage and charge the covered organizations.

Key Issue

Even if a church or nonprofit organization is exempt from workers' compensation, the voluntary purchase of the coverage or the securing of additional general liability coverage may be prudent. This is because other types of insurance typically exclude work-related accidents: health, accident, disability, auto, and general liability insurance policies are some examples.

Overtime and minimum pay

The Fair Labor Standards Act (FLSA) provides protection for employees engaged in interstate commerce concerning minimum wages, equal pay, overtime pay, recordkeeping, and child labor (some states even have more restrictive versions of the FLSA). Any employee who makes less than $455 per week, full-time or part-time, is generally entitled to overtime pay. Overtime pay is required regardless of whether an employee is paid on an hourly or salary basis. For employees to be exempt from the overtime and minimum wage requirements, they must meet the $455 per week threshold and be paid on a salary basis. In other words, employees paid on an hourly basis do not meet the exemption requirements.

The employees of nonprofit organizations involved in commerce or in the production of goods for commerce are generally considered covered by the provisions of the FLSA. Commerce is defined by the FLSA as "trade, commerce, transportation, transmission, or communication among several states or between any state and any place outside thereof." Conversely, nonprofits that are not engaged in commerce or fall below the $500,000 annual gross sales volume requirement are generally exempt from the Act.

Are ministers exempt from the Fair Labor Standards Act? Generally, yes under the ministerial exception. This common law doctrine received prominent exposure by the U.S. Supreme Court in its unanimous decision in the *Hosanna Tabor* case. One should note that this doctrine likely applies more broadly than the tax determination of who qualifies as a minister. Organizations should consult with their legal counsel in analyzing this potential exemption.

The FLSA applies to schools regardless of whether they are nonprofit entities operated by religious organizations. However, there are special rules for teachers. Church-operated day care centers and elementary and secondary schools are generally considered subject to the FLSA.

> **Warning**
>
> There is significant confusion over "compensatory time," or giving time off in lieu of paying overtime. If an employee is covered under the Fair Labor Standards Act, providing compensatory time is not an option. Payment for the overtime must be made in cash.

Many local churches and small nonprofits do not meet the $500,000 threshold (see above). However, individual employees are generally covered under the FLSA if they send or receive just a few emails each year across state lines. Therefore, most churches and nonprofits should follow the FLSA regulations as a precaution against possible action by the Department of Labor. Ministers are generally exempt under the professional provisions of this exemption.

The current FLSA minimum wage is $7.25 per hour. (Caution: Several states have established minimum wages that exceed the federal rate.) Teenagers may be paid a training wage of any amount above $4.25 per hour for the first 90 days of employment. Minors under age 14 generally cannot be hired.

Any employee paid over $455 per week must meet the duties test in order to be classified as an exempt employee. The duties tests are divided into employee type categories. These categories are executive, administrative, and professional employees. For specific information on these exemptions, go to www.dol.gov/whd/overtime/fs17a_overview.pdf.

Please note, this topic has received significant attention lately. A change in the threshold is possible. Organizations should monitor the latest legislation related to this matter to assure full compliance with the law.

Nondiscrimination Rules

To qualify for exclusion from income, many fringe benefits must be nondiscriminatory. This is particularly true for many types of benefits for certain key employees. Failure to comply with the nondiscrimination rules does not disqualify a fringe benefit plan entirely. The benefit is simply fully taxable for the highly compensated or key employees.

The nondiscrimination rules apply to the following types of fringe benefit plans: qualified tuition and fee discounts, eating facilities on or near the employer's premises, educational assistance benefits, dependent care assistance plans, tax-sheltered annuities (TSAs), 401(k) plans, and other deferred compensation plans, group-term life insurance benefits, self-insured medical plans, health savings accounts (including health reimbursement arrangements), and cafeteria plans (including a flexible spending account dependent care plan and a health care flexible spending account).

Fringe benefit plans that limit benefits only to officers or highly compensated employees are clearly discriminatory. An officer is an employee who is appointed, confirmed, or elected by the board of the employer. A highly compensated employee for 2019 is someone who was paid more than $125,000, or if the employer elects, was in the top 20% of paid employees for compensation for the previous year.

Paying Employee Expenses

An accountable plan is a reimbursement or expense allowance arrangement that requires (1) a business purpose for the expenses, (2) employees to substantiate the expenses, and (3) the return of any excess reimbursements. This documented plan is required for reimbursement of expenses to be excluded from taxable income for employees.

The substantiation of expenses and return of excess reimbursements must be handled within a reasonable time. The following methods meet the "reasonable time" definition:

➤ The fixed date method applies if:

☐ an advance is made within 30 days of when an expense is paid or incurred

☐ an expense is substantiated to the employer within 60 days after the expense is paid or incurred, and

☐ any excess amount is returned to the employer within 120 days after the expense is paid or incurred

➤ The periodic statement method applies if:

☐ the employer provides employees with a periodic statement that sets forth the amount paid under the arrangement in excess of substantiated expense

☐ statements are provided at least quarterly, and

☐ the employer requests that the employee provide substantiation for any additional expenses that have not yet been substantiated and/or return any amounts remaining unsubstantiated within 120 days of the statement

If employees substantiate expenses and return any unused excess payments to the church or nonprofit organization on a timely basis, payments to the employee for business expenses have no impact on tax reporting. They are not included on Form W-2 for the employee.

The timing of documenting expenses for reimbursement is of utmost importance. Under the fixed date method (see above), the IRS provides a safe harbor of 60 days after the expense is paid or incurred. In other words, the IRS may contest a reimbursement, based on timeliness of submitting the documentation, if the documentation is not provided to the employer. Does this mean that the IRS will disallow expenses reimbursed on the 61st day? Not necessarily. It simply means 60 days is a safe harbor as a "reasonable time."

> **Example:** A church approves $50,000 of compensation for the pastor and tells her to let the church know at the end of the year how much she has spent on business expenses, and they will show the net amount on Form W-2. Is this valid? No. The salary must be established separately from expense reimbursements. Further, even if an accountable expense reimbursement plan is used, the annual submission of expense documentation would fail the timeliness test for expenses incurred in all but the last portion of the year.

Per diem allowance

Church and nonprofit employers that help their employees cover business travel expenses have two basic options: (1) The employer can pay employees the precise amount of their expenses, or (2) the employer can opt for convenience and pay a set "per diem" allowance for each day of business travel.

The standard per diem rates for travel within the continental United States (CONUS) are $94 for lodging and $55 for meals and entertainment (based on October 1, 2018, to September 30, 2019). Federal per diem rates for travel outside CONUS, including Alaska, Hawaii, Puerto Rico, the northern Mariana Islands, U.S. possessions, and all other foreign localities, are published by the U.S. Department of State.

> **Tip**
>
> With a per diem, the organization doesn't need receipts for each meal; the documents showing the organization paid the per diem are proof of expense, if it is at the federal rate.

Given the efficiency and administrative advantages of the per diem approach, some churches and nonprofits choose to make per diem payments to volunteers within the IRS limits based on location. However, unlike in the case of employees, volunteers must include in income any part of per diem allowances that exceed deductible travel expenses.

Sample Accountable Expense Reimbursement Plan

Whereas, Income tax regulations provide that an arrangement between an employee and employer must meet the requirements of business connection, substantiation, and return of excess payments in order to be considered a reimbursement;

Whereas, Plans that meet the three requirements listed above are considered to be accountable plans, and the reimbursed expenses are generally excludable from an employee's gross compensation;

Whereas, Plans that do not meet all the requirements listed above are considered nonaccountable plans, and payments made under such plans are includable in gross employee compensation; and

Whereas, First Church desires to establish an accountable expense reimbursement policy in compliance with the income tax regulations;

Resolved, That First Church establishes an expense reimbursement policy effective _____, 20___, whereby employees serving the church may receive advances for, or reimbursement of, expenses if:

A. There is a stated business purpose of the expense related to the ministry of the church, and the expenses would qualify for deductions for federal income tax purposes if the expenses were not reimbursed

B. The employee provides adequate substantiation to the church for all expenses, and

C. The employee returns all excess reimbursements within a reasonable time

Resolved, That the following methods will meet the "reasonable time" definition:

A. An advance is made within 30 days of when an expense is paid or incurred

B. An expense is substantiated to the church within 60 days after the expense is paid or incurred

C. An excess amount is returned to the church within 120 days after the expense is paid or incurred

Resolved, That substantiation of business expenses will include business purpose, business relationship (including names of persons present), cost (itemized accounting), time, and place of any individual non-lodging expense of $75 or more and for all lodging expenses. Auto mileage reimbursed must be substantiated by a daily mileage log separating business and personal miles. The church will retain the documentation related to the expenses substantiated.

Note: The above resolution includes the basic guidelines for an accountable expense reimbursement plan. If the employer desires to place a dollar limit on reimbursements to be made under the plan employee-by-employee, a separate resolution may be adopted for this purpose.

Reimbursing Medical Expenses

Medical expenses that are not eligible for reimbursement under a health insurance plan are deductible on Schedule A as itemized deductions. However, many employees may take a standard deduction and not itemize and those that do complete the Schedule A generally have their medical expenses subject to a limitation of only amounts over 7.5% of adjusted gross income for 2018 and 10% for 2019 and future years. There are multiple options employers may use to assist in the reimbursement of medical expenses including:

➤ **Health Savings Account (HSA).** These are individual portable, tax-free, interest-bearing accounts through which individuals with high-deductible health insurance can save for medical expenses. The purpose of an HSA is to pay what basic coverage would ordinarily pay. Within limits, HSA contributions made by employers are excludable from income tax and social security wages or contributions may be funded through a salary reduction agreement. The 2018 annual deductible contribution limits to an HSA are $3,450 for an individual and $6,900 for a family. The limits apply to combined employer and employee contributions. Earnings on amounts in an HSA are not currently taxable, and HSA distributions used to pay for medical expenses are not taxable. Distributions from HSAs which are not used for qualified medical expenses are subject to an additional tax of 20 percent on the amount includible in gross income.

➤ **Flexible Spending Account (FSA).** An FSA may be established with or without any other cafeteria plan options. It allows an employee to pre-fund medical and dental expenses in pre-tax dollars using a salary reduction election.

If an FSA only covers medical expenses, it is commonly referred to as a health care FSA. These plans cannot reimburse for over-the-counter drugs except for insulin. Salary reductions for FSAs were limited to $2,650 in 2018. The 2019 limit is projected to be $2,700.

Some employers provide a grace period for an FSA. If so, the grace period begins the day following the end of the plan year and lasts for two and a half months. It is designed to allow employees the opportunity to take full advantage of their non-taxable contributions when expenses fall short of what was originally projected. If a grace period is offered, a rollover (see "Tip" above) of $500 from one plan year to the next may not be provided and vice versa.

Tip

Up to $500 in unused funds can roll over into the following plan year. While the employer can elect to allow less than $500 to be rolled over, the same rollover limit must apply to all plan participants.

➤ **Health Reimbursement Arrangement (HRA).** Under an HRA (Section 105), an employer may reimburse medical expenses up to a maximum dollar amount for the coverage period. HRAs do not provide a salary reduction election.

Compensation Steps of Excellence

- **Prepare a compensation philosophy statement** – This should take into account the present situation as well as long-term goals and objectives. Broad categories may include (1) attraction, (2) retention, and (3) motivation and reward.

- **Be certain that pastoral or executive compensation is determined by the board** or a board-appointed committee, independently of the individual.

- **Board notification of family members receiving compensation.** For appropriate transparency with the board, the board should be notified at least annually of all family member compensation.

- **Determine comparable compensation** – Consider what other organizations pay for similar roles.

- **Consider all compensation, not just wages** – Fringe benefits should be considered as part of compensation and may include (1) taxable, (2) non-taxable, and (3) tax deferred. Compensation may also include forgiveness of debt, bonuses, deferred compensation arrangements, or other non-wage related amounts.

- **Adopt an accountable reimbursement plan.**

- **Maximize the minister's housing exclusion, when appropriate.**

- **Ensure compensation is fair and reasonable.**

- **Compensation should be reviewed periodically** to determine if there are needed changes to the structure or benefits based on changes in the organization or from outside influences.

INTEGRITY*Points*

- **Qualifying for the housing allowance.** Determining which individuals qualify for ministerial status (and, therefore, qualify for a housing allowance designation) can be a challenging issue for the employing church or other nonprofit organization—it's always the employer's decision, not the employee's. It's fairly simple to make this determination for a local church and for religious denominations.

  When we move beyond local churches and denominations, ministerial status is more murky. It requires an understanding of assignment of ministers and perhaps what constitutes performing significant sacerdotal functions. Then there are the processes for ordaining, licensing, or commissioning of ministers by churches and the question of whether these practices are valid. All in all, a high degree of integrity must be applied to this process.

- **Fringe benefits, stewardship, and compliance.** The decision of which fringe benefits to offer staff is often indicative of a ministry's stewardship. It isn't just how much an employee is paid, it's also *how* compensation is paid. Are tax-free and tax-deferred opportunities maximized? And then there is the proper reporting of taxable fringe benefits which reflects a ministry's willingness to comply with tax law. For example, providing a vehicle to a key employee is an excellent fringe benefit from the employee's compensation view, but there are compliance issues to be followed with respect to personal miles.

- **Fair Labor Standards Act (FLSA) issues.** The overtime and minimum wage rules included in the FLSA are often overlooked and abused by churches and other charities. Many churches and most other ministries are subject to the FLSA. With the Department of Labor's generous interpretation of "interstate commerce," just a few emails sent across state lines each year by an employee will often qualify that employee for FLSA coverage even if the organization is not covered. Another common FLSA abuse is "paying" overtime by giving employees "compensatory" time off. While Congress periodically considers compensatory time off with respect to the FLSA, it has never passed.

4 Employer Reporting

In This Chapter

- Classification of workers
- Reporting compensation
- Payroll tax withholding

- Depositing withheld payroll taxes
- Filing quarterly payroll tax forms
- Filing annual payroll tax forms

Withholding and reporting requirements that employers must comply with are complicated. The special tax treatment of qualified ministers simply adds another level of complexity.

Churches and nonprofit organizations are generally required to withhold federal (and state and local, as applicable) income taxes and social security taxes and to pay employer social security tax on all wages paid to all full-time or part-time employees (except qualified ministers).

Classification of Workers

Whether an individual is classified as an employee or independent contractor has far-reaching consequences. This decision determines an organization's responsibility under the Federal Insurance Contributions Act (FICA), income tax withholding responsibilities, potential coverage under the Fair Labor Standards Act (FLSA) (see pages 64–65), and coverage under an employer's benefit plans. Misclassification can lead to significant penalties.

Questions frequently arise about the classification of certain nonprofit workers. Seasonal workers and those working less than full-time such as secretaries, custodians, and musicians require special attention for classification purposes. If a worker receives pay at an hourly rate, it will be difficult to justify independent contractor status. This conclusion holds true even if the workers are part-time.

Since 1935, the IRS has relied on certain common law rules (pages 73–74) to determine whether workers are employees or independent contractors. Pressure continues to build on Congress and the IRS to provide clearer guidance on who can be an independent contractor and when the classification applies, especially in light of employer responsibilities under the Affordable Care Act.

Employees

If a worker is a nonministerial employee, the employer must withhold federal income tax (and state income tax, if applicable) and Federal Insurance Contributions Act (FICA) taxes, match the employee's share of FICA taxes, and unless exempted, pay unemployment taxes on the employee's wages. In addition, the employer may incur obligations for employee benefit plans such as vacation, sick pay, health insurance, and retirement plan contributions.

"Control" is the primary factor in determining whether an individual is an employee or an independent contractor. Among other criteria, employees comply with instructions, have a continuous relationship, perform work personally, work full-time or part-time, are subject to dismissal, can quit without incurring liability, are often reimbursed for expenses, and must submit reports.

Key Issue

The employee vs. independent contractor decision is one of the most fundamental issues facing an employer making payments to workers. If a worker is truly an employee but is treated as an independent contractor, this can result in not withholding the appropriate income and FICA-type social security tax amounts.

Independent contractors

If the worker is classified as an independent contractor, quarterly estimated income taxes and social security taxes under the Self-Employment Contributions Act (SECA) are paid by the worker. There is no unemployment tax liability or income or social security tax withholding requirement for independent contractors.

Independent contractors normally set the order and sequence of work, set their hours of work, work for others at the same time, are paid by the job, offer their services to the public, have an opportunity for profit or loss, furnish their own tools, may do work on another's premises, and there is often substantial investment by the worker.

Independent Contractor Status Myths

- *Myth:* A written contract will characterize a person as an independent contractor.
  Fact: It is the substance of the relationship that governs.

- *Myth:* Casual labor or seasonal workers are independent contractors, or their classification is a matter of choice.
  Fact: There is never a choice. The classification is determined by the facts and circumstances.

- *Myth:* If a person qualifies as an independent contractor for federal payroll tax purposes, he or she is automatically exempt for workers' compensation and state unemployment tax purposes.
  Fact: State workers' compensation and unemployment tax laws are often broader, and an individual may actually be covered under these laws even though qualifying as an independent contractor for federal payroll tax purposes.

Common law rules

Defining a worker as an employee or an independent contractor depends on the degree of control over the worker to establish an employer-employee relationship. The IRS identifies three general ways an organization may exercise such control: behavioral control, financial control, and through the organization-worker relationship. As a church analyzes these factors, it is safest to start from the assumption that a worker is an employee unless the factors clearly indicate independent contractor status. No single factor is determinative, rather all forms of control must be analyzed.

➤ **Behavioral control.** Factors relating to behavioral control include:

1. **Types of instructions** – An employee is generally subject to the employer's instructions about the when, where, and how work is to be performed.

2. **Degree of instructions** – An employee is generally subject to more detailed instructions than an independent contractor.

3. **Evaluation systems** – A system that evaluates how a worker performs a job is indicative of an employment relationship, whereas a contractor relationship will generally just focus on the result.

> **Key Issue**
>
> The amount of control and direction the employer has over a worker's services is the most important issue in deciding whether a worker is an employee or an independent contractor.

4. **Training** – Generally an employer does not provide training to a contractor.

➤ **Financial control.** Factors under financial control include:

1. **Significant investment** – An employer will usually provide all equipment and resources to an employee, but a contractor will provide their own.

2. **Unreimbursed expenses** – Contractors are more likely to have unreimbursed expenses than an employee.

3. **Opportunity for profit or loss** – A contractor generally has an opportunity for loss as well as an opportunity for profit.

4. **Services available to the public** – An employee tends to only work for one organization, whereas a contractor tends to work for a number of different organizations.

5. **Method of payment** – A contractor is generally contracted for a flat fee for a job. However, there are some professions where contractors are also paid on an hourly basis.

➤ **Relationship of the parties.** Factors here generally include:

1. **Written contract** – While there can be contracts between an employee and an employer, a contract generally tends to indicate a type of contractor relationship.

2. **Employee benefits** – Does the worker receive benefits that would be more typical of an employment relationship?

3. **Permanency of the relationship** – A contractor is typically hired with a set time frame in mind, whereas an employee relationship is more likely open-ended.

4. **Services provided as a key activity of the organization** – The more central a worker's actions are to the core activities of the organization, the more likely the organization will exercise a higher degree of control over their operations.

Once an organization has analyzed these factors to determine the nature of the relationship between the worker and the organization, it's time to review the overall level of behavioral control and financial control along with nature of the relationship to determine if it is an employment situation or if the relationship qualifies as an independent contractor. Remember to be conservative; you will want to start from the assumption that there is an employment relationship.

➤ **Correcting a misclassification.** For the past several years, the IRS has offered a Voluntary Classification Settlement Program (VCSP) for employers that need to reclassify workers as employees for employment tax purposes. The program, generally available to those organizations that are not already under an audit, allows an employer to pay 10 percent of the employment tax liability for the most recent tax years in exchange for not being liable for interest and penalties on that amount and will not be subject to an employment tax audit for prior years for the worker being reclassified. This is completed on Form 8952 and more information is available at IRS.gov.

The classification of ministers

It is important that the organization decide whether the services of ministers employed by the organization qualify for special tax treatment as ministerial services.

Most ordained, commissioned, or licensed ministers serving local churches are eligible for six special tax provisions with respect to services performed in the exercise of ministry. The IRS and courts apply certain tests to ministers serving local churches, including whether the minister administers the sacraments, conducts worship services, is considered a spiritual leader by the church, and performs management services in the "control, conduct, or maintenance of a religious organization." It may not be necessary for a minister to meet all of these factors to qualify for the special tax treatment. For a complete discussion of this topic, see the 2019 edition of the *Zondervan Minister's Tax & Financial Guide*.

Ordained, commissioned, or licensed ministers not serving local churches may qualify as ministers for federal tax purposes without meeting additional tests if their duties include the following (see also pages 48–52):

➤ Administration of church denominations and their integral agencies, including teaching or administration in parochial schools, colleges, or universities that are under the authority of a church or denomination

➤ Performing services for an institution that is not an integral agency of a church pursuant to an assignment or designation by ecclesiastical superiors, but only if the services relate to the assigning church's purposes

---

Special Tax Provisions for Ministers

- Exclusion for income tax purposes of the housing allowance and the fair rental value of ministry-owned housing provided rent-free to clergy.

- Exemption of clergy from self-employment tax under very limited circumstances.

- Treatment of clergy (who do not elect social security exemption) as self-employed for social security tax purposes for income from ministerial services.

- Exemption of clergy compensation from mandatory income tax withholding.

- Eligibility for a voluntary income tax withholding arrangement between the minister-employee and the employer.

- Potential double benefit of mortgage interest and real estate taxes as itemized deductions and as housing expenses for housing allowance purposes.

If a church does not assign the minister's services, they will be qualified services only if they substantially involve performing sacerdotal functions or conducting religious worship (including preaching, leading Bible studies, spiritual counseling, etc.).

Sample Board Resolution for Ministerial Assignment

Whereas, _____Name of assigning church_____ recognizes the calling of ___Name of minister assigned___ as a minister and is (ordained, licensed, or commissioned); and

Whereas, We believe that the assignment of ___Name of minister assigned___ will further the efforts and mission of our church and we desire to provide support and encouragement;

Resolved, That _____Name of minister assigned_____ is hereby assigned to _____Name of ministry to which assigned_____ effective_____, 20___ to serve as _____Position Title_____; and

Resolved, That this assignment is made for a period of one year upon which time it will be reviewed and may be renewed; and

Resolved, That this assignment is contingent upon the quarterly submission of activity and financial reports by ___Name of minister assigned___ to our church.

Reporting Compensation

Minister-employees

Forms W-2 are annually provided to minister-employees. There is no requirement to withhold income taxes, but they may be withheld under a voluntary agreement. Social security taxes should not be withheld.

Nonminister-employees

If an employee does not qualify as a minister for tax purposes, the organization is liable to withhold and pay FICA and income taxes. Certain FICA tax exceptions are discussed below.

Nonemployees

Self-employed recipients of compensation should receive Form 1099-MISC instead of Form W-2 (if the person has received compensation of at least $600 for the year).

Payroll Tax Withholding

FICA social security

Most churches and nonprofit organizations must withhold FICA taxes from their employees' wages and pay them to the IRS along with the employer's share of the tax. Minister-employees are an exception to this rule.

FICA includes both a social security and Medicare tax component. In 2018, employers and employees each pay social security tax at a rate of 6.2% (12.4% total) on the social security wage base of up to $128,400.

> **Warning**
>
> FICA-type social security taxes should never be withheld from the compensation of a qualified minister. Ministers are self-employed for social security purposes, even when performing ministerial duties for a parachurch organization. They must file Schedule SE to compute self-employment social security tax, unless they have opted out of social security.

The employer and employee also must each pay a 1.45% Medicare tax rate (2.9% total) on all employee wages (unlike social security, there is no wage base limit for Medicare tax). Additionally, under the health care reform law, employers are responsible for withholding an additional 0.9% Medicare tax on all employee wages in excess of $200,000.

There are a few exceptions to the imposition of FICA. Generally, wages of less than $100 paid to an employee in a calendar year are not subject to FICA. Services excluded from FICA include:

> ➤ services performed by a minister of a church in the exercise of ministry or by a member of a religious order in the exercise of duties required by such order

➤ services performed in the employ of a church or church-controlled organization that opposes for religious reasons the payment of social security taxes (see later discussion of filing Form 8274)

➤ services performed by a student in the employ of a school, college, or university

Churches and church-controlled organizations opposed to social security taxes

Very few churches and church-controlled organizations are exempt from payment of FICA taxes. An organization must certify opposition for religious reasons to the payment of employer social security taxes.

Organizations in existence on September 30, 1984 were required to file Form 8274 by October 30, 1984 to request exemption from payment of FICA taxes. Any organization created after September 30, 1984 must file before the first date on which a quarterly employment tax return is due from the organization.

Organizations desiring to revoke their exemption made earlier by filing Form 8274 should file Form 941 with full payment of social security taxes for that quarter.

Federal income tax

Most nonprofit organizations are exempt from the payment of federal income tax on the organization's income (see pages 22–29 for the tax on unrelated business income). But they must withhold and pay federal, state, and local income taxes on the wages paid to each employee. Minister-employees are an exception to this rule.

A minister-employee may have a voluntary withholding agreement with a church or nonprofit employer relating to the minister's income taxes (or he or she may file Form 1040-ES, or both). An agreement to withhold income taxes from wages must be in writing. There is no required form for the agreement. A minister may request voluntary withholding by submitting Form W-4 (Employee Withholding Allowance Certificate) to the employer, indicating the amount to be withheld, or the written request may be in another format.

Caution

Social security taxes (FICA) should never be withheld from the salary of a minister-employee. But under a voluntary withholding agreement for ministers' federal income taxes, additional federal income tax may be withheld sufficient to cover the minister's self-employment tax liability. This withholding must be identified as "federal income tax withheld" (not as social security taxes withheld).

Federal income taxes for all employees (except ministers) are calculated based on the chart and tables shown in IRS Publication 15. State and local income taxes are usually required to be withheld according to state withholding tables.

Form **W-4**	**Employee's Withholding Allowance Certificate**	OMB No. 1545-0074
Department of the Treasury Internal Revenue Service	▶ Whether you're entitled to claim a certain number of allowances or exemption from withholding is subject to review by the IRS. Your employer may be required to send a copy of this form to the IRS.	**2018**

1 Your first name and middle initial	Last name	2 Your social security number
Walter R.	Knight	511-02-7943

Home address (number and street or rural route)	3 ☐ Single ☒ Married ☐ Married, but withhold at higher Single rate.
601 Oakridge Boulevard	**Note:** If married filing separately, check "Married, but withhold at higher Single rate."
City or town, state, and ZIP code	4 If your last name differs from that shown on your social security card,
Vinton, VA 24179	check here. You must call 800-772-1213 for a replacement card. ▶ ☐

5	Total number of allowances you're claiming (from the applicable worksheet on the following pages) . . .	5	4
6	Additional amount, if any, you want withheld from each paycheck	6	$
7	I claim exemption from withholding for 2018, and I certify that I meet **both** of the following conditions for exemption.		
	• Last year I had a right to a refund of **all** federal income tax withheld because I had **no** tax liability, **and**		
	• This year I expect a refund of **all** federal income tax withheld because I expect to have **no** tax liability.		
	If you meet both conditions, write "Exempt" here . . . . ▶	7	

Under penalties of perjury, I declare that I have examined this certificate and, to the best of my knowledge and belief, it is true, correct, and complete.

Employee's signature
(This form is not valid unless you sign it.) ▶ *Walter R. Knight*   Date ▶ 1/01/18

8 Employer's name and address (**Employer:** Complete boxes 8 and 10 if sending to IRS and complete boxes 8, 9, and 10 if sending to State Directory of New Hires.)	9 First date of employment	10 Employer identification number (EIN)

For Privacy Act and Paperwork Reduction Act Notice, see page 4.   Cat. No. 10220Q   Form **W-4** (2018)

This form must be completed by all lay employees, full- or part-time. Your exemption for 2018 expires February 15, 2019. If a minister completes this form, it can be the basis to determine income tax withholding under a voluntary agreement.

➤ **Form W-4.** All employees, part-time or full-time, must complete a W-4 form. (Ministers are an exception to this requirement unless a voluntary withholding arrangement is used.) The withholding allowance information completed on this form gives the basis to determine the amount of income tax to be withheld.

Churches and nonprofits must file all Forms W-4 with the IRS on any employees who claim exempt status from withholding (and the employees' wages would normally exceed $200 weekly) or claim more than 10 withholding allowances.

➤ **Form W-7.** Certain individuals who are not eligible for a social security number (SSN) may obtain an individual taxpayer identification number. The following individuals may file Form W-7: (1) nonresident aliens who are required to file a U.S. tax return, (2) nonresident aliens who are filing a U.S. tax return only to claim a refund, (3) individuals being claimed as dependents on U.S. tax returns and who are not eligible to obtain a social security number, (4) individuals being claimed as husbands or wives for exemptions on U.S. tax returns and who are not eligible to obtain an SSN, and (5) U.S. residents who must file a U.S. tax return but are not eligible for an SSN.

Personal liability for payroll taxes

Church and nonprofit officers and employees may be personally liable if payroll taxes are not withheld and paid to the IRS. If the organization has willfully failed to withhold and

Form **W-7**
(Rev. September 2016)
Department of the Treasury
Internal Revenue Service

Application for IRS Individual
Taxpayer Identification Number

▶ **For use by individuals who are not U.S. citizens or permanent residents.**
▶ **See separate instructions.**

OMB No. 1545-0074

An IRS individual taxpayer identification number (ITIN) is for federal tax purposes only.

Before you begin:

• **Don't submit** this form if you have, or are eligible to get, a U.S. social security number (SSN).

• *Getting an ITIN doesn't change your immigration status or your right to work in the United States and doesn't make you eligible for the earned income credit.*

Application Type (Check one box):
☐ Apply for a New ITIN
☒ Renew an Existing ITIN

Reason you're submitting Form W-7. Read the instructions for the box you check. **Caution:** If you check box b, c, d, e, f, or g, you **must file a U.S. federal tax return with Form W-7 unless you meet one of the exceptions** (see instructions).

a ☐ Nonresident alien required to get an ITIN to claim tax treaty benefit

b ☐ Nonresident alien filing a U.S. federal tax return

c ☒ U.S. resident alien **(based on days present in the United States)** filing a U.S. federal tax return

d ☐ Dependent of U.S. citizen/resident alien ⎱ Enter name and SSN/ITIN of U.S. citizen/resident alien (see instructions) ▶ _____

e ☐ Spouse of U.S. citizen/resident alien

f ☐ Nonresident alien student, professor, or researcher filing a U.S. federal tax return or claiming an exception

g ☐ Dependent/spouse of a nonresident alien holding a U.S. visa

h ☐ Other (see instructions) ▶ _____

Additional information for **a** and **f**: Enter treaty country ▶ _____ and treaty article number ▶ _____

Name (see instructions)	**1a** First name Liam	Middle name Ethan	Last name Martin
Name at birth if different . . ▶	**1b** First name	Middle name	Last name

Applicant's mailing address	**2** Street address, apartment number, or rural route number. **If you have a P.O. box, see separate instructions.** 1200 Palm Street
	City or town, state or province, and country. Include ZIP code or postal code where appropriate. Sarasota, FL 34234

Foreign (non-U.S.) address (if different from above) (see instructions)	**3** Street address, apartment number, or rural route number. **Don't use a P.O. box number.** 121 Maple Run
	City or town, state or province, and country. Include ZIP code or postal code where appropriate. Toronto, ON M5A 2N4

Birth information	**4** Date of birth (month / day / year) 6/20/1975	Country of birth Canada	City and state or province (optional) Toronto, ON	**5** ☒ Male ☐ Female

Other information	**6a** Country(ies) of citizenship Canada	**6b** Foreign tax I.D. number (if any)	**6c** Type of U.S. visa (if any), number, and expiration date Religious Workers

6d Identification document(s) submitted (see instructions) ☒ Passport ☐ Driver's license/State I.D.
☐ USCIS documentation ☐ Other _____
Issued by: Canada No.: 12345678 Exp. date: 6 / 1 / 2022 Date of entry into the United States (MM/DD/YYYY): 5 / 1 / 2018

6e Have you previously received an ITIN or an Internal Revenue Service Number (IRSN)?
☒ **No/Don't know.** Skip line 6f.
☐ **Yes.** Complete line 6f. If more than one, list on a sheet and attach to this form (see instructions).

6f Enter ITIN and/or IRSN ▶ **ITIN** ☐☐☐-☐☐-☐☐☐☐ **IRSN** ☐☐☐-☐☐-☐☐☐☐ and name under which it was issued ▶ _____
First name | Middle name | Last name

6g Name of college/university or company (see instructions) First Baptist Church
City and state Sarasota, FL Length of stay 6 months

Sign Here Keep a copy for your records.	Under penalties of perjury, I (applicant/delegate/acceptance agent) declare that I have examined this application, including accompanying documentation and statements, and to the best of my knowledge and belief, it is true, correct, and complete. I authorize the IRS to share information with my acceptance agent in order to perfect this Form W-7, Application for IRS Individual Taxpayer Identification Number.

▶ Signature of applicant (if delegate, see instructions)
Liam Ethan Martin
Date (month / day / year) 5 / 1 / 18
Phone number 914-123-1234

Name of delegate, if applicable (type or print)
Delegate's relationship to applicant ☐ Parent ☐ Court-appointed guardian ☐ Power of Attorney

Acceptance Agent's Use ONLY	▶ Signature	Date (month / day / year) / /	Phone Fax
	▶ Name and title (type or print)	Name of company	EIN Office Code	PTIN

For Paperwork Reduction Act Notice, see separate instructions. Cat. No. 10229L Form **W-7** (Rev. 9-2016) pay the taxes, the IRS has the authority to assess a 100% penalty of withheld income and social security taxes.

This penalty may be assessed against the individual responsible for withholding and paying the taxes, even if the person is an unpaid volunteer such as a church treasurer.

Depositing Withheld Payroll Taxes

The basic rules for depositing withheld payroll taxes are as follows:

➤ If your total accumulated and unpaid employment tax (income tax withheld, social security tax withheld and matched by the organization) is less than $2,500 in a calendar quarter, taxes can be paid directly to the IRS when the organization files Form 941. These forms are due one month after the end of each calendar quarter.

➤ If payroll taxes are over $2,500 for a quarter, payroll tax deposits must be made monthly or before the 15th day of each month for the payroll paid during the preceding month. Large organizations with total employment taxes of over $50,000 per year are subject to more frequent deposits.

To determine if an organization is a monthly depositor, you must determine if the accumulated liabilities in the "look-back period" reached a threshold of $50,000. Those with an accumulated liability of $50,000 or less in the look-back period are generally monthly depositors (except those qualifying for quarterly deposits with liabilities of $1,000 or less).

> **Remember**
>
> A new organization (or one filing payroll tax returns for the first time) will be required to file monthly until a "look-back period" is established. A look-back period begins on July 1 and ends on June 30 of the preceding calendar year.

The cost of missing deposit deadlines can be very high. Besides interest, the organization can be hit with penalties at progressively stiffer rates. These range from 2% if you deposit the money within 5 days of the due date to 15% if it is not deposited within 10 days of the first delinquency notice or on the day that the IRS demands immediate payment, whichever is earlier.

Only very small organizations are exempted from depositing electronically—employers with $2,500 or less in quarterly employment taxes who pay their liability when filing their returns. All other coupon users must switch to making deposits by wire using the Treasury's Electronic Federal Tax Payment System (EFTPS): www.eftps.gov or call 800-555-3453.

Using EFTPS is a free and convenient way to make federal tax payments online or by telephone, 24/7. To enroll in this system, you merely need your taxpayer identification number, bank account number, routing number, and address and name as they appear on your IRS tax documents. After you enter the requested information online, you will receive your PIN. Call 1-800-982-3526 to get a temporary internet password. Then you are ready to make a payment online or by telephone.

Page 2

Name (not your trade name): **Barnett Ridge Church**
Employer identification number (EIN): **35 - 2017883**

950217

Part 2: Tell us about your deposit schedule and tax liability for this quarter.

If you are unsure about whether you are a monthly schedule depositor or a semiweekly schedule depositor, see section 11 of Pub. 15.

16 Check one:

☐ Line 12 on this return is less than $2,500 or line 12 on the return for the prior quarter was less than $2,500, and you didn't incur a $100,000 next-day deposit obligation during the current quarter. If line 12 for the prior quarter was less than $2,500 but line 12 on this return is $100,000 or more, you must provide a record of your federal tax liability. If you are a monthly schedule depositor, complete the deposit schedule below; if you are a semiweekly schedule depositor, attach Schedule B (Form 941). Go to Part 3.

☒ You were a monthly schedule depositor for the entire quarter. Enter your tax liability for each month and total liability for the quarter, then go to Part 3.

Tax liability:	Month 1	2,201 .
	Month 2	2,493 .
	Month 3	2,448 .
	Total liability for quarter	7,142 .	Total must equal line 12.

☐ You were a semiweekly schedule depositor for any part of this quarter. Complete Schedule B (Form 941), Report of Tax Liability for Semiweekly Schedule Depositors, and attach it to Form 941.

Part 3: Tell us about your business. If a question does NOT apply to your business, leave it blank.

17 If your business has closed or you stopped paying wages . . . . ☐ Check here, and
enter the final date you paid wages . . . . _____

18 If you are a seasonal employer and you don't have to file a return for every quarter of the year . . . . ☐ Check here.

Part 4: May we speak with your third-party designee?

Do you want to allow an employee, a paid tax preparer, or another person to discuss this return with the IRS? See the instructions for details.

☐ Yes. Designee's name and phone number _____

Select a 5-digit Personal Identification Number (PIN) to use when talking to the IRS. _____

☐ No.

Part 5: Sign here. You MUST complete both pages of Form 941 and SIGN it.

Under penalties of perjury, I declare that I have examined this return, including accompanying schedules and statements, and to the best of my knowledge and belief, it is true, correct, and complete. Declaration of preparer (other than taxpayer) is based on all information of which preparer has any knowledge.

Sign your name here — *David Baker*

Print your name here: **David Baker**
Print your title here: **Office Manager**

Date 4 /15/ 19   Best daytime phone: **334-873-1754**

Paid Preparer Use Only   Check if you are self-employed . . . ☐

Preparer's name		PTIN	
Preparer's signature		Date	/ /
Firm's name (or yours if self-employed)		EIN	
Address		Phone	
City		State	ZIP code	

✗

Page 2   Form **941** (Rev. 1-2019)

Page 1

Form **941 for 2019:** **Employer's QUARTERLY Federal Tax Return**
(Rev. January 2019)
Department of the Treasury — Internal Revenue Service

950117
OMB No. 1545-0029

Employer identification number (EIN) **3 5 - 2 0 1 7 8 8 3**

Name (not your trade name) **Barnett Ridge Church**

Trade name (if any) _____

Address **PO Box 517**
Number   Street   Suite or room number
Selma   **AL**   **36704**
City   State   ZIP code

Foreign country name   Foreign province/county   Foreign postal code

Report for this Quarter of 2019
(Check one.)

☒ 1: January, February, March
☐ 2: April, May, June
☐ 3: July, August, September
☐ 4: October, November, December

Go to www.irs.gov/Form941 for instructions and the latest information.

Read the separate instructions before you complete Form 941. Type or print within the boxes.

Part 1: Answer these questions for this quarter.

1 Number of employees who received wages, tips, or other compensation for the pay period including: Mar. 12 (Quarter 1), June 12 (Quarter 2), Sept. 12 (Quarter 3), or Dec. 12 (Quarter 4)	1	1
2 Wages, tips, and other compensation	2	24,811 .
3 Federal income tax withheld from wages, tips, and other compensation	3	4,642 .
4 If no wages, tips, and other compensation are subject to social security or Medicare tax		☐ Check and go to line 6.

	Column 1	Column 2
5a Taxable social security wages . . .	16,340 . × 0.124 =	2,026 .
5b Taxable social security tips	. × 0.124 =	.
5c Taxable Medicare wages & tips . . .	16,340 . × 0.029 =	474 .
5d Taxable wages & tips subject to Additional Medicare Tax withholding	. × 0.009 =	.

5e Add Column 2 from lines 5a, 5b, 5c, and 5d	5e	2,500 .
5f Section 3121(q) Notice and Demand—Tax due on unreported tips (see instructions)	5f	.
6 Total taxes before adjustments. Add lines 3, 5e, and 5f	6	7,142 .
7 Current quarter's adjustment for fractions of cents	7	.
8 Current quarter's adjustment for sick pay	8	.
9 Current quarter's adjustments for tips and group-term life insurance	9	.
10 Total taxes after adjustments. Combine lines 6 through 9	10	7,142 .
11 Qualified small business payroll tax credit for increasing research activities. Attach Form 8974	11	.
12 Total taxes after adjustments and credits. Subtract line 11 from line 10	12	7,142 .
13 Total deposits for this quarter, including overpayment applied from a prior quarter and overpayments applied from Form 941-X, 941-X (PR), 944-X, or 944-X (SP) filed in the current quarter	13	7,142 .
14 Balance due. If line 12 is more than line 13, enter the difference and see instructions	14	0 .

15 Overpayment. If line 13 is more than line 12, enter the difference _____ Check one: ☐ Apply to next return. ☐ Send a refund.

► You MUST complete both pages of Form 941 and SIGN it.   Next ►

For Privacy Act and Paperwork Reduction Act Notice, see the back of the Payment Voucher.   Cat. No. 17001Z   Form **941** (Rev. 1-2019)

File this form to report social security (FICA) and Medicare taxes and federal income tax withheld.

Form **941-X:** Adjusted Employer's QUARTERLY Federal Tax Return or Claim for Refund
(Rev. April 2017) Department of the Treasury — Internal Revenue Service

OMB No. 1545-0029

Employer identification number (EIN) 3 5 – 6 3 0 9 2 9 4

Name (not your trade name) Little Valley Church

Trade name (if any)

Address 4865 Douglas Road
Number   Street   Suite or room number

Springfield   OH   45504
City   State   ZIP code

Foreign country name   Foreign province/county   Foreign postal code

Return You're Correcting ...
Check the type of return you're correcting.

[X] 941

[ ] 941-SS

Check the ONE quarter you're correcting.

[X] 1: January, February, March

[ ] 2: April, May, June

[ ] 3: July, August, September

[ ] 4: October, November, December

Enter the calendar year of the quarter you're correcting.
2018   (YYYY)

Enter the date you discovered errors.
05 / 10 / 2018
(MM / DD / YYYY)

Read the separate instructions before completing this form. Use this form to correct errors you made on Form 941 or 941-SS. Use a separate Form 941-X for each quarter that needs correction. Type or print within the boxes. You MUST complete all three pages. Don't attach this form to Form 941 or 941-SS.

Part 1:   Select ONLY one process. See page 4 for additional guidance.

[X] **1. Adjusted employment tax return.** Check this box if you underreported amounts. Also check this box if you overreported amounts and you would like to use the adjustment process to correct the errors. You must check this box if you're correcting both underreported and overreported amounts on this form. The amount shown on line 21, if less than zero, may only be applied as a credit to your Form 941, Form 941-SS, or Form 944 for the tax period in which you're filing this form.

[ ] **2. Claim.** Check this box if you overreported amounts only and you would like to use the

Use this form to correct income, social security (FICA), and Medicare tax information reported on Form 941. It may be necessary to issue Form W-2c to employees relating to prior year data. The Form 941-X has three pages.

Filing Quarterly Payroll Tax Forms

Employers must report covered wages paid to their employees by filing Form 941, Employer's Quarterly Federal Tax Return, with the IRS.

Form 941

Church and other nonprofit employers that withhold income tax and both social security and medicare taxes must file Form 941 quarterly. There is no requirement to file Form 941 if your organization has not been required to withhold payroll taxes even if you have one or more minister-employees. However, if the only employee is a minister and voluntary federal income tax has been withheld, Form 941 must be filed.

Most common errors made on Form 941

The IRS has outlined the most common errors discovered during the processing of Form 941 and the best ways to avoid making these mistakes.

> **Idea**
>
> Do not file more than one Form 941 per quarter even if you deposit payroll taxes monthly. If you have multiple locations or divisions, you must file only one Form 941 per quarter. Filing more than one return may result in processing delays and require correspondence with the IRS.

A checklist for avoiding errors follows:

➤ Do not include titles or abbreviations, such as Dr., Mr., or Mrs.

➤ On line 2, do not include amounts designated as housing allowance for qualified ministers.

➤ Make sure that taxable social security wages and the social security tax on line 5a and the taxable Medicare wages and the Medicare tax on line 5c are reported separately. Most employers will need to complete both lines 5a and 5c.

➤ The preprinted form sent by the IRS should be used. If the return is prepared by a third-party preparer, make certain that the preparer uses exactly the name that appears on the preprinted form that was sent.

➤ Check the math for lines 5e, 10, and 12.

➤ Make sure the social security tax on line 5a is calculated correctly (social security wages x 12.4%).

➤ Make sure the Medicare tax on line 5c is calculated correctly (Medicare wages x 2.9%).

➤ Be sure to use the most recent Form 941 that the IRS sends. The IRS enters the date the quarter ended after the employer identification number. If the form is used for a later quarter, the IRS will have to contact the employer.

➤ Make sure there is never an entry on both lines 14 and 15. There cannot be a balance due and a refund.

Filing Annual Payroll Tax Forms

Form W-2

By January 31, each employee must be given a Form W-2. Be sure to reconcile the data reflected on Forms W-2, W-3, and 941 before distributing Forms W-2 to employees. If these forms do not reconcile, the IRS generally sends a letter to the employer requesting additional information. For additional help, call 866-455-7438.

Make all entries without a dollar sign or comma but with a decimal point and cents (do not use whole dollars).

Void. Put an X in this box when an error has been made on this W-2.

Box 1 – Wages, tips, other compensation. Items to include in Box 1 (before any payroll deductions) are:

➤ total wages paid during the year (including love offerings paid by the church or nonprofit organization to a minister or other employee)

➤ the value of noncash payments, including taxable fringe benefits

➤ business expense payments under a nonaccountable plan

➤ payments of per diem or mileage allowance paid for business expense purposes that exceed the IRS-specified rates

➤ payments made by a church or nonprofit organization to an employee's Individual Retirement Account

➤ payments for moving expenses

➤ all other compensation, including taxable fringe benefits ("Other compensation" represents amounts an organization pays to an employee from which federal income tax is not withheld. If you prefer, you may show other compensation on a separate Form W-2.)

➤ the cash housing allowance or the fair market rental value of housing and utilities, which must be reported as taxable income for lay employees (non-ministerial employees), unless lodging is furnished on the employer's premises and the employee is required to accept the lodging as a condition of employment

Exclude the following:

➤ the fair rental value of a church-provided parsonage or a properly designated housing allowance for ministers

➤ auto and business expense reimbursements paid through an accountable expense plan

➤ contributions to 403(b) tax-sheltered annuities or 401(k) plans

Box 2 – Federal income tax withheld. Enter the total federal income tax withheld according to the chart and tables in IRS Publication 15.

A minister-employee may enter into a voluntary withholding arrangement with the employing organization. Based on Form W-4 or other written withholding request, federal income tax withholding may be calculated from the chart and tables in Publication 15, excluding any housing allowance amount.

The minister may request that an additional amount of income tax be withheld to cover self-employment tax. However, the additional amount withheld is reported as income tax withheld on the quarterly Form 941 and in Box 2 of Form W-2.

An organization that provides additional compensation to the employee-minister to cover part or all of the self-employment tax liability may:

➤ pay the additional compensation directly to the IRS by entering that amount on the organization's Form 941 and in Boxes 1 and 2 of Form W-2, or

Remember

One of an employer's primary challenges is to determine if all of an employee's compensation is reported on Form W-2. Taxable compensation that is often erroneously omitted includes life insurance premiums paid for the employee (only group-term life up to $50,000 is tax-free) and expense allowances (only expenses reimbursed under an accountable plan are tax-free).

➤ pay the additional compensation to the minister, with the minister being responsible for remitting the amounts to the IRS with a Form 1040-ES. If this procedure is followed, the organization reports this amount only as additional compensation on Form 941 and only in Box 1 of Form W-2.

Box 3 – Social security wages. Show the total wages paid (before payroll deductions) subject to employee social security tax (FICA). This amount must not exceed $128,400 in 2018 (the maximum social security tax wage base). Include nonaccountable employee business expenses reported in Box 1. Generally, all cash and noncash payments reported in Box 1 must also be shown in Box 3. Voluntary salary reduction tax-sheltered annuity contributions for nonminister employees are included in Box 3.

Box 3 should be blank for a qualified minister (an individual who meets the ministerial factors of the IRS).

Box 4 – Social security tax withheld. Show the total FICA social security tax (not including the organization's share) withheld or paid by the organization for the employee. The amount shown must equal 6.2% of the amount in Box 3 and must not exceed $7,960.80 for 2018. Do not include the employer portion of FICA tax (6.2%).

Checklist for Completing Box 1 of Form W-2

Data Included for			
Minister Only	Both	Nonminister Only	
	yes		Salary
no		yes	Housing/furnishings allowance (designated in advance)
no		yes	Parsonage rental value
no		yes	Parsonage utilities paid by church or nonprofit
	yes		Social security/Medicare "allowance" or reimbursement
	no		Transportation/travel and other business and professional expense reimbursements only if paid under a board-adopted accountable reimbursement plan
	yes		"Reimbursements" if not paid under an accountable reimbursement plan
	yes		Love offerings or cash gifts in excess of $25
	no		Contributions to a tax-sheltered annuity plan
	no		Group qualified health/dental/long-term care insurance premiums paid directly by the employer
	no		Group-term life insurance premiums (for up to $50,000 coverage) paid directly by the employer
	yes		Moving expenses paid for or reimbursed to an employee
	yes		Value of personal and nonbusiness use of organization's vehicle

22222	Void ☐	**a** Employee's social security number 517-38-6451	For Official Use Only ▶ OMB No. 1545-0008		
b Employer identification number (EIN) 35-2948039			**1** Wages, tips, other compensation 93800.00	**2** Federal income tax withheld 7000.00	
c Employer's name, address, and ZIP code ABC Charity 2870 North Hull Road Traverse City, MI 49615			**3** Social security wages 95000.00	**4** Social security tax withheld 5890.00	
			5 Medicare wages and tips 95000.00	**6** Medicare tax withheld 1377.50	
			7 Social security tips	**8** Allocated tips	
d Control number			**9** Verification code	**10** Dependent care benefits	
e Employee's first name and initial Last name Suff. Michael A Black			**11** Nonqualified plans	**12a** See instructions for box 12 E 1200.00	
			13 Statutory employee ☐ Retirement plan ☐ Third-party sick pay ☐	**12b**	
15550 Cleveland Avenue Traverse City, MI 49615			**14** Other	**12c**	
				12d	
f Employee's address and ZIP code					

15 State MI	Employer's state ID number 6309294	**16** State wages, tips, etc. 93800.00	**17** State income tax 700.00	**18** Local wages, tips, etc.	**19** Local income tax	**20** Locality name

Form W-2 Wage and Tax Statement   **2018**

Copy A For Social Security Administration — Send this entire page with Form W-3 to the Social Security Administration; photocopies are **not** acceptable.

Department of the Treasury—Internal Revenue Service
For Privacy Act and Paperwork Reduction Act Notice, see the separate instructions.
Cat. No. 10134D

Do Not Cut, Fold, or Staple Forms on This Page

Form W-2 must be filed for each employee who received taxable compensation or for whom income tax or FICA-type social security tax was withheld. The example shown above is for a lay employee.

Some organizations pay the employee's share of FICA tax for some or all nonminister employees instead of deducting it from the employee's wages. These amounts paid by the organization must be included in Boxes 1, 3, and 5.

Box 4 should be blank for qualified ministers. Any amount of withholding to meet the minister's SECA tax liability must be reported in Box 2, not in Box 4 or Box 6.

Box 5 – Medicare wages. The wages subject to Medicare tax are the same as those subject to social security tax (Box 3), except there is no wage limit for the Medicare tax.

> **Example:** A *nonminister* employee is paid wages of $130,000. The amount shown in Box 3 (social security wages) should be $128,400, but the amount shown in Box 5 (Medicare wages) should be $130,000. If the wages are less than $128,400, the amounts entered in Boxes 3 and 5 will be the same.

Box 5 should be blank for qualified ministers. Nonaccountable business expense reimbursements for lay employees are included in Box 5.

Box 6 – Medicare tax withheld. Enter the total employee Medicare tax (not the ministry's share) withheld or paid by the ministry for the employee. The amount shown must equal 1.45% of the amount in Box 5. Box 6 should be blank for qualified ministers.

Box 9 – Advance EIC payment. Show the total paid to the employee as advance earned income credit payments.

Box 10 – Dependent care benefits. Show the total amount of dependent care benefits under Section 129 paid or incurred by the organization for the employee, including any amount over the $5,000 exclusion. Also include in Box 1, Box 3, and Box 5 any amount over the $5,000 exclusion.

Box 11 – Nonqualified plans. Enter the total amount of distributions to the employee from a nonqualified deferred compensation plan. Nonqualified plans do not include a tax-sheltered annuity or a "Rabbi Trust." Include an amount in Box 11 only if it is also includible in Box 1 or Boxes 3 and 5.

Box 12 – Additional entries. The following items are most frequently inserted in Box 12 by churches and other nonprofit organizations:

C – If the organization provided the employee more than $50,000 of group-term life insurance, show the cost of the premiums for coverage over $50,000. Also include the amount in Box 1 (also in Boxes 3 and 5 if a lay employee).

DD – Value of employer-provided health coverage. This data is required for employers issuing 250 or more Form W-2s.

E – Section 403(b) voluntary salary reduction agreement to purchase an annuity contract. This amount would not be included in Box 1 for either ministerial or lay employees. This amount would be included in Boxes 3 and 5 for a lay employee.

L – Generally, payments made under an accountable plan are excluded from the employee's gross income and are not required to be reported on Form W-2. But if the organization pays a per diem or mileage allowance, and the amount paid exceeds the amount substantiated under IRS rules, wages must be reported on Form W-2 the amount in excess of the amount substantiated. Report the amount substantiated (the nontaxable portion) in Box 12. In Box 1, show the portion of the reimbursement that is more than the amount treated as substantiated. For lay employees the excess amount is subject to income tax withholding, social security tax, Medicare tax, and possibly federal unemployment tax.

> **Example 1:** An employee receives mileage reimbursement at the rate of 54.5 cents per mile for 2018 and substantiates the business miles driven to the organization. The mileage reimbursement is not reported on Form W-2.

> **Example 2:** An employee receives a mileage allowance of $2,000 per year and does not substantiate the business miles driven. The $2,000 allowance is includible in Box 1 as compensation for a minister and Boxes 1, 3, and 5 for a lay employee.

Payments made to *nonminister employees* under a nonaccountable plan are reportable as wages on Form W-2 and are subject to income tax withholding, social security tax, Medicare tax, and possibly federal unemployment tax.

Payments made to *minister-employees* under a nonaccountable plan are reportable as wages on Form W-2 and may be subject to income tax withholding under a voluntary agreement, but they are not subject to mandatory withholding or social security (FICA) or Medicare tax.

P – Report moving expense reimbursements and payments in Box 1 for either ministerial or lay employees. This amount is also included in Boxes 3 and 5 for lay employees.

R – Employer contributions to an Archer medical savings account.

S – Salary reductions to a savings incentive match plan for employees with a SIMPLE retirement account.

T – Employer payments under an adoption assistance plan.

Y – Deferrals under a section 409A nonqualified deferred compensation plan.

Z – Income under a section 409A nonqualified deferred compensation plan.

Box 13 – Check the appropriate boxes. The box that may apply to employees of churches and nonprofit organizations is the retirement plan box. Mark this check box if the employee was an active participant (for any part of the year) in any of the following: (1) a qualified pension plan described in section 401(a), including a 401(k) plan, (2) an annuity plan described in section 403(a), (3) an annuity contract or custodial account described in section 403(b), or (4) a simplified employee pension (SEP) plan described in section 408(k).

Box 14 – Other. You may use this box for any other information the employer wishes to provide to an employee. Label each item and include information such as health insurance premiums deducted or educational assistance payments.

> **Filing Tip**
>
> The minister's housing allowance could be included in Box 14 with the words "Housing Allowance." However, some employers prefer to provide the minister with a separate statement reflecting the housing allowance amount.

If the organization owns or leases a vehicle for an employee's use, the value of the personal use of the vehicle is taxable income. The value of the use of the vehicle is established by using one of the methods described on pages 56–58. The amount of the personal use must be included in Box 1 (and in Boxes 3 and 5 if a lay employee) or on a separate statement to the employee. The employee is required to maintain a mileage log or similar records to substantiate business and personal use of the vehicle and submit this to the employer. If its use is not substantiated, the employer must report 100% of the use of the vehicle as taxable income.

> **Caution**
>
> Do not include any per diem or mileage allowance or other reimbursements for employee business expenses under an accountable plan in Boxes 1 or 14 if the total reimbursement is less than or equal to the amount substantiated.

If the employee fully reimburses the employer for the value of the personal use of the vehicle, then no value would be reported in either Box 1 or in Box 14. Reimbursement of the amount spent for gas on personal trips does not constitute a reimbursement of the full value of the personal use of the vehicle.

Form W-3

A Form W-3 is submitted to the IRS as a transmittal form with Forms W-2. Form W-3 and all attached W-2s must be submitted to the Social Security Administration Center by January 31. No money is sent with Form W-3.

Forms W-2c and W-3c

Use Form W-2c to correct errors on a previously filed Form W-2. Use Form W-3c to transmit corrected W-2c forms to the Social Security Administration. If you are correcting only an employee's name or social security number, you do not have to file Form W-3c with Form W-2c. File Forms W-2c and W-3c as soon as possible after you discover an error. Also provide Form W-2c to employees as soon as possible.

If you are correcting only an employee's name and/or social security number, complete Form W-2c through Box g, as appropriate. Do not complete Boxes 1 through 20.

Wages paid in error in a prior year remain taxable to the employee for that year. This is because the employee received and had use of those funds during that year. The employee is not entitled to file an amended return (Form 1040X) to recover the income tax on these wages. Instead, the employee is entitled to a deduction for the repaid wages on his or her Form 1040 for the year of repayment.

Unemployment taxes

The federal and state unemployment systems provide temporary unemployment compensation to workers who have lost their jobs. Employers provide the revenue for this program by paying federal unemployment taxes, under the Federal Unemployment Tax Act (FUTA), and state unemployment taxes. These are strictly employer taxes, and no deductions are taken from employees' wages.

The current federal unemployment tax law exempts from coverage:

➤ services performed in the employment of a church, a convention, or an association of churches, or an organization that is operated primarily for religious purposes (to qualify for exemption, employees must be performing strictly religious duties)

➤ services performed by an ordained, commissioned, or licensed minister of a church in the exercise of ministry, or by a member of a religious order in the exercise of duties required by such order

➤ services performed in the employment of an unincorporated church-controlled elementary or secondary school

DO NOT STAPLE

33333	a Control number	For Official Use Only ▶ OMB No. 1545-0008

b Kind of Payer (Check one)	941 ☒	Military ☐	943 ☐	944 ☐	Kind of Employer (Check one)	None apply ☐	501c non-govt. ☒	Third-party sick pay (Check if applicable) ☐
	CT-1 ☐	Hshld. emp. ☐	Medicare govt. emp. ☐			State/local non-501c ☐	State/local 501c ☐ Federal govt. ☐	

c Total number of Forms W-2 20	d Establishment number	1 Wages, tips, other compensation 243987.00	2 Federal income tax withheld 39142.00
e Employer identification number (EIN) 35-2948039		3 Social security wages 236431.00	4 Social security tax withheld 14659.00
f Employer's name **ABC Charity**		5 Medicare wages and tips 243987.00	6 Medicare tax withheld 3538.00
2870 North Hull Road Traverse City, MI 49615		7 Social security tips	8 Allocated tips
		9	10 Dependent care benefits
		11 Nonqualified plans	12a Deferred compensation
g Employer's address and ZIP code		13 For third-party sick pay use only	12b
h Other EIN used this year			

15 State MI	Employer's state ID number 6309294	14 Income tax withheld by payer of third-party sick pay
16 State wages, tips, etc. 243987.00	17 State income tax 4387.00	18 Local wages, tips, etc.	19 Local income tax

Employer's contact person **Daniel L. Lewis**	Employer's telephone number **231-435-2201**	For Official Use Only
Employer's fax number **231-435-2205**	Employer's email address **dlewis@gmail.com**	

Under penalties of perjury, I declare that I have examined this return and accompanying documents and, to the best of my knowledge and belief, they are true, correct, and complete.

Signature ▶ *Daniel L. Lewis*   Title ▶ **Treasurer**   Date ▶ **1/31/19**

Form **W-3** Transmittal of Wage and Tax Statements   **2018**   Department of the Treasury Internal Revenue Service

Form W-3 is the "cover sheet" or transmittal form for all Forms W-2.

DO NOT CUT, FOLD, OR STAPLE THIS FORM

44444 For Official Use Only ▶ OMB No. 1545-0008	c Tax year/Form corrected 2018 / W-2	d Employee's correct SSN 404-82-1034
a Employer's name, address, and ZIP code **Little Valley Church** 4865 Douglas Road Springfield, OH 45504	e Corrected SSN and/or name (Check this box and complete boxes f and/or g if incorrect on form previously filed.) ☐	
	Complete boxes f and/or g only if incorrect on form **previously filed** ▶	
	f Employee's **previously reported** SSN	
b Employer's Federal EIN 35-6309294	g Employee's **previously reported** name	
	h Employee's first name and initial **Norman R.**	Last name **Tice**	Suff.
Note. Only complete money fields that are being corrected (exception: for corrections involving MQGE, see the General Instructions for Forms W-2 and W-3, under Specific Instructions for Form W-2c, boxes 5 and 6).	418 Trenton Street Springfield, OH 45504	
	i Employee's address and ZIP code	

Previously reported	Correct information	Previously reported	Correct information
1 Wages, tips, other compensation 10000.00	1 Wages, tips, other compensation 12500.00	2 Federal income tax withheld 4800.00	2 Federal income tax withheld 2000.00
3 Social security wages 10000.00	3 Social security wages 12500.00	4 Social security tax withheld 820.00	4 Social security tax withheld 775.00
5 Medicare wages and tips 10000.00	5 Medicare wages and tips 12500.00	6 Medicare tax withheld 145.00	6 Medicare tax withheld 181.25
7 Social security tips	7 Social security tips	8 Allocated tips	8 Allocated tips
9	9	10 Dependent care benefits	10 Dependent care benefits
11 Nonqualified plans	11 Nonqualified plans	12a See instructions for box 12	12a See instructions for box 12
13 Statutory employee ☐ Retirement plan ☐ Third-party sick pay ☐	13 Statutory employee ☐ Retirement plan ☐ Third-party sick pay ☐	12b	12b
14 Other (see instructions)	14 Other (see instructions)	12c	12c
		12d	12d

Form W-2c is used to submit changes to data previously filed on Form W-2.

➤ services performed in the employment of an incorporated religious elementary or secondary school if it is operated primarily for religious purposes and is operated, supervised, controlled, or principally supported by a church, a convention, or an association of churches

➤ services performed in the employment of an elementary or secondary school that is operated primarily for religious purposes and is not operated, supervised, controlled, or principally supported by a church, a convention, or an association of churches

States may expand their coverage of unemployment taxes beyond the federal minimum. In many states, exemption is also provided for:

➤ services performed in the employ of a separately incorporated church school if the school is operated primarily for religious purposes and is operated, supervised, controlled, or principally supported by a church, a convention, or an association of churches

Unemployment reporting requirements

Nonprofit organizations that are liable for FUTA taxes are required to file Form 940, or 940-EZ Employer's Annual Federal Unemployment Tax Return, due on January 31, if one of the following tests apply:

➤ The organization paid wages of $1,500 or more in any calendar quarter in the current or prior year, or

➤ The organization had one or more employees for at least some part of a day in any 20 or more different weeks in the current or prior year

> **Filing Tip**
>
> Recent court cases reflect attempts by states to subject religious organizations, including churches, to state unemployment taxes. Except for an Oregon case and a New York case, most courts have held that churches are not subject to state unemployment tax.

Although Form 940 covers a calendar year, the organization may have to make deposits of the tax before filing the return. Generally, deposit FUTA tax quarterly if the FUTA tax exceeds $500.

The taxable wage base under FUTA is $7,000 for 2018. (The state wage base may be different.) The tax applies to the first $7,000 paid to each employee as wages during the year. For example, if there was only one employee for the year and the salary was $20,000, only $7,000 is subject to FUTA. The gross FUTA tax rate is 6.0% for 2018.

Generally, organizations can take a credit against the FUTA tax for amounts paid into the state unemployment funds. This credit cannot be more than 5.4% of taxable wages. The credit is reduced for organizations that have not repaid loans from the federal jobless fund.

Use Form 940 or 940-EZ to report this tax. The organization may be able to use Form 940-EZ instead of Form 940 if (1) unemployment taxes ("contributions") were paid to only one state, (2) state unemployment taxes were paid by the due date of Form 940 or 940-EZ, and (3) all wages that were taxable for FUTA tax purposes were also taxable for the state's unemployment tax.

INTEGRITY*Points*

- **Worker classification issues.** Classifying workers correctly is very important in the minds of two important federal government agencies: the Department of Labor (DOL) and the IRS. The DOL's interest relates to being sure workers who are employees are classified as such because of the implications for the Fair Labor Standards Act (minimum wage and overtime), workers' compensation, and other fringe benefit purposes. The IRS wants to see federal income tax and FICA-type social security tax (for lay employees) withheld for all workers who qualify as employees. The employer mandate under the Affordable Care Act also brings increased scrutiny to worker classification issues.

  Too often churches and nonprofits make a decision on employee vs. independent contractor based on what the FICA social security cost (and perhaps other paper-work costs) will be for the organization. Actually, the social security cost factor has no relationship to an appropriate employee vs. independent contractor decision. Integrity requires proper evaluation of worker classification to ensure workers receive the benefits to which they are entitled.

- **Ministers and social security.** One of the most common mistakes made by churches and nonprofits is to withhold FICA-type social security tax from a qualified minister. The employing organization may inappropriately give a minister a choice (of FICA withholding or paying their own social security). A minister may also inappropriately request that FICA tax be withheld because it was done this way by his or her previous employer. Unfortunately, there is no choice on this issue.

  Qualified ministers must pay their own social security by completing Schedule SE, filed with their Form 1040. If an employer withholds and matches FICA-type social security tax from the pay of a minister, then it has not correctly reported the minister's taxable compensation, because the matched portion of the FICA tax escapes income tax when it is fully taxable for a minister. Organizations must apply these rules with integrity, sometimes in spite of pressure from employees to do otherwise.

CHAPTER 5 Information Reporting

In This Chapter

- General filing requirements
- Reporting on the receipt of funds
- Reporting on the payment of funds

- Summary of payment reporting requirements

Information reporting to the IRS is required for almost all nonprofit organizations. The key issues to consider for information reporting are:

➤ **Classifying payments to workers.** An organization generally makes many payments to individuals providing services to the organization. Some of the recipient individuals are employees and others are independent contractors. The organization must first make a determination as to which workers are independent contractors before proceeding with information reporting with respect to these workers. Payments of $600 or more in a calendar year to an independent contractor trigger filing Form 1099-MISC.

➤ **Information filing for other payments.** Certain payments other than to independent contractors also trigger information reporting such as payments of interest or royalties and payments to annuitants and nonresident aliens.

➤ **Information filing for receipt of funds.** The receipt of certain funds qualify for information reporting such as the receipt of interest on mortgages.

General Filing Requirements

Information forms (1098 and 1099) must be provided to the payees/recipients on or before January 31 following the calendar year that the funds were paid or received. Copies of the forms (or electronic media) must be filed with the IRS by January 31 following the year that the funds were paid or received.

An extension of time to file may be requested by filing Form 8809, Application for Extension of Time to File Information Returns, by the due date of the returns.

Form **W-9**
(Rev. October 2018)
Department of the Treasury
Internal Revenue Service

**Request for Taxpayer
Identification Number and Certification**

▶ Go to *www.irs.gov/FormW9* for instructions and the latest information.

Give Form to the
requester. Do not
send to the IRS.

1 Name (as shown on your income tax return). Name is required on this line; do not leave this line blank.
Richard K. Bennett

2 Business name/disregarded entity name, if different from above

3 Check appropriate box for federal tax classification of the person whose name is entered on line 1. Check only **one** of the following seven boxes.

[X] Individual/sole proprietor or single-member LLC
[ ] C Corporation
[ ] S Corporation
[ ] Partnership
[ ] Trust/estate

[ ] Limited liability company. Enter the tax classification (C=C corporation, S=S corporation, P=Partnership) ▶

Note: Check the appropriate box in the line above for the tax classification of the single-member owner. Do not check LLC if the LLC is classified as a single-member LLC that is disregarded from the owner unless the owner of the LLC is another LLC that is not disregarded from the owner for U.S. federal tax purposes. Otherwise, a single-member LLC that is disregarded from the owner should check the appropriate box for the tax classification of its owner.

[ ] Other (see instructions) ▶

4 Exemptions (codes apply only to certain entities, not individuals; see instructions on page 3):

Exempt payee code (if any) _____

Exemption from FATCA reporting code (if any) _____

(Applies to accounts maintained outside the U.S.)

5 Address (number, street, and apt. or suite no.) See instructions.
829 Garner Street

Requester's name and address (optional)

6 City, state, and ZIP code
Thomasville, SC 27360

7 List account number(s) here (optional)

Part I **Taxpayer Identification Number (TIN)**

Enter your TIN in the appropriate box. The TIN provided must match the name given on line 1 to avoid backup withholding. For individuals, this is generally your social security number (SSN). However, for a resident alien, sole proprietor, or disregarded entity, see the instructions for Part I, later. For other entities, it is your employer identification number (EIN). If you do not have a number, see *How to get a TIN*, later.

Note: If the account is in more than one name, see the instructions for line 1. Also see *What Name and Number To Give the Requester* for guidelines on whose number to enter.

Social security number
4 0 3 – 9 9 – 1 2 9 7

or

Employer identification number

Part II **Certification**

Under penalties of perjury, I certify that:

1. The number shown on this form is my correct taxpayer identification number (or I am waiting for a number to be issued to me); and

2. I am not subject to backup withholding because: (a) I am exempt from backup withholding, or (b) I have not been notified by the Internal Revenue Service (IRS) that I am subject to backup withholding as a result of a failure to report all interest or dividends, or (c) the IRS has notified me that I am no longer subject to backup withholding; and

3. I am a U.S. citizen or other U.S. person (defined below); and

4. The FATCA code(s) entered on this form (if any) indicating that I am exempt from FATCA reporting is correct.

Certification instructions. You must cross out item 2 above if you have been notified by the IRS that you are currently subject to backup withholding because you have failed to report all interest and dividends on your tax return. For real estate transactions, item 2 does not apply. For mortgage interest paid, acquisition or abandonment of secured property, cancellation of debt, contributions to an individual retirement arrangement (IRA), and generally, payments other than interest and dividends, you are not required to sign the certification, but you must provide your correct TIN. See the instructions for Part II, later.

Sign Here

Signature of U.S. person ▶ *Richard K. Bennett*   Date ▶ 1/2/19

Use this form to obtain the taxpayer identification number in non-employee situations.

Do Not Staple   6969

Form **1096**

Department of the Treasury
Internal Revenue Service

**Annual Summary and Transmittal of
U.S. Information Returns**

OMB No. 1545-0108

20**19**

FILER'S name
ABC Charity

Street address (including room or suite number)
2870 North Hull Street

City or town, state or province, country, and ZIP or foreign postal code
Traverse City, MI 49615

Name of person to contact	Telephone number
Marianne Smith	**231-435-2201**
Email address	Fax number
marsmith@msn.com	**231-435-2205**

For Official Use Only

1 Employer identification number	2 Social security number	3 Total number of forms	4 Federal income tax withheld	5 Total amount reported with this Form 1096
35-2946039		**10**	$	$ **9843.00**

6 Enter an "X" in only one box below to indicate the type of form being filed.

7 Form 1099-MISC with NEC in box 7, check . . . . ▶ [ ]

W-2G 32	1097-BTC 50	1098 81	1098-C 78	1098-E 84	1098-F 03	1098-Q 74	1098-T 83	1099-A 80	1099-B 79	1099-C 85	1099-CAP 73	1099-DIV 91	1099-G 86	1099-INT 92	1099-K 10	1099-LS 16
[ ]	[ ]	[ ]	[ ]	[ ]	[ ]	[ ]	[ ]	[ ]	[ ]	[ ]	[ ]	[ ]	[ ]	[ ]	[ ]	[ ]

1099-LTC 93	1099-MISC 95	1099-OID 96	1099-PATR 97	1099-Q 31	1099-QA 1A	1099-R 98	1099-S 75	1099-SA 94	1099-SB 43	3921 25	3922 26	5498 28	5498-ESA 72	5498-QA 2A	5498-SA 27	
[ ]	[X]	[ ]	[ ]	[ ]	[ ]	[ ]	[ ]	[ ]	[ ]	[ ]	[ ]	[ ]	[ ]	[ ]	[ ]	

Return this entire page to the Internal Revenue Service. Photocopies are not acceptable.

Under penalties of perjury, I declare that I have examined this return and accompanying documents and, to the best of my knowledge and belief, they are true, correct, and complete.

Signature ▶ *Daniel L. Lewis*   Title ▶ Treasurer   Date ▶ 1/13/19

This form is the "cover sheet" or transmittal form that must accompany all Forms 1099-MISC and other information forms.

Obtaining correct identification numbers

Organizations required to file information returns with the IRS must obtain the correct taxpayer identification number (TIN) to report real estate transactions, mortgage interest paid to or by the organization, and certain other transactions.

Form W-9, Request for Taxpayer Identification Number and Certification, is used to furnish the correct TIN to the organization and in certain other situations to:

➤ certify that the TIN furnished is correct

➤ certify that the recipient of the income is not subject to backup withholding, or

➤ certify exemption from backup withholding

> **Remember**
>
> If the recipient does not furnish a completed Form W-9, the church or nonprofit organization is required to withhold 28% of the payment for amounts paid, deposit the withholding with Form 8109 or 8109-B, and report amounts withheld on Form 1099-INT, 1099-MISC, or 1099-R, as applicable.

Reporting on the Receipt of Funds

Receipt of interest on mortgages

Use Form 1098, Mortgage Interest Statement, to report mortgage interest of $600 or more received by an organization during the year from an individual, including a sole proprietor. There is no requirement to file Form 1098 for interest received from a corporation, partnership, trust, estate, or association. A transmittal Form 1096 must accompany one or more Forms 1098.

Reporting on the Payment of Funds

Payments of interest

File Form 1099-INT, Interest Income, for each person to whom an organization paid interest reportable in Box 1 of at least $10 in any calendar year. This form is also required if any federal income tax was withheld under the backup withholding rules (28% is the 2018 rate), regardless of the amount of the payment. In certain instances, the $10 limit increases to $600. There is no requirement to file Form 1099-INT for payments made to a corporation or another tax-exempt organization.

The $10 limit applies if the interest is on "evidences of indebtedness" (bonds and promissory notes) issued by a corporation in "registered form." A note or bond is in "registered form" if its transfer must be effected by the surrender of the old instrument and either the corporation's reissuance of the old instrument to the new holder or its reissuance of a new instrument to the new holder.

9292	☐ VOID	☐ CORRECTED			

PAYER'S name, street address, city or town, state or province, country, ZIP or foreign postal code, and telephone no.	Payer's RTN (optional)	OMB No. 1545-0112		**Interest Income**
	1 Interest income	**2018**		
Lancaster Community Church 1425 Spencer Avenue Logansport, IN 46958	$ 913.00	Form **1099-INT**		
	2 Early withdrawal penalty			Copy A
	$			
PAYER'S TIN	RECIPIENT'S TIN	3 Interest on U.S. Savings Bonds and Treas. obligations		For **Internal Revenue Service Center**
35-7921873	307-20-6590	$		
RECIPIENT'S name		4 Federal income tax withheld	5 Investment expenses	File with Form 1096.
James R. Moore		$	$	
		6 Foreign tax paid	7 Foreign country or U.S. possession	For Privacy Act and Paperwork Reduction Act Notice, see the **2018 General Instructions for Certain Information Returns.**
Street address (including apt. no.)		$		
804 Linden Avenue		8 Tax-exempt interest	9 Specified private activity bond interest	
City or town, state or province, country, and ZIP or foreign postal code		$	$	
Wabash, IN 46992		10 Market discount	11 Bond premium	
	FATCA filing requirement ☐	$	$	
		12 Bond premium on Treasury obligations	13 Bond premium on tax-exempt bond	
Account number (see instructions)	2nd TIN not. ☐	$	$	
		14 Tax-exempt and tax credit bond CUSIP no.	15 State 16 State identification no. 17 State tax withheld	
			$	
			$	

Form **1099-INT**   Cat. No. 14410K   www.irs.gov/Form1099INT   Department of the Treasury - Internal Revenue Service

Do Not Cut or Separate Forms on This Page — Do Not Cut or Separate Forms on This Page

Use this form to report certain interest payments to the recipients.

Example 1: Sleepy Hollow Church financed a new church by issuing registered bonds. A 1099-INT form must be provided to each bond investor receiving $10 or more in interest during any calendar year.

If Sleepy Hollow engaged a bond broker to handle the issuance of the bonds, the broker would issue 1099-INT forms. If Sleepy Hollow issued the bonds without using a bond broker, the church would issue the 1099-INT forms.

Example 2: Sleepy Hollow Church borrows funds from church members. The notes are transferable. There is no requirement to return the bonds to the church for reissuance. The $600 limit applies for the issuance of 1099-INT forms for the payment of interest on these notes.

Payments to annuitants

File Form 1099-R for each person to whom the organization made a designated distribution that is a total distribution from a retirement plan or a payment to an annuitant of $1 or more. If part of the distribution is taxable and part is nontaxable, Form 1099-R should reflect the entire distribution.

Example: ABC Charity makes payments of $1,000 during the year to one of its annuitants, Mary Hughes. (Several years earlier, Mary entered into the charitable gift annuity agreement by giving a check to ABC.)

A portion of each annuity payment is a tax-free return of principal, and the remainder is annuity income for Mary. ABC will generally report the entire

9898	☐ VOID	☐ CORRECTED				
PAYER'S name, street address, city or town, state or province, country, ZIP or foreign postal code, and phone no.			1 Gross distribution	OMB No. 1545-0119		Distributions From Pensions, Annuities, Retirement or Profit-Sharing Plans, IRAs, Insurance Contracts, etc.
ABC Charity 8049 Riverside Blvd. Sacramento, CA 95831			$ 1000.00	2018		
			2a Taxable amount	Form 1099-R		
			$			
			2b Taxable amount not determined ☒	Total distribution ☐		Copy A For Internal Revenue Service Center
PAYER'S TIN 35-0179214	RECIPIENT'S TIN 945-77-2540		3 Capital gain (included in box 2a)	4 Federal income tax withheld		File with Form 1096.
			$	$		
RECIPIENT'S name Mary Hughes			5 Employee contributions/ Designated Roth contributions or insurance premiums	6 Net unrealized appreciation in employer's securities		For Privacy Act and Paperwork Reduction Act Notice, see the 2018 General Instructions for Certain Information Returns.
			$	$		
Street address (including apt. no.) PO Box 942			7 Distribution code(s)	IRA/ SEP/ SIMPLE ☐	8 Other $ %	
City or town, state or province, country, and ZIP or foreign postal code El Toro, CA 92609			9a Your percentage of total distribution %	9b Total employee contributions $		
10 Amount allocable to IRR within 5 years $	11 1st year of desig. Roth contrib.	FATCA filing requirement ☐	12 State tax withheld $ $	13 State/Payer's state no.	14 State distribution $ $	
Account number (see instructions)		Date of payment	15 Local tax withheld $	16 Name of locality	17 Local distribution $	

Form **1099-R** Cat. No. 14436Q   www.irs.gov/Form1099R   Department of the Treasury - Internal Revenue Service

Do Not Cut or Separate Forms on This Page — Do Not Cut or Separate Forms on This Page

Use this form for retirement or annuity payments.

$1,000 in Box 1 on Form 1099-R and check Box 2b unless ABC determines the taxable amount for the year.

Form W-4P, Withholding Certificate for Pension or Annuity Payments, should be completed by recipients of income from annuity, pension, and certain other deferred compensation plans to inform payers whether income tax is to be withheld and on what basis.

Payments to nonresident aliens

Payments for personal services made to noncitizens who are temporarily in this country (nonresident aliens) are often subject to federal income tax withholding at a 30% rate. Some payments may be exempt from income tax withholding if the person is from a country with which the United States maintains a tax treaty. A nonresident alien is a person who is neither a U.S. citizen nor a resident of the United States. Salary payments to nonresident aliens employed in the United States are subject to income tax withholding based on the regular withholding tables.

Single, nonrecurring, fixed, or determinable payments to nonresident aliens are generally not subject

Caution

Generally, 30% must be withheld from the gross amount paid to a foreign payee unless the payment can be reliably associated with valid documentation that establishes the payee is a U.S. person. If there is no documentation or if the documentation is believed to be unreliable or incorrect, the presumption rules outlined in IRS Publication 515 must be followed.

to withholding. Honoraria paid to visiting speakers usually fit this definition. It is not clear if love offerings are subject to withholding.

All payments to nonresident aliens, other than expense reimbursements and amounts reported on Form W-2, must be reported on Forms 1042 and 1042-S. These forms are filed with the IRS Service Center in Philadelphia by March 15 for the previous calendar year, and a copy of Form 1042-S must be sent to the nonresident alien.

Payments of royalties and for other services

An organization must file Form 1099-MISC for each recipient (other than corporations) to whom it has paid:

➤ at least $10 in royalties, or

➤ at least $600 in rents (for example, office rent or equipment rent), payments for services (nonemployee compensation), or medical health care payments

Payments of attorneys' fees to a lawyer or law firm must be included, generally in Box 7, even if the firm providing the legal services is incorporated.

Caution

There is more misunderstanding about the use of the Form 1099-MISC than about most IRS forms. Payments of $600 or more per calendar year to non-corporate providers of services trigger the filing of this form. This form should not be used for employee compensation payments, so typically an organization should not report clergy compensation (or the housing allowance) on this form.

Example: A charity has established a written, nondiscriminatory employee health reimbursement arrangement under which the charity pays the medical expenses of the employee, spouse, and dependents.

If $600 or more is paid in the calendar year to a doctor or other provider of health care services, a Form 1099-MISC must be filed. Amounts paid to an employee under a health reimbursement arrangement (or health care flexible spending account) are not reportable on Form W-2 or 1099-MISC.

Benevolence payments to nonemployees are not reportable on Form 1099-MISC (or any other information form). Benevolence payments to employees are reportable on Form W-2.

Do not include the payment of a housing allowance to a minister on Form 1099-MISC. Advances, reimbursements, or expenses for traveling and other business expenses of an employee are not reportable on Form 1099-MISC. These payments may be reportable on Form W-2 if they do not comply with the accountable expense plan rules.

Advances, reimbursements, or expenses for traveling and other business expenses of a self-employed person are not reportable on Form 1099-MISC if made under an accountable expense reimbursement plan. Under this type of plan, expenses are reimbursed *only* if they are substantiated as to amount, date, and business nature, and any excess reimbursements must be returned to the organization.

On Form 1099-MISC, report all advances, reimbursements, or expenses for traveling and other business expenses of a self-employed person for income tax purposes that are *not* substantiated to the paying organization.

Example 1: ABC Ministry organizes a seminar and engages a speaker. The speaker is paid a $750 honorarium, and ABC reimburses the travel expenses of $200 upon presentation of proper substantiation by the speaker. Form 1099-MISC should be issued to the speaker for $750.

Example 2: Same facts as Example 1, except $250 of the $750 payment is designated for travel expenses and the speaker substantiates to ABC for the travel. Since the honorarium is $500, after excluding the substantiated payments, and therefore is less than the $600 limit, there is no requirement to issue a Form 1099-MISC to the speaker.

If ABC paid an honorarium to the same speaker during the same calendar year of $100 or more, bringing the total for the year to the $600 level, a Form 1099-MISC should be issued.

Example 3: ABC Ministry contracts for janitorial services with an unincorporated janitorial service and pays $2,000 during the year for this service. ABC should issue a Form 1099-MISC for these payments.

9595	☐ VOID	☐ CORRECTED		
PAYER'S name, street address, city or town, state or province, country, ZIP or foreign postal code, and telephone no. ABC Charity 110 Harding Avenue Cincinnati, OH 45963	**1 Rents** $ **2 Royalties** $	OMB No. 1545-0115 20**18** Form **1099-MISC**	**Miscellaneous Income**	
	3 Other income $	**4 Federal income tax withheld** $	**Copy A** For **Internal Revenue Service Center**	
PAYER'S TIN 35-1148942	RECIPIENT'S TIN 389-11-8067	**5 Fishing boat proceeds** $	**6 Medical and health care payments** $	**File with Form 1096.**
RECIPIENT'S name Mark A. Mitchell	**7 Nonemployee compensation** $ 2400.00	**8 Substitute payments in lieu of dividends or interest** $	For Privacy Act and Paperwork Reduction Act Notice, see the **2018 General Instructions for Certain Information Returns.**	
Street address (including apt. no.) 512 Warren Avenue	**9 Payer made direct sales of $5,000 or more of consumer products to a buyer (recipient) for resale ▶** ☐	**10 Crop insurance proceeds** $		
City or town, state or province, country, and ZIP or foreign postal code Norwood, OH 45212	**11**	**12**		
Account number (see instructions)	FATCA filing requirement ☐	2nd TIN not. ☐	**13 Excess golden parachute payments** $	**14 Gross proceeds paid to an attorney** $
15a Section 409A deferrals $	**15b Section 409A income** $	**16 State tax withheld** $ $	**17 State/Payer's state no.**	**18 State income** $ $

Form **1099-MISC** Cat. No. 14425J www.irs.gov/Form1099MISC Department of the Treasury - Internal Revenue Service
Do Not Cut or Separate Forms on This Page — Do Not Cut or Separate Forms on This Page

Use this form to report royalty and nonemployee services payments.

Payments to volunteers

Payments to volunteers that represent a reimbursement under an accountable business expense reimbursement plan for expenses directly connected with the volunteer services are not reportable by the organization to the volunteer. With proper substantiation, unreimbursed volunteer expenses may be claimed as charitable contributions.

> **Remember**
>
> Legislation is almost annually introduced to allow tax-free mileage reimbursements to volunteers at the business mileage rate. To date, this provision has not been enacted.

Payments for auto mileage up to the maximum IRS rate for charitable miles are tax-free for volunteers. When an organization provides liability insurance for its volunteers, the value of the coverage can be excluded from the volunteer's income as a working condition fringe benefit.

Payments to or on behalf of volunteers that are not business expenses are reported on Form W-2 or Form 1099-MISC, depending on whether or not a common law employee relationship exists. When the relationship takes the form of an employer-employee relationship, payments other than expense reimbursement are reported on Form W-2. Payments to nonemployee volunteers for medical, educational, or personal living expenses must be reported as nonemployee compensation on Form 1099-MISC. Tax-free payments to volunteers for lodging, meals, and incidental expenses are limited to actual expenses (including use of the charitable mileage rate).

Moving expenses

Moving expenses an employer pays to a third party on behalf of the employee (for example, to a moving company) and services that an employer furnishes in kind to an employee are reported on Form W-2.

Racial nondiscrimination

Form 5578, *Annual Certification of Racial Nondiscrimination for a Private School Exempt from Federal Income Tax*, must be filed by churches and other charities that operate, supervise, or control a private school. The form must be filed by the 15th day of the fifth month following the end of the organization's calendar year or fiscal period. For organizations that must file Form 990, there is no requirement to file Form 5578 since the information is included in Schedule E.

The "private school" definition includes preschools, primary, secondary, preparatory, and high schools, and colleges and universities, whether operated as a separate legal entity or an activity of a church.

| Form **5578**
(Rev. August 2013)
Department of the Treasury
Internal Revenue Service | **Annual Certification of Racial Nondiscrimination
for a Private School Exempt From Federal Income Tax**
▶ Information about Form 5578 and its instructions is at *www.irs.gov/form5578*.
(For use by organizations that do not file Form 990 or Form 990-EZ) | OMB No. 1545-0213
Open to Public Inspection
For IRS Use Only ▶ |

| For the period beginning | July 1, 2017 | , and ending | June 30, 2018 | , |

1a Name of organization that operates, supervises, and/or controls school(s).	1b Employer identification number
Fellowship Church	**73-0896893**

Address (number and street or P.O. box no., if mail is not delivered to street address)	Room/suite
East Main Street	

City or town, state, and ZIP + 4 (If foreign address, list city or town, state or province, and country. Include postal code.)

Lamont, KS 66855

2a Name of central organization holding group exemption letter covering the school(s). (If same as 1a above, write "Same" and complete 2c.) If the organization in 1a holds an individual exemption letter, write "Not Applicable."	2b Employer identification number

Address (number and street or P.O. box no., if mail is not delivered to street address)	Room/suite	2c Group exemption number (see instructions under *Definitions*)

City or town, state, and ZIP + 4 (If foreign address, list city or town, state or province, and country. Include postal code.)

3a Name of school. (If more than one school, write "See Attached," and attach a list of the names, complete addresses, including postal codes, and employer identification numbers of the schools.) If same as 1a, write "Same."	3b Employer identification number, if any
Fellowship Christian School	**Same**

Address (number and street or P.O. box no., if mail is not delivered to street address)	Room/suite
Same	

City or town, state, and ZIP + 4 (If foreign address, list city or town, state or province, and country. Include postal code.)

Same

Under penalties of perjury, I hereby certify that I am authorized to take official action on behalf of the above school(s) and that to the best of my knowledge and belief the school(s) has (have) satisfied the applicable requirements of sections 4.01 through 4.05 of Rev. Proc. 75-50, 1975-2 C.B. 587, for the period covered by this certification.

(Signature)	Ralph Winzeler, Superintendent (Type or print name and title.)	5/26/18 (Date)

| For Paperwork Reduction Act Notice, see instructions. | Cat. No. 42658A | Form **5578** (Rev. 8-2013) |

Immigration control

The Immigration Reform and Control Act (IRCA) prohibits all employers from hiring unauthorized aliens, imposes documentation verification requirements on all employers, and provides an "amnesty" program for certain illegal aliens. The law also prohibits employers with three or more employees from discriminating because of national origin. An I-9 Form (see page102) must be completed and retained on file by all employers for each employee. The form must be available for inspection at any time. Form I-9 may be obtained by calling 800-375-5283 or at http://uscis.gov/i-9.

The Form I-551, Alien Registration Card (Green Card), issued after August 1, 1989, is the exclusive registration card issued to lawful permanent residents as definitive evidence of identity and U.S. resident status.

Employment Eligibility Verification
Department of Homeland Security
U.S. Citizenship and Immigration Services

USCIS
Form I-9
OMB No. 1615-0047
Expires 08/31/2019

► START HERE: Read instructions carefully before completing this form. The instructions must be available, either in paper or electronically, during completion of this form. Employers are liable for errors in the completion of this form.

ANTI-DISCRIMINATION NOTICE: It is illegal to discriminate against work-authorized individuals. Employers CANNOT specify which document(s) an employee may present to establish employment authorization and identity. The refusal to hire or continue to employ an individual because the documentation presented has a future expiration date may also constitute illegal discrimination.

Section 1. Employee Information and Attestation (Employees must complete and sign Section 1 of Form I-9 no later than the first day of employment, but not before accepting a job offer.)

Last Name (Family Name)	First Name (Given Name)	Middle Initial	Other Last Names Used (if any)
Hendricks	Fred	W.	

Address (Street Number and Name): 408 Forest Avenue
Apt. Number:
City or Town: Cincinnati
State: OH
ZIP Code: 45980

Date of Birth (mm/dd/yyyy): 06-12-1959
U.S. Social Security Number: 5 1 4 - 4 2 - 9 0 8 7
Employee's E-mail Address: fhend@hotmail.com
Employee's Telephone Number: 513-641-5950

I am aware that federal law provides for imprisonment and/or fines for false statements or use of false documents in connection with the completion of this form.

I attest, under penalty of perjury, that I am (check one of the following boxes):

[X] 1. A citizen of the United States
[ ] 2. A noncitizen national of the United States (See instructions)
[ ] 3. A lawful permanent resident (Alien Registration Number/USCIS Number):
[ ] 4. An alien authorized to work until (expiration date, mm/dd/yyyy):

Some aliens may write "N/A" in the expiration date field. (See instructions)

Aliens authorized to work must provide only one of the following document numbers to complete Form I-9:
An Alien Registration Number/USCIS Number OR Form I-94 Admission Number OR Foreign Passport Number.

1. Alien Registration Number/USCIS Number:
OR
2. Form I-94 Admission Number:
OR
3. Foreign Passport Number:
Country of Issuance:

QR Code - Section 1
Do Not Write in This Space

Signature of Employee: Fred W. Hendricks
Today's Date (mm/dd/yyyy): 01/03/2019

Preparer and/or Translator Certification (check one):
[ ] I did not use a preparer or translator. [ ] A preparer(s) and/or translator(s) assisted the employee in completing Section 1.
(Fields below must be completed and signed when preparers and/or translators assist an employee in completing Section 1.)

I attest, under penalty of perjury, that I have assisted in the completion of Section 1 of this form and that to the best of my knowledge the information is true and correct.

Signature of Preparer or Translator:
Today's Date (mm/dd/yyyy):

Last Name (Family Name)	First Name (Given Name)

Address (Street Number and Name):
City or Town:
State:
ZIP Code:

Form I-9 07/17/17 N

Employer Completes Next Page

Page 1 of 3

Employment Eligibility Verification
Department of Homeland Security
U.S. Citizenship and Immigration Services

USCIS
Form I-9
OMB No. 1615-0047
Expires 08/31/2019

Section 2. Employer or Authorized Representative Review and Verification
(Employers or their authorized representative must complete and sign Section 2 within 3 business days of the employee's first day of employment. You must physically examine one document from List A OR a combination of one document from List B and one document from List C as listed on the "Lists of Acceptable Documents.")

Employee Info from Section 1	Last Name (Family Name)	First Name (Given Name)	M.I.	Citizenship/Immigration Status
	Hendricks	Fred	W	Citizen

List A Identity and Employment Authorization	OR	List B Identity	AND	List C Employment Authorization
Document Title		Document Title: Driver's License		Document Title: Birth Certificate
Issuing Authority		Issuing Authority: Ohio		Issuing Authority: Ohio
Document Number		Document Number: 514-42-9087		Document Number:
Expiration Date (if any)(mm/dd/yyyy)		Expiration Date (if any)(mm/dd/yyyy): 6/30/20		Expiration Date (if any)(mm/dd/yyyy):
Document Title		Additional Information		QR Code - Sections 2 & 3 Do Not Write In This Space
Issuing Authority				
Expiration Date (if any)(mm/dd/yyyy)				
Document Title				
Issuing Authority				
Document Number				
Expiration Date (if any)(mm/dd/yyyy)				

Certification: I attest, under penalty of perjury, that (1) I have examined the document(s) presented by the above-named employee, (2) the above-listed document(s) appear to be genuine and to relate to the employee named, and (3) to the best of my knowledge the employee is authorized to work in the United States.

The employee's first day of employment (mm/dd/yyyy): _____ (See instructions for exemptions.)

Signature of Employer or Authorized Representative: David L. Brown
Today's Date (mm/dd/yyyy): 01/03/2019
Title of Employer or Authorized Representative: Business Manager

Last Name of Employer or Authorized Representative: Brown
First Name of Employer or Authorized Representative: David L.
Employer's Business or Organization Name: Fairfield Church

Employer's Business or Organization Address (Street Number and Name): 110 Harding Avenue
City or Town: Cincinnati
State: OH
ZIP Code: 45960

Section 3. Reverification and Rehires (To be completed and signed by employer or authorized representative.)

A. New Name (if applicable)			B. Date of Rehire (if applicable)
Last Name (Family Name)	First Name (Given Name)	Middle Initial	Date (mm/dd/yyyy)

C. If the employee's previous grant of employment authorization has expired, provide the information for the document or receipt that establishes continuing employment authorization in the space provided below.

Document Title:
Document Number:
Expiration Date (if any) (mm/dd/yyyy):

I attest, under penalty of perjury, that to the best of my knowledge, this employee is authorized to work in the United States, and if the employee presented document(s), the document(s) I have examined appear to be genuine and to relate to the individual.

Signature of Employer or Authorized Representative:
Today's Date (mm/dd/yyyy):
Name of Employer or Authorized Representative:

Form I-9 07/17/17 N

Page 2 of 3

This form must be completed and retained on file by all employers for employees hired after November 6, 1986. (For more information on completing this form, go to www.uscis.gov.)

Summary of Payment Reporting Requirements

Below is an alphabetical list of some payments and the forms necessary to report them. It is not a complete list of payments, and the absence of a payment from the list does not suggest that the payment is exempt from reporting.

Types of Payment	Report on Form
Advance earned income credit	W-2
Annuities, periodic payments	1099-R
* Attorneys' fees	1099-MISC
** Auto, personal use of employer-owned vehicle	W-2
Auto reimbursements (nonaccountable plan):	
Employee	W-2
Nonemployee	1099-MISC
Awards:	
Employee	W-2
Nonemployee	1099-MISC
Bonuses:	
Employee	W-2
Nonemployee	1099-MISC
Cafeteria/flexible benefit plan	5500, 5500-C, or 5500-R
Christmas bonuses:	
Employee	W-2
Nonemployee	1099-MISC
Commissions:	
Employee	W-2
Nonemployee	1099-MISC
Compensation:	
Employee	W-2
Nonemployee	1099-MISC
Dependent care payments	W-2
Education expense reimbursement (nonaccountable plan):	
Employee	W-2
Nonemployee	1099-MISC
Employee business expense reimbursement (nonaccountable plan)	W-2

Types of Payment	Report on Form
Fees:	
Employee	W-2
Nonemployee	1099-MISC
Group-term life insurance (PS 58 costs)	W-2 or 1099-R
Interest, other than mortgage	1099-INT
Long-term care benefits	1099-LTC
Medical expense reimbursement plan (employee-funded)	5500, 5500-C, or 5500-R
Mileage (nonaccountable plan):	
Employee	W-2
Nonemployee	1099-MISC
Mortgage interest	1098
Moving expense:	
Employee	W-2
Nonemployee	1099-MISC
Prizes:	
Employee	W-2
Nonemployee	1099-MISC
Real estate proceeds	1099-S
Rents	1099-MISC
Royalties	1099-MISC
Severance pay	W-2
Sick pay	W-2
Supplemental unemployment	W-2
Vacation allowance:	
Employee	W-2
Nonemployee	1099-MISC

* The exemption from reporting payments made to corporations does not apply to payments to a lawyer or a law firm for legal services, even if the provider of the legal services is incorporated.

** Or, the value may be reported on a separate statement to the employee.

Integrity**Points**

- **Obtaining a completed Form W-9.** The proper completion of forms in the 1099 series all starts with obtaining a completed Form W-9 before the applicable payments are made by the church or nonprofit. Unless the Form W-9 is obtained before payments are made, it may be very difficult to obtain the form at a later date and could complicate the filing of the appropriate 1099 form. Integrity requires having procedures to obtain a Form W-9 at the beginning of the relationship with a recipient of certain charity payments.

- **Reporting of payments to independent contractors.** Because there is generally no tax to withhold, it is easy for a church or nonprofit to overlook the filing of Form 1099-MISC. When an organization fails to file a required Form 1099-MISC, it may be inadvertently giving an independent contractor a license to not report taxable income. Integrity requires the proper filing of Form 1099-MISC and all other forms in the 1099 series, if applicable.

- **Reporting of payments to noncitizens.** Churches and other nonprofits often make payments to individuals who are not U.S. citizens and are temporarily in the U.S. The proper reporting to the IRS is often overlooked. For example, payments might be made by a church to a national worker (noncitizen) visiting the church to report on the effectiveness of gifts made by a church to an international mission field.

  While reimbursements made under an accountable expense reimbursement plan are not reportable, other payments must be reported on Form 1042-S, and some payments are even subject to federal income tax withholding. Integrity requires organizations to understand the rules relating to payment to noncitizens before the payments are made.

6 Financial Management and Reporting

In This Chapter

- Recordkeeping of income and expenses
- Accounting records
- Financial reports
- Budgeting
- Audits and other related services
- Fraud

One does not have to look far to find examples of organizations that have suffered because their financial records and reporting systems were deficient. Sound financial recordkeeping is invaluable to churches and other nonprofit organizations in these three ways:

➤ **Helps board and staff make well-informed decisions.** Only from a quality set of financial records may good reports be prepared which reflect the financial condition of the organization. These reports are vital to allow the board and staff to assess the overall financial health of the organization, determine financial trends, measure financial outcomes, and project future budgetary needs. Informed decisions may only be made based on solid financial records.

➤ **Helps the organization keep running smoothly.** Without a sound accounting system, it will not be possible for an organization to keep on track financially. Quality financial records keep order from turning into chaos. Imagine the challenges that would face an organization if its records did not clearly reflect its liabilities, if it did not know how much had been expended of a giver's temporarily restricted gift, or if the accounting records had not been reconciled to the bank statement. Yes, a smoothly running organization requires good accounting records.

➤ **Helps the organization demonstrate financial accountability.** Churches and nonprofit organizations must demonstrate accountability in a variety of ways. Church members anticipate at least annual financial data on the church's operations. Most nonprofit organizations other than churches must file Form 990 and perhaps Form 990-T with the Internal Revenue Service. Grant funders anticipate appropriate reporting on the use of grant funds. Accountability to the organization's board is a given. Good financial records are the basis for accountability to all constituents.

Recordkeeping of Income and Expenses

A good chart of accounts is the starting point for recording income and expenses. Finding the balance between too few and too many accounts in the chart is the key. Too few accounts will restrict reporting capabilities, while too many accounts leads to cumbersome recording processes and excessive time spent in analyzing and reconciling accounts. A sample chart of accounts for a church is reflected on page 107, and it could be adapted for other organizations as well.

In terms of accounting for income, adequate internal controls to safeguard these assets are very important. Offerings are the financial lifeblood of churches, and these funds must be handled with care. Pages 129–32 reflect key guidelines for handling church offerings. Many of these principles apply to handling gifts to other nonprofits and income of various types.

When it comes to disbursing funds, one of the most important principles is to pay almost all expenses by check or electronic means. The use of a petty cash fund should be the only exception to payment by check. Cash from a deposit should never be used to pay expenses.

> **Caution**
>
> Checks should not be written until near the time when funds are available to cover them. Some organizations write checks when bills are due without regard to available cash. Checks are then held for days, weeks, or sometimes months until they are released for payment. This is an extremely confusing practice that makes it very difficult to determine the actual checkbook balance.

Use preprinted, consecutively numbered checks. All spoiled checks should be marked "void" and kept on file with the canceled checks.

In some instances, it may be wise to require two signatures on every check or on checks over a certain amount. In other situations, one signature may be appropriate. The level of controls over the funds will help determine if more than one signature is necessary. Access to a checking account should generally be limited to no more than two or three individuals. For example, the pastor of a church should not have access to the checking account. Checks should never be signed and delivered to anyone without completing the payee and the amount.

The use of check request forms, including approval by the appropriate person, is often a good expense-control procedure. Large organizations often use a formal purchase order system. In either case, oral requests for funds should not be permitted.

Every check should have some type of written document to support it—an invoice, petty cash receipt, payroll summary, and so on (a sample cash expense report is shown on page 109). If such support is not available for a valid reason, a memo should be written to support the expenditure. For example, an honorarium paid to a visiting speaker would not be supported by an invoice but should be documented by indicating the speaker's name, the date of the speaking engagement, and the event.

Sample Chart of Accounts

Note: Fund numbers could be used as a prefix to the account numbers

Assets (100)
101   Cash and cash equivalents
110   Prepaid expenses
120   Short-term investments
         Land, buildings, and equipment
160   Buildings
162   Furnishings
180   Long-term investments

Liabilities (200)
201   Accounts payable
210   Notes payable

Net Assets (300)
301   Unrestricted
302   Board designated
310   Temporarily restricted

Revenues and Support (400)
         Contributions
401   Regular offerings
402   Sunday school offerings
403   Missions offerings
404   Building fund offerings
419   Other offerings
         Investment income
421   Interest income
422   Rental income
         Other income
431   Book sales
439   Other income

Expenses (500–600)
         Salaries and wages
501   Salary including cash housing allowance
502   Social security (SECA) reimbursement
         Benefits
511   Pension
512   Tax-deferred payments (TSA)
513   Social security (FICA)

514   Medical expense reimbursement
515   Insurance premiums
         Supplies
521   Postage
522   Literature and printing
523   Office supplies
524   Maintenance supplies
530   Advertising
         Travel and entertainment
541   Airline
542   Vehicle rental
543   Mileage
544   Meals
545   Hotel
549   Other travel expense
550   Continuing education
         Insurance
561   Workers' Compensation
562   Health insurance
563   Property insurance
569   Other insurance
         Benevolences
571   Denominational budgets
579   Other benevolences
         Services and professional fees
581   Speaking honoraria
582   Custodial services
583   Legal and audit fees
589   Other fees
         Office and occupancy
591   Rent
592   Telephone
593   Utilities
594   Property taxes
599   Other office and occupancy
600   Depreciation
610   Interest expense

Suffix digits may be used to indicate the functional expense category, such as:

Church example		Nonprofit example	
- 10	Administration	- 10	Feeding program
- 20	Pastoral	- 20	Bible distribution
- 30	Youth	- 30	Crusades
- 40	Children	- 40	Training
- 50	Men's	- 50	Child sponsorship
- 60	Women's	- 60	Disaster relief
- 70	Music and worship	- 70	Administration
- 80	Missions	- 80	Development
- 90	Membership and evangelism		

Cash Count Summary

March 4 _____ , 20 18

	Sunday School	Sunday A.M.	Sunday P.M.	Received During Week	TOTAL
Coins	83.12	21.82	10.42		115.36
Currency	320.00	431.00	108.00		859.00
Checks	25.00	1,855.00	360.00	185.00	2,425.00
TOTALS	428.12	2,307.82	478.42	185.00	3,399.36

Breakdown by Type of Gift

	Sunday School	Sunday A.M.	Sunday P.M.	Received During Week	TOTAL
Regular Tithes and Offerings		1,942.82	368.42	140.00	2,451.24
Sunday School	428.12				428.12
Building Fund		85.00	50.00	15.00	150.00
Missions		100.00	30.00	20.00	150.00
Other Designated Funds:					
Benevolence Fund		40.00			40.00
School Project		30.00	10.00		40.00
Choir Robes		50.00			50.00
Youth Trip		40.00	20.00	10.00	70.00
Parking Lot		20.00			20.00
TOTALS	428.12	2,307.82	478.42	185.00	3,399.36

Counted by: *Mike Anderson*
Helen David
Bob Wells

Deposited on: March 6 _____ , 20 18

Contributions by Donor

March 4 _____ , 2018 _____ (X) A.M. ( ) P.M. ( )

Name of Contributor	Regular Tithes & Offerings	Sunday School	Building Fund	Missions	Other Description	Other Amount
Wilson, M/M Mark	150.00		10.00	20.00		
Young, Frank	35.00					
Jackson, Ellen	60.00		15.00			
Avery, Lori	40.00					
Floyd, M/M Mike	200.00	10.00			Benevolence	40.00
Long, M/M Harold	45.00		50.00			
Martin, Mary	75.00			10.00		
Ross, M/M Steve	80.00			50.00		
Harris, M/M Joe	65.00		5.00		School Project	40.00
York, Kelly	150.00					
Walker, Peggy	30.00					
Franklin, M/M Bob	75.00	5.00		15.00		
Gilles, Don	40.00		10.00			
Shields, Lou	500.00					
White, M/M Ron	80.00		20.00			
Howe, Art	100.00		20.00		Choir Robes	50.00
Plunkett, M/M Stan	60.00	10.00				
Robbins, Nancy	75.00				Youth Trip	70.00
Lyon, M/M Bill	50.00			5.00		
Clark, M/M David	80.00		20.00			
Bowers, James	40.00				Parking Lot	20.00
Burr, Cindy	60.00			40.00		
Anonymous	361.24	403.12		10.00		
TOTALS	2,451.24	428.12	150.00	150.00		220.00

CASH EXPENSE REPORT

Name: _____ Pastor Frank Morris _____

Address: _____ 3801 North Florida Avenue _____

_____ Miami, FL 33168 _____

Period Covered: From: __7/1/18__ To: __7/14/18__

| DATE | TRAVEL | | | | | | | | OTHER * | | ACCOUNT to be Charged |
	City	Purpose of Travel	Brkfast	Lunch	Dinner	Snack	Lodging	Trans.	Description	Amount	
7/2/18									Lunch w/Bob Cox	18.21	544-20
7/6/18	Atlanta, GA	Continuing Ed. Sem.		10.80	13.40	2.10	90.50	265.08	Tips	8.00	549-20
7/6/18	" "	" " "	6.40								544-20
7/6/18									Lunch w/Al Lane	12.80	544-80
7/14/18									Lunch w/Sam Lee	11.12	544-40
	TOTAL CASH EXPENSES		6.40	10.80	13.40	2.10	90.50	265.08		50.13	

*If this is entertainment, please use the entertainment worksheet on the back of this form.

Frank Morris __7/16/18__
Signature (person requesting reimbursement) Date

Bob Davis __7/16/18__
Approved by Date

Total cash expenses	438.41
Personal auto business mileage (Complete worksheet on the back of this form.)	106.28
195 miles X 54.5¢ per mile	
Less travel advance	(300.00)
Balance due	244.69
Refund due organization	

PERSONAL AUTO BUSINESS MILEAGE			
Date	Purpose/Destination	Miles	Account to be charged
7-01-18	Calls/Valley View Rest Home	23	543-20
7-02-18	Brown Funeral Home/Harold Boone	18	"
7-03-18	Calls/Various Homes	20	"
7-06-18	Calls/Memorial Hospital	15	"
7-05-18	Kiwanis Speaker/Pat's Cafeteria	25	"
7-07-18	Calls/Various Homes	10	"
7-08-18	Calls/St. Luke's Hospital	17	"
7-09-18	Calls/Cannon Nursing Home	12	"
7-10-18	Calls/Various Homes	8	"
7-12-18	Calls/Memorial Hospital	15	"
7-15-18	Ministerial Convention/Webb City	32	"
	TOTAL MILES TRAVELED	195	

To mileage summary on page one ←

ENTERTAINMENT WORKSHEET				
(Expenses paid in behalf of individual(s) other than the person filing this expense report.)				
Date	Persons Entertained	Purpose of Entertainment	Place	Amount
7-03-18	M/M Bob Cox	Prospective Members	Olive Garden	18.21
7-06-18	Al Lane	Discuss Ch. Bldg Plans	Chi-Chi's	12.80
7-14-18	Sam Lee	Church Goals w/Bd. Chair	Damon's	11.12
	TOTAL AMOUNT SPENT			42.13

To "other" expense column on page one ←

Occasionally, it may be necessary to advance funds before supporting documentation is available (for example, a travel advance for future travel). In these instances, a system must be devised to ensure documentation is provided on a timely basis and any excess funds are returned.

Accounting Records

Accounting systems differ in shape, size, complexity, and efficiency. The objectives of the system should be to measure and control financial activities and to provide financial information to an organization's governing body, a congregation, and givers. In choosing the accounting system for your organization, the most important consideration is the ability of the individual(s) keeping the records.

Cash and accrual methods

Most small-to-medium-size churches and nonprofit organizations use the cash or modified cash basis of accounting. These methods do not conform to U.S. generally accepted accounting principles (GAAP). When the accrual basis of accounting is required for audit purposes, the cash basis is often used throughout the year with the conversion to accrual at year-end.

Advantages of cash method

Under the cash method, revenue is recorded only when cash is received, and expenses are recorded when they are paid. For example, office supplies expense is shown in the month when the bill is paid, even though the supplies were received and used in the previous month. Pledges are not recorded as receivables, and the revenue from pledges is recorded as the cash is received.

The primary advantage of the cash method is its simplicity. It is easier for non-accountants to understand and keep records on this basis. When financial statements are required, the treasurer just summarizes the transactions from the checkbook stubs or runs the computer-prepared financial statements with fewer adjusting entries required. For smaller organizations, the difference between financial results on the cash and on the accrual basis is often not significant.

Advantages of accrual method

Many organizations use the accrual method of accounting when the cash basis does not accurately portray the financial picture. Under the accrual method, revenue is recorded when earned. For example, a church charges a fee for the use of the fellowship hall for a wedding. Under accrual

Idea

Even when obtaining an accrual basis audit, you can keep your books on the cash basis during the year and record journal entries on the last day of the year to convert to accrual. Too many organizations struggle to keep their books on the accrual basis (recording accounts receivable, accounts payable, etc.) when their financial life would be much simpler if the cash basis were used.

accounting, the revenue is recorded in the month earned even though the cash might not be received until a later month.

Under accrual accounting, expenses are recorded when incurred. For example, telephone expense is recorded in the month when the service occurs although the bill may not be paid until the next month.

U.S. generally accepted accounting principles for nonprofit organizations require the use of accrual basis accounting. Organizations that have their books audited by Certified Public Accountants (CPAs) and want the CPAs to report that the financial statements appear according to "U.S. generally accepted accounting principles" (GAAP) must either keep their records on the accrual basis or make the appropriate adjustments at the end of the year to convert to this basis. Financial statements prepared on a cash or other comprehensive basis may qualify under GAAP if the financial statements are not materially different from those prepared on an accrual basis.

Modified cash method

The modified cash method of accounting is a combination of certain features of the cash and accrual methods. For example, accounts payable may be recorded when a bill is received although other payables or receivables are not recorded. The modified cash method portrays the financial picture more accurately than the cash method but not as well as the full accrual method.

Depreciation

Cash basis financial statements will not show property and equipment assets and therefore will not show depreciation. However, accrual statements will require this presentation and modified cash statements will typically include these assets as well to better reflect what the ministry owns. Depreciation is calculated over the expected useful life of the asset and therefore can be useful from a budgeting perspective to build in replacement reserves. If these amounts are set aside, there should not be a need to obtain financing for items such as air conditioning units or roof replacements.

Fund accounting

Fund accounting (or accounting by classes of net assets) provides an excellent basis for stewardship reporting. It is a system of accounting in which separate records are kept for resources donated to an organization that are restricted by givers or outside parties for certain specified purposes or uses.

GAAP requires that net assets be broken down into the following three classes, based on the presence or absence of giver-imposed restrictions and their nature:

Remember

Fund accounting does not necessarily require multiple bank accounts. One bank account is all that is usually necessary. However, it may be appropriate to place restricted funds into a separate bank account to ensure the funds are not inadvertently spent for other purposes.

Net assets with donor restrictions

➤ **Permanently restricted.** These assets are not available for program expenses, payments to creditors, or other organizational needs. An example is an endowment gift with a stipulation that the principal is permanently not available for spending but the investment income from the principal may be used in current operations.

➤ **Temporarily restricted.** These assets may be restricted by purpose or time, but the restrictions are not permanent. An example of the purpose-restricted gift is a gift for a certain project or for the purchase of some equipment. An example of a time-restricted gift is a contribution in the form of a trust, annuity, or term endowment (the principal of the gift is restricted for a certain term of time).

Net assets without donor restrictions

➤ These net assets may be used for any of the organization's purposes. According to accounting standards, "The only limits on unrestricted net assets are broad limits

---

Sample Record Retention and Destruction Policy

The following is a partial listing of recommended retention times for several types of records. Churches and nonprofit organizations will retain many of these documents on their computer network. These apply to both physical and electronic documents. If no physical copy of an electronic document is retained, the means to "read" the electronic document must also be retained. For all records maintained electronically, be certain there is a backup that is tested and can be restored.

Record Type	Retention Period
A. Accounting and Finance	
Accounts payable and accounts receivable ledgers and schedules	7 years
Annual audit reports and financial statements	Permanent
Annual audit records, including workpapers and other documents that relate to the audit	7 years after completion of audit
Bank statements and canceled checks	7 years
Credit card numbers	Full credit card numbers should not be retained any longer than immediate business needs and merchant account agreements dictate
Employee expense reports	7 years
General ledgers	Permanent
Notes receivable ledgers and schedules	7 years
Investment records	7 years after sale of investment
B. Contracts	
Contracts and related correspondence (including any proposal that resulted in the contract and all other documentation)	7 years after expiration or termination

Comment: Some states may require longer retention periods generally, or for specific types of contracts. A local attorney should be consulted.

Record Type	Retention Period

C. Corporate Records

Corporate records (minutes books, signed minutes of the board and all committees, corporate seals, articles of incorporation, bylaws, annual corporate reports) — Permanent

Licenses and permits — Permanent

D. Electronic Documents

Electronic mail: Retention of emails depends on the subject matter.
- All email—from internal or external sources—is generally deleted after 12 months.
- The organization will archive email for six months after the staff has deleted it, after which time the email will be permanently deleted.
- Staff should not store or transfer organization-related email to non-work-related computers except as necessary or appropriate for organization purposes.

Electronic Documents: Retention of electronic documents (including Microsoft Office, PDF files, etc.) depends on the subject matter.

Web page files - Internet cookies: At all workstations, the internet browser should be scheduled to delete Internet cookies once per month.

Comment: This section may be the appropriate place to include other policies regarding email retention, usage, or subject matter. Whether the paper or electronic document is the "official document" would be determined by each organization.

E. Payroll Documents

Employee deduction authorizations	4 years after termination
Payroll deductions	Termination + 7 years
W-2 and W-4 forms	Termination + 7 years
Garnishments, assignments, attachments	Termination + 7 years
Payroll registers (gross and net)	7 years
Time cards/sheets	2 years
Unclaimed wage records	6 years

F. Personnel Records

Commissions/bonuses/incentives/awards	7 years
EEO-1/EEO-2 – Employer information reports	2 years after superseded or filing (whichever is longer)
Employee earnings records	Separation + 7 years
Employee handbooks	1 copy kept permanently
Employee personnel records (including individual attendance records, application forms, job or status change records, performance evaluations, termination papers, withholding information garnishments, test results, training and qualification records)	6 years after separation
Employment contracts – individual	7 years after separation
Employment records – correspondence with employment agencies and advertisements for job openings	3 years from date of hiring decision
Employment records – all non-hired applicants (including all applications and resumes – whether solicited or unsolicited, results of post-offer, pre-employment physicals, results of background investigations, if any, related correspondence)	2–4 years (4 years if file contains any correspondence which might be construed as an offer)
Job descriptions	3 years after superseded

Record Type	Retention Period
Personnel count records	3 years
Forms I-9	3 years after hiring, or
	1 year after separation if later

Comment: Many employment and employment tax-related laws have both state and federal law requirements. A local attorney should be consulted.

G. Property Records

Correspondence, property deeds, assessments, licenses, rights of way	Permanent
Property insurance policies	Permanent

H. Tax Records

Tax exemption documents and related correspondence	Permanent
IRS rulings	Permanent
Excise tax records	7 years
Payroll tax records	7 years
Tax bills, receipts, statements	7 years
Tax returns – income, franchise, property	Permanent
Tax workpaper packages – originals	7 years
Sales/use tax records	7 years
Annual information returns – federal and state	Permanent
IRS or other government audit records	Permanent

Comment: Retention period for sales taxes and property taxes are determined by state law. A local accountant or attorney should be consulted.

I. Contribution Records

Records of contributions	7 years
Documents evidencing terms, conditions, or restrictions on gifts	7 years after funds are expended

resulting from the nature of the organization and the purposes specified in its articles of incorporation or bylaws."

Giver-imposed restrictions normally apply to the use of net assets and not to the use of specific assets. Only givers or outside parties may "restrict" funds given to a nonprofit organization. The organization's board may not "restrict" monies—they may only "designate" funds. For example, if a giver donates money for a new church organ, the funds should be placed in a restricted fund. If the church board sets funds aside in a debt retirement fund, this is a designated fund, a subdesignation of unrestricted net assets.

Records retention and destruction

Proper maintenance of corporate documents and records is critical from both a management and a legal perspective. An organization's preparedness for a financial or IRS audit, legal action and/or response, public inquiry, and loss by theft or natural catastrophe, among other things, depends largely on keeping accurate records for as long as necessary.

Financial Reports

In preparing financial reports, there is one basic rule: Prepare different reports for different audiences. For example, a church board would normally receive a more detailed financial report than the church membership. Department heads in a nonprofit organization might receive reports that relate only to their department.

Financial statements should:

Key Issue

"Dashboard" financial reporting is increasingly used by nonprofits. It gets its name because it's like a financial dashboard—with gauges, redlines, and warning lights. It cuts through the barrage of uninterrupted data and delivers a clear view of the organization's performance. It often includes a visualization of historical information and personalized reports for key staff members.

➤ be easily comprehensible so that any person taking the time to study them will understand the financial picture

➤ be concise so that the person studying them will not get lost in detail

➤ be all-inclusive in scope and embrace all activities of the organization

➤ have a focal point for comparison so that the person reading them will have some basis for making a judgment (usually this will be a comparison with a budget or data from the corresponding period of the previous year)

➤ be prepared on a timely basis (the longer the delay after the end of the period, the longer the time before corrective action can be taken)

Dashboard reports present a quick, comprehensible overview of an organization's financial status (dashboard reports can also reflect other critical measures of organizational performance and mission effectiveness). When dashboard reports present key indicators in consistent formats, board members and staff can readily spot changes and trends in these measurements. Like the dashboard inside a car, these reports often display the equivalent of warning lights that only flare up when there is an impending problem or when certain variables are outside of predetermined limits.

For additional reading, see *Financial and Accounting Guide for Not-for-Profit Organizations* by John A. Mattie, John H. McCarthy, and Nancy E. Shelmon (John Wiley & Sons, Inc.).

Statement of financial position

A statement of financial position shows assets, liabilities, and net assets as of the end-of-period date. This statement is also called a balance sheet because it shows how the two sides of the accounting equation (assets minus liabilities equals net assets) "balance" in the organization.

Financial Questions for Boards

Financial reporting to the organization's board should answer the following questions:

1. Is our cash flow projected to be adequate? (This question presumes the organization prepares cash flow projections.)

2. What is the trend of cash in terms of number of days or number of months of cash on hand (excluding cash related to temporarily and permanently restricted net assets)? What is the organization's goal in terms of the number of days or months of cash in hand?

3. Do we have sufficient net assets (reserves)? (This question presumes the organization has established goals for net assets so that measurement is possible.) The ECFA eBook *9 Essentials of Church Cash Reserves* may be a useful resource.

4. Did total net assets increase or decrease, and is this a significant change from last year?

5. Did unrestricted net assets increase or decrease, and is it a significant change from last year?

6. Have any funds related to temporarily or permanently restricted net assets been borrowed for operational or capital needs?

7. Is the financial activity compared with the operating and capital budgets? (This question presumes the organization prepares both operating and capital budgets.)

8. Are there any significant differences between actual and budgeted data? If so:
   a. Why did they occur?
   b. Do they need to be addressed, and if so, how?

9. Are there any significant differences between this year-to-date and prior year-to-date actual data? If so:
   a. Are trends reflected by major revenue categories, e.g., contributions?
   b. Are trends reflected by major expense categories, e.g., salaries and fringe benefits?

10. If investments show major changes, does the Statement of Cash Flows show significant sales or purchases?

11. Were there significant purchases of property or equipment during the year?

12. Has long-term and/or short-term debt significantly increased or decreased?

13. Are payroll tax payments up-to-date and always timely made?

14. Are federal, state, and local filings up-to-date, e.g., 941s, W-2s, 1099s, etc.?

15. Are any vendor accounts in over-30-day status?

Anything an organization owns that has a monetary value is an asset. Cash, land, buildings, furniture, and fixtures are examples of assets. Anything the organization owes is a liability. Liabilities might include amounts owed to suppliers (accounts payable) or to the bank (notes payable and other amounts due).

Common Nonprofit Financial Statement Errors

Statement of Financial Position

- **Omitting net assets by class.** Net assets must be categorized by net assets with and without donor restrictions. When net assets without donor restrictions are subdivided into components such as net investment in plant, board-designated, and other, a total for all the components must be shown.

- **Reflecting negative balances in net assets with donor restrictions.** It is improper to show either a negative total of net assets with donor restrictions or a component of this net asset class, perhaps in a footnote to the financial statements. When the balance in such an account has been totally released, additional expenditures must be charged to the unrestricted class.

Statement of Activities

- **Reporting exchange transactions as with donor restrictions revenue.** All earned income should be reported as without donor restrictions. Contributions with specific giver restrictions as to time or purpose and investment return relating to the investment of temporarily restricted contributions are the only types of revenue that should be reported with donor restrictions.

- **Reporting fundraising events, conferences, thrift shops, etc. as a net amount.** It is appropriate to show the two gross numbers (gross proceeds of an activity less expenses of activity equals net revenue from activity) for each activity in the statement of activities. The display of the gross data is typically shown in the revenue section of the statement unless expenses exceed revenue for this activity. In this case, the display is generally shown in the expense section.

- **Failure to recognize all gifts-in-kind revenue.** Examples of revenue that should be reflected include free rent and services provided by another organization.

- **Failure to report qualifying contributed services of volunteers.** All contributed services must be recorded unless the services do not meet the recognition criteria in FASB Accounting Standards Codification 958-605-25-16 or there is no reasonable way to assign a value to the services.

- **Failure to disclose fundraising expense.** Fundraising expenses must be disclosed except in the very rare circumstances where these expenses are immaterial.

- **Failure to properly allocate expenses functionally.** Expenses must be allocated and reported functionally—e.g., program, general and administration, fundraising. Depreciation, interest, and occupancy expenses must be functionally allocated unless the amounts are immaterial.

- **Reporting expenses in either of the restricted classes of net assets.** Although losses may be reported in any class, all expenses should be reported as decreases in net assets without donor restrictions.

Statement of activities

The statement of activities (also referred to as a statement of revenues and expenses) reflects an organization's support and revenue, expenses, and changes in net assets for a certain period of time. It shows the sources of an organization's income and how the resources were used. The form of the statement will depend on the type of organization and accounting method used. But the statement must present the change in net assets with and without donor restrictions as well as total net assets.

Many smaller organizations will have several lines for support and revenue such as contributions, sales of products, investment income, and so on. Expenses are often listed by natural classification such as salaries, fringe benefits, supplies, and so on.

Organizations desiring to meet GAAP accounting standards must reflect functional expenses (for example, by program, management and general, fundraising, and membership development) in the statement of activities or footnotes. Organizations will also show expenses by natural classification in the statement of activities, in the footnotes, or in a separate schedule/statement.

Statement of cash flows

The statement of cash flows provides information about the cash receipts and disbursements of your organization and the extent to which resources were obtained from, or used in, operating, investing, or financing activities. The direct method of presenting a cash flow statement starts by listing all sources of cash from operations during the period and deducts all operating outflows of cash to arrive at the net cash flow. The indirect method begins with the change in net assets and adjusts backwards to reconcile the change in net assets to net cash flows.

Statement of functional expenses

A statement of functional expenses provides information about the nature and amount of costs associated with each of the program services and supporting activities (administration, fundraising, etc.) carried out by the organization.

Currently, only voluntary health and welfare organizations must provide a statement of functional expenses as a basic statement. However, as noted below, upcoming changes may result in more organizations preparing this statement.

New nonprofit accounting standards

The Financial Accounting Standards Board's (FASB) Accounting Standards Update (ASU) 2016-14, *Presentation of Financial Statements of Not-for-Profit Entities,* is effective for all nonprofit organizations. The significant components of these standards are reflected here:

Net asset classifications. The three existing classes of net assets (unrestricted, temporarily restricted, and permanently restricted) will be reported as two:

- Net assets without donor restrictions
- Net assets with donor restrictions

To enhance readers' understanding of the donor restrictions, footnote disclosures are required to include the timing and nature of the restrictions, as well as the composition of net assets with donor restrictions at the end of the period. The disclosures continue to show an analysis by time, purpose, and perpetual restrictions.

Underwater endowments. As part of the change to classification of net assets, endowments that have a current fair value that is less than the original gift amount (or amount required to be retained by donor or by law), known as "underwater" endowments, are now classified in net assets with donor restrictions, instead of the current classification in unrestricted net assets. Expanded disclosures are required to include the following information:

- The original amount of the endowment
- The nonprofit's policy relating to spending from these funds
- Whether that policy was followed

Board-designated net assets. At times, a nonprofit's governing board may make designations or appropriations that result in self-imposed limits on the use of resources without donor restrictions, known as board-designated net assets. Enhanced disclosure information are required on the amounts and purposes of these designations.

Long-lived assets. Gifts for construction or acquisition of long-lived assets must now have the related restrictions released when the asset is placed in service unless there are explicit donor instructions to handle the gift differently. The option to imply a time restriction and release the restriction over an asset's useful life is no longer permitted.

Transparency and utility of liquidity information. Quantitative and qualitative information about liquidity is required for the purpose of providing financial statement users with an understanding of an entity's exposure to risks, as well as how an entity manages its liquidity risk, and information about the availability of assets to meet cash needs for general expenditures within one year of the balance sheet (statement of financial position) date. The discussion may include information on budgeting, reserve policies, and the ability to meet expenses for the next 12 months. The inclusion of a current ratio (current assets vs. current liabilities) would describe quantitatively the liquidity of the organization.

Presentation of investment expenses. Investment return (income) is now reported net of investment expenses. A disclosure of the components of investment expense is no longer required.

Expenses classified by function and nature. An analysis of expenses by both function and natural classification is required for all nonprofits on a separate statement, on the face of the statement of activities, or in the footnotes. While a separate statement of functional expenses is not required (including voluntary health and welfare organizations), it may be the most effective presentation option for nonprofits with more than one program. Investment expenses that have been netted against investment return are not permitted to be included in that analysis. Additional disclosures are required regarding specific methodologies used to allocate costs among program and support functions.

Presentation for cash flow information. Under the new standard, nonprofits may continue to present cash flows from operations using either the direct or indirect method. However, nonprofits are no longer required to present the indirect method reconciliation if the direct method is used. The intent of this change is to allow an organization to select the presentation method that best serves the needs of the entity, providing greater flexibility in financial reporting.

Restricted Cash

FASB's Accounting Standards Update (ASU) 2016-18 *Restricted Cash* was released on November 17, 2016. It is effective for annual financial statements issued for fiscal years beginning after December 15, 2018 and early adoption is permitted. The primary purpose of this standard is to clarify that changes to cash and restricted cash are to be shown in total on the statement of cash flows and will no longer reflect transfers between the two classifications.

The nature of any restrictions must be disclosed including the (1) purpose of the restriction, (2) duration of the restriction, (3) source of restrictions, and (4) amount. Restricted cash includes accounts such as bond sinking funds in addition to minimum balance requirements and accounts held for debt covenants, as examples. A reconciliation of the statement of cash flow cash and cash equivalents as compared to cash and cash equivalent accounts on the statement of financial position is required.

Leases

On February 25, 2016, FASB issued ASU 2016-02, *Leases*. Generally, it is effective for fiscal years beginning after December 15, 2019. While this may seem to be long-term rather than an immediate change, consider that the application will be retroactive so any leases an organization may currently be obligated to that have terms extending past this date will be impacted.

The basic premise of this new standard will result in most leases being classified as capital rather than operating with an asset and corresponding liability reflected on the statement of financial position. The impact to the statement of activities will be minimal because the amounts expensed each year will likely be similar under the existing and new standards. This standard will apply to accrual based financial statements as well as most modified cash basis financial statements but will not impact cash basis financials. For specifics surrounding an organization's leases, we recommend working directly with a knowledgeable CPA.

Budgeting

A budget is an effective tool for allocating financial resources and planning and controlling spending even for smaller organizations. A budget matches anticipated inflows of resources with outflows of resources. Preparing a budget requires considerable effort. It includes looking back at revenue and expense trends. Projected plans and programs must be converted into estimated dollar amounts. Too many organizations budget expenses with some degree of precision and then set the income budget at whatever it takes to cover the total expenses. This is often a disastrous approach. A list of key considerations is included in the ECFA eBooks *10 Essentials of Church Budgeting* and *10 Essentials of Ministry Budgeting*.

Separate budgets should be prepared for all funds of an organization. Even capital and debt-retirement funds should be budgeted. The separate budgets are then combined into a unified budget.

Line-item budgets within each fund reflect the projected cost of salaries, fringe benefits, utilities, maintenance, debt retirement, and other expenses. The line-item approach is generally used in reporting to department heads or other responsible individuals.

Program budgets are often presented to the board of a nonprofit organization or a church's membership. In this approach, the cost of a program is reflected rather than the cost of specific line-items such as salaries or fringe benefits.

Cash Reserves

Budgeting should not only include planning for the next year's income and expenses but should include consideration of future needs as well. Reserves for operating expenses, program expansion, and capital replacements are common. It is recommended an organization have 60-90 days of operating expenses on hand in case of emergency or a sudden decline in contributions. Having funds set aside for program expansion allows ministries to pursue unexpected opportunities. Reserves for capital replacements may prevent an organization from requiring debt financing to purchase a new HVAC system or roof when an unexpected problem occurs.

The planning of reserves is important. Without budgeting for such amounts, any excess in a year is likely spent or committed. An intentional setting aside of resources will put the organization in a better financial position and allow for flexibility in the future.

Audits and Other Related Services

An annual audit, review, or compilation of the financial statements and the disclosure of the financial statements are key components of transparency, both within a church or other nonprofit and to givers and the public. This flows directly from biblical principles: "This is the verdict: Light has come into the world, but men loved darkness instead of light because their deeds were evil. Everyone who does evil hates the light, and will not come into the light for fear that his deeds will be exposed" (John 3:19–20).

External audits, reviews, and compilations should be performed by an independent CPA who has no impairing relationship to the organization and has maximum objectivity. Internal audits are generally performed by members or those closely associated with the organization.

External services

Selecting the level of service for an organization requires an understanding of the desired outcome. An audit may be necessary because of criteria such as a requirement in the organization's bylaws or a debt covenant. It may also be that the organization is large enough that an audit is a good internal control and provides more accountability and transparency to the constituents. A review may be helpful for a smaller organization that desires to have a third party involved but doesn't have the size or complexity to require a full audit. If an organization chooses to have a compilation they may want to consider including some agreed-upon procedures testing at the same time or at another time during the year. It is a cost-effective way to gain greater confidence in certain areas of operations.

An **audit** is a formal examination of financial statements intended to assess the accuracy and thoroughness of financial records. An independent CPA performs this procedure on a set of financial statements in order to render an opinion based on the accounting records provided. An unmodified audit opinion states that the financial statements are in conformity with accounting principles generally accepted in the United States (GAAP). Audits are performed according to auditing standards generally accepted in the United States (GAAS). An audit is more expensive than a review or compilation because an opinion on the accuracy of financial statements requires significantly more work than that involved in either a review or a compilation. The result should be an audit report in addition to a management comment letter describing any material weaknesses or significant deficiencies that may exist in the organization's systems or processes.

A **review** is the performance of limited procedures as a basis for expressing limited assurance on financial statements. Although not as comprehensive as an audit, a review provides some assurance compared to no assurance provided with respect to a compilation. A review report states that: (1) the accountants do not express an opinion on the financial statements, and (2) based on their review, they are not aware of any material modifications that should be made to the financial statements. A review is less expensive than an audit but more expensive than a compilation. In performing this accounting service, the accountant must conform to the American Institute of Certified Public Accountants (AICPA) Statements on Standards for Accounting and Review Services (SSARS).

> ### Remember
>
> Independence is the cornerstone of the external CPA. The independent CPA should have no ties to management and no responsibility for governance or finance. The public can place faith in the audit or review function because an independent CPA is impartial and recognizes an obligation of fairness.

A **compilation** is the gathering of financial information and the creation of financial statements for an organization. A compilation involves no assurance on the financial statements, as the accountant simply assembles the financial statements for the organization. In performing this accounting service, the accountant must conform to SSARS.

Agreed-upon procedures may be appropriate when an audit, review, or compilation is not required or selected. An independent CPA is engaged to report findings on specific procedures performed on a particular subject matter. For example, an agreed-upon procedures engagement might be performed to evaluate an organization's internal control procedures, cash handling procedures, or worker classification procedures.

A good choice for a CPA firm is one that:

➤ is thoroughly knowledgeable about current accounting standards and one that understands the organization's niche of Christ-centered nonprofits

➤ routinely prepares value-added management letters for its audit clients

➤ helps minimize fees

➤ understands the organization's accounting system

Preparing for an external service. Any external involvement in an organization's finances causes an additional level of work. It can seem overwhelming especially the first time. Here are some keys to simplify the process:

• Clear, upfront and ongoing communication with the CPA will minimize unnecessary work or possible frustration. Ask questions along the way.

• Perform reconciliations throughout the year. Accounts such as cash, investments, contributions, and payroll should be reconciled monthly rather than waiting to do it at year-end.

• Consider making copies of invoices that may be needed, such as fixed asset purchases, and putting them in a separate folder to reduce the amount of filing during the engagement.

• Prepare all requested items before the CPA begins work. What may take hours to prepare will only take minutes to review.

• Determine what staff will be involved in the engagement and be certain they are available during the scheduled time.

• If an organization has never gathered information related to its fixed assets, the organization can begin by reviewing the accounting records for the previous five years and gathering information on furniture and equipment that has been purchased. For buildings that are older and where invoices may not exist, staff can work with the CPA, but usually a value can be determined based on information such as previous board minutes or past county assessor's records.

Internal audits

Members of the organization may form an audit committee to perform an internal audit to determine the validity of the financial statements. (Sample internal audit guidelines are shown on pages 128–35.) If the committee takes its task seriously, the result may be significant improvements in internal control and accounting procedures. A key concept of an internal audit is to *test* a sample of transactions, not to *review* all the transactions.

Fraud

Internal controls and preventing fraud

Fraud and misuse of givers' funds in churches and nonprofits can create some of the most sensational news. When this happens, it is generally attributed to all nonprofits and churches. Sadly, this causes a diminished witness of the Gospel in the sight of skeptics.

So why don't we eliminate the possibility of any fraud being committed? The simple answer is that we just cannot. The processes necessary to eliminate all fraud are nothing short of having a small army of employees rotating through different jobs as they separately review each transaction, with checks and balances that would bring any organization to a grinding halt. This would not be effective stewardship. Therefore, our goal should not be to eliminate all fraud but to find a reasonable balance between preventive efforts and risks.

An additional perspective in fraud prevention is to consider what happens when a staff member is subjected to inaccurate accusations of fraud. If the organization has not allowed for adequate controls in this situation, that person may be without any means to disprove the accusations, resulting in a grave injustice to the staff member of a nonprofit or a church.

ECFA has developed a webpage specifically on fraud awareness, recent news, and prevention at ECFA.org/Fraud. See also the ECFA eBooks *10 Essentials of Church Internal Controls* and *10 Essentials of Internal Controls for Ministries.*

Understanding why fraud happens

In the aftermath of a fraud discovery, guilty parties often indicate that they did not believe they were doing something wrong. In short, this is a result of a progression of rationalizations that causes a person to believe he or she is doing something that is appropriate, or that does not hurt anyone.

A situation of fraud generally occurs when there are three elements combined:

1. **A need or pressure develops.** A person has either internal or external motivation to acquire additional resources. This could include medical needs, a divorce, or even just trying to impress someone.

2. **An opportunity forms.** A person is presented with an opportunity to acquire funds or assets and becomes convinced he or she will not get caught. Hardly anyone commits a crime thinking there will be consequences.

3. **A rationalization is created.** A person is able to rationalize away what he or she is doing and so become comfortable committing the fraud. This could be a perception of being unappreciated, under-compensated, or even thinking it will be only a short-term loan.

When one or more of these three elements are present, it may be just a matter of time until a fraud is committed—the more elements present, the more likely the fraud. Of these three elements, the only one that an organization has control over is the opportunity element.

Different types of fraud

There are generally two types of fraud that are committed: those generated externally and those caused from within an organization. External fraud situations are frequently a type of Ponzi investment scheme. The organization will be offered a handsome rate of return in exchange for depositing or investing the funds with that person for a period of time. Other examples of external fraud can include external check manipulation, billing scams, and technology related crimes.

Internal fraud can include fraudulent use of checks, manipulation of invoices or expenses, mishandling of cash, mishandling of gifts-in-kind or other assets, misuse of organizational credit cards, and manipulation of computer systems.

As technology continues to leap forward, the nature and the types of fraud situations will continue to become more complex and will leverage these technologies. Organizations should be vigilant in keeping up with these technologies and conduct full due diligence when adopting new technologies to help prevent unknown vulnerabilities. For example, receiving funds or paying funds electronically can increase transaction complexity and make it much more difficult to identify fraudulent transactions.

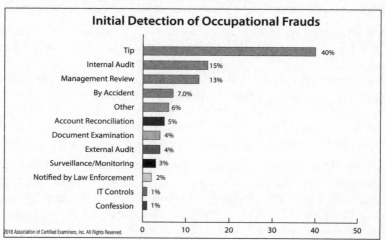

Initial Detection of Occupational Frauds

Detection Method	Percentage
Tip	40%
Internal Audit	15%
Management Review	13%
By Accident	7.0%
Other	6%
Account Reconciliation	5%
Document Examination	4%
External Audit	4%
Surveillance/Monitoring	3%
Notified by Law Enforcement	2%
IT Controls	1%
Confession	1%

How to detect fraud

The latest report from the Association of Certified Fraud Examiners shows that merely relying on one fraud detection tool is ineffective in uncovering fraud. It also highlights the importance of equipping personnel with a means to effectively report suspicions without fear of retribution, especially when the job market is tight. For this reason, each organization should have a whistleblower policy in place.

The frequency of discovering fraud is also higher, for instance, when an organization's management has taken proactive steps to look for fraud. Management reviews of systems and transactions, internal audits, reconciliations, reviewing documentations, and other monitoring senior staff may conduct will help prevent unnecessary steps in operations as well as enhance fraud prevention and detection. It is important that an organization's leadership sets this example from the top down, rather than trivializing these important steps. Note: Looking for fraud in a public manner on a regular basis is also a good deterrent as it helps decrease the likelihood of an opportunity for fraud, since potential perpetrators are more likely to believe they would get caught.

Looking for fraud can take a variety of forms, and it is helpful if this process is modified periodically to prevent measures from being easily anticipated. A leader will want to:

➤ **Review and check procedures.** In reviewing processes, a leader may find procedures that are antiquated or ineffective to accomplish the goal. A leader should be able to provide a logical reason for any step in the process. If expressing this reason is problematic, then the procedure should be reviewed to see if it is necessary.

➤ **Look for uncorrected errors.** If an error goes unnoticed by anyone in an office, this could form the opportunity element for an employee, just waiting for pressure and rationalization. As long as we are human there will always be errors that occur. However, if there are errors that are not caught by a review process, this poses a bigger problem. If a leader discovers an uncorrected error, especially a substantial one, then the review process should be evaluated to prevent this from reoccurring.

➤ **Look for gaps.** As a leader is reviewing different procedures and processes, he or she should take a step back from the process and see if there are gaps that could be manipulated. It could be the nature of the organization has changed in such a way that there are new exposure risks. For example, have procedures been developed to oversee electronic giving programs? It may be that a leader will need to prioritize these gaps depending on the staff available to assist in the controls. The key principle here is that a leader will need to review the cost of the procedure, even if it is just staff time, in light of the risk posed to the organization if fraud were to occur.

➤ **Look for trends, abnormalities, or inconsistencies.** A leader should review inconsistencies or changes to see if there are correlations to a certain worker. For example, every time a certain pair of workers counts funds, there appears to be a drop in gifts received. These abnormalities can be elusive, but the possibility of fraud should be considered when faced with such situations.

➤ **Look for unwillingness to let others help.** It is fairly common for frauds or errors to be discovered when someone goes on leave or takes a vacation. Frequently fraudsters will avoid being detected by preventing others from getting too close to certain information or even refuse to take vacations for fear that a fraud would be discovered. This is a good reason, among others, to consider job cross-training and mandatory vacations for employees.

How to prevent fraud

As previously discussed, one method in preventing fraud is to look for it. This step and internal controls in general should all be structured to prevent any person from developing the opportunity to commit fraud undetected. See additional practical steps in the ECFA eBook *9 Essentials of Avoiding Church Fraud* and *9 Essentials of Avoiding Ministry Fraud.*

Surveys show that weaknesses creating an opportunity for fraud mostly relate to either not having sufficient controls in place or a lack of leadership to adequately review, update, and test controls to ensure effectiveness. This equates to a double impact for organizations. First, it indicates a vulnerability to fraud opportunities. Second, it's likely that resources have been ineffectively expended in trying to prevent the fraud. It is important for leaders to continually review fraud prevention efforts and to maintain a balance between prevention and program operations. This is a process, not just a one-time event.

The importance of finding an appropriate balance between efficiency and effectiveness of fraud prevention efforts cannot be underestimated. It provides a reasonable assurance that fraud is not happening. Either too many or too few controls for an organization is not prudent management. Therefore, controls an organization utilizes must be custom tailored for that organization rather than just utilizing a template. One size does not fit all. The internal control and internal audit guidelines on the following pages are just examples that should be viewed in light of the organization's needs before being adopted.

What to do when fraud is discovered

When fraud is discovered, time is of the essence as there may be time limitations for pursuing legal recourse or recovering the funds before they or related records disappear. A ministry should consider working through the following steps in a timely manner:

1. **Discuss with the insurance company.**
2. **Contact an attorney.**
3. **Consider engaging a certified fraud examiner.**
4. **Investigate the complaint swiftly and thoroughly with expert help.**
5. **Consider protecting other organizations by notifying law enforcement.**

Many ministries have insurance for employee theft and dishonesty. They should understand that to collect on this policy in the event of a fraud occurrence, it is probable the insurance company will require the matter be referred to law enforcement authorities.

Internal Control and Internal Audit Guidelines

Financial statements

☐ Are monthly financial statements prepared on a timely basis and submitted to the ministry's board?

☐ Do the financial statements include all funds (with and without donor restrictions)?

☐ Do the financial statements include a statement of financial position and statement of activities?

☐ Do the financial statements provide sufficient explanatory notes to provide context for financial data?

☐ Are account balances in the financial records reconciled with amounts presented in financial reports?

Guidelines for Handling Digital Cash Receipts

Thefts of physical offerings may include cash or checks because of the possibility of misdirecting deposits.

However, with digital gifts it may be as simple for the fraudster as redirecting the flow of the digital funds and covering up the missing funds.

Gifts flood in through ministries' websites and other portals, as givers use debit and credit cards, ACH (Automated Clearing House) debits to their bank accounts, electronic checks, charges to their cellular accounts, and even virtual currency, using a variety of devices, including their computers, tablets, and smart phones.

To understand how to prevent a ministry from being a victim of digital theft, the organization must first understand the basics of how electronic giving is set up. There are three basic elements in establishing digital giving:

1. **Giving platform.** Typically, the ministry collects credit card information and possibly bank account information through an online giving platform such as PushPay or SecureGive.

    To ensure your giving platform is secure, look for SSL (Secure Sockets Layer) encryption, which establishes an encrypted link, allowing data to be transmitted securely between browsers and web servers (look for "https" in the web address instead of just "http").

2. **Payment processor.** The giving platform is in between the giver and the payment processor (also called the merchant account provider), which processes the gift and delivers it to the ministry's financial institution. It is usually a third-party service using a system of computer processes to receive, verify, and accept or decline credit card transactions on behalf of the ministry through secure internet connections.

3. **Giver management system.** While some giving platforms have the option of processing giving records, many organizations host giving records on their own IT systems, which may or may not easily integrate with a giving platform.

Strong internal controls for digital giving include:

- **Building a strong, multi-person payment processor relationship.** Digital giving involves interaction with at least one outside vendor—the payment processor. Who should have the initial and ongoing interaction with this and other vendors in the digital giving process?

  While one person must initially establish an account with each payment processor, multiple staff members, including a high-ranking ministry staffer, should verify the initial set-up.

- **Limit authorized changes to payment processor accounts.** After initially establishing a payment processor relationship, changes to the account routing number should be limited to high-ranking ministry staff, none of whom participate in the reconciliation of digital funds or have access to the giver management system.

- **Set notifications to be sent any time changes are made to payment processor accounts.** Each payment processor should be requested to immediately notify a high-ranking ministry leader of any change to the bank routing information.

- **Verify that the payment processor has internal controls in place.** How do you evaluate the quality of the internal controls employed by your payment-processing vendor? Only by insisting it has a SSAE 16 Type 2 (also commonly referred to as a SOC 1 Type 2) report issued by an independent auditing firm covering its internal controls.

- **Require regular payment processor transaction reports.** All payment processor transaction monthly reports should be received by a high-ranking ministry leader, in addition to a staff member more directly involved with the transactions. Use the reports to confirm the proper routing number was used.

- **Reconcile digital giving accounts regularly.** A high-ranking ministry official should begin each examination of digital gifts with the following reconciliations:

  - ✓ Bank accounts to payment processor transaction reports. This reconciliation ensures that all digital gifts were deposited in the appropriate bank account.

  - ✓ Giving records to payment processor transaction reports. This reconciliation verifies that all digital gifts are recorded in the giver management system (this is in addition to verifying that all non-digital gifts are recorded).

  - ✓ Giving records to bank accounts. This reconciliation verifies that all digital gifts deposited into bank accounts are reflected in the giving records.

Guidelines for Handling Physical Donations

- **Adopt policies to prevent problems.** Written policies are the "ounce of prevention" that could avoid serious problems at your church. Adopt a series of detailed policies that outline the procedures to be followed from the time the money goes into the offering plate—in worship services, Sunday school classes, other services, received in the mail, or delivered to the church—until the money is deposited in the bank. Other ministries need to consider similar procedures for amounts collected at events and conferences.

- **Make accountability and confidentiality dual goals.** Too many ministries focus so much on confidentiality that accountability takes too low a priority. True, some confidentiality is sacrificed when good accountability exists. But the ministry that does not balance confidentiality and accountability is treading on dangerous ground.

- **Use confidentiality statements.** Counters should sign a written statement of confidentiality before participating in the counting process. If the commitment of confidentiality is broken, the individual(s) should be removed from the team of counters.

- **Always follow the principle of two.** When a ministry leaves the donations in control of a single person—even for a short time period—before the count has been recorded or the uncounted funds have been dropped at the bank, it is a blatant invitation for problems. When sole access to the funds is allowed, most people will not take any money. However, for some, the temptation may be too great.

- **Encourage the use of offering envelopes.** Churches should encourage members to use offering envelopes. The envelopes provide a basis for recording contributions in the church's giver records.

- **Have counters complete offering tally sheets.** Tally sheets should be completed that separately account for loose checks and cash that were placed in offering envelopes. Checks or cash placed in blank, unidentified offering envelopes should be recorded with the loose funds. This separation of money serves as a control for the later posting to giver records.

- **Use a secure area for counting.** For safety of the counting team, confidentiality, and avoidance of interruptions, provide a secure area in which the donations can be counted. (When amounts are significant, consider providing armed security when donations are transported to the bank.) The counters should have an adding machine, coin wrappers, offering tally sheets, and other supplies. The adding machine should have a tape (instead of a paperless calculator) so the counting team can run two matching adding machine tapes of the offering.

- **Deposit all offerings intact.** Donations should always be counted and deposited intact. Depositing intact means not allowing cash to be used for the payment of church expenses or to be exchanged for other cash or a check.

  If donations are not deposited intact, an unidentified variance between the count and the deposit could occur. Additionally, if an individual is permitted to cash a check from donated funds, the ministry may inadvertently provide the person with a canceled check that could be used in claiming a charitable tax deduction.

- **Properly identify giver-restricted funds.** All giver restrictions should be carefully preserved during the counting process. These restrictions are usually noted on an offering envelope or response device, but they can take the form of an instruction attached to a check or simply a notation on the check.

- **Place donations in a secure location when they are stored at the organization.** If donations are stored in the church or ministry, even for short periods of time, the use of a secure location is important. A locked safe implies security, while an unlocked desk drawer connotes lack of security. But defining security is often not that easy.

  Follow these steps:
  - ✓ Use a safe with two locks.
  - ✓ In a church, the head usher and the assistant should bag the gifts and seal the bag before it is transported to the safe.

    ✓ Members of the same family should not transport the donations to the safe or open the safe at the same time.

    ✓ Require two individuals to open the safe, one with the key and the other with the combination.

    ✓ No one is permitted to have both the combination and the key to the safe.

    ✓ Change the combination at regular intervals.

    ✓ After placing funds in the safe, each individual must sign the safe opening log (names, date, time of opening).

Ideally, in churches, offerings are counted during or after the service, and a deposit is made as soon as possible. Alternately, the cash portion of the offering is recorded, and the uncounted offerings are immediately transported to the bank drop box by two people. When these two preferable options are not used, the offerings are generally stored at the church for a period of time on Sunday or perhaps until Monday morning. This process requires a secure storage location, preferably a safe, and highly structured controls over access to locked bank bags and the safe.

Ministries should also deposit amounts timely and not allow large balances to be maintained on site for an extended period of time.

- **Use proper controls when dropping uncounted funds at the bank.** If the church drops uncounted offerings at the bank, several key principles should be followed:

    ✓ All individuals transporting funds should have a current background check on file (updated within the last two years).

    ✓ The funds should be placed in locked bank bags with careful control of the number of persons who have keys to the bags.

    ✓ Two individuals should transport the funds to the bank.

    ✓ Two people should pick up the funds from the bank on the next business day, count the funds, and make the deposit.

- **Segregate duties when recording individual contributions.** Someone other than a member of the counting team should record individual gifts in giver records. This segregation of duties reduces the possibility of misappropriation of gifts.

General Cash Safeguards

    ❑ Are cash handling procedures in writing?

    ❑ Has the bank been notified to never cash checks payable to the organization?

    ❑ Are procedures established to care for contributions delivered or mailed during the week and on weekends?

Donation counting

    ❑ Are at least two individuals present when contributions are counted? (The persons counting the money should not include a pastor of a church, the church treasurer, business administrator, controller, or other individuals in supervisory positions.)

❐ Do money counters verify the contents of the offering envelopes are identical to the amounts written on the remittance devices (envelopes, postcards, etc.)?

❐ Are all checks stamped with a restrictive endorsement stamp immediately?

❐ Are money counters rotated so the same people are not handling the funds at all times?

❐ Are giver-restricted funds properly identified during the process of counting contributions?

Depositing of funds

❐ Are all funds promptly deposited? Are receipt records compared with bank deposits?

❐ Are all contributions deposited intact? Contribution monies should not be used to pay cash expenses.

Restricted funds

❐ Are donations for restricted purposes properly recorded in the accounting records?

❐ Are restricted funds held for the intended purpose(s) and not spent on operating needs?

Donation records/receipting

❐ Are individual giver records kept as a basis to provide giver acknowledgments for all cash contributions and all other single contributions of $250 or more?

❐ If no goods or services (other than intangible religious benefits) were provided in exchange for a gift, does the receipt include a statement to this effect?

❐ If goods or services (other than intangible religious benefits) were provided in exchange for a gift, does the receipt:

- inform the giver that the amount of the contribution that is deductible for federal income tax purposes is limited to the excess of the amount of any money and the value of any property contributed by the giver over the value of the goods and services provided by the organization, and

- provide the giver with a good-faith estimate of the value of such goods and services?

❐ Are the donations reconciled from counting sheets to the giver records for a selected time period?

Cash disbursements

❐ Are all disbursements paid by check or electronic payments (except for minor expenditures paid through the petty cash fund)?

❐ Is written documentation available to support all disbursements?

❐ Is there an accountable reimbursement plan for expenses?

- Do employees report and substantiate expenses within 60 days of incurring the expense?

- Does the substantiation include original receipts and documentation of the time, place, amount, and purpose of expenditure?

❏ Is a petty cash fund used for disbursements of small amounts? If so, is the fund periodically reconciled and replenished based on proper documentation of the cash expenditures?

❏ If a petty cash fund is used, are vouchers prepared for each disbursement from the fund?

❏ Are prenumbered checks used? Account for all the check numbers, including voided checks.

❏ Are blank checks or check authorization forms ever signed in advance? This should never be done.

Information reporting

❏ Has the organization filed Form 990 or received written confirmation that it is exempt from the Form 990 filing requirement?

❏ Has the organization filed Form 990-T for gross unrelated business income over $1,000 per fiscal year, if required?

❏ Were payments made to recipients (other than corporations) of at least $10 in royalties or at least $600 in rents, payments for services, prizes and awards, or medical and health care payments?

  • Did the organization obtain Form W-9 for all applicable recipients and file Form 1099-MISC?

❏ Was a Form 1099-INT provided to each recipient of interest totaling $600 or more during the calendar year?

❏ If operating a preschool or private school which is not separately incorporated, did the organization file Form 5578 concerning a statement of racial nondiscrimination with the IRS?

Payroll tax reporting

❏ Does the organization withhold and pay the employee's share of FICA taxes for all nonministerial employees?

❏ Does the organization pay the employer's share of FICA taxes for all nonministerial employees?

❏ Were timely deposits of employment taxes made?

❏ Was a Form 941 filed for each quarter of the previous calendar year?

❏ Were the totals from the four quarterly Forms 941 verified with the totals on Form W-3 prepared at year-end?

❏ Was a Form W-2 given to all persons classified as employees (including ministers) by January 31?

❏ Were Form W-2 and Transmittal Form W-3 provided to the IRS for all persons classified as employees (including ministers) by January 31?

Bank statement reconciliation

❏ Are written bank reconciliations prepared on a timely basis? Test the reconciliation for the last month in the fiscal year. Trace transactions between the bank and the books for completeness and timeliness.

❏ Are there any checks that have been outstanding over three months?

❏ Are there any unusual transactions in the bank statement immediately following year-end? Obtain the bank statement for the first month after year-end directly from the bank for review by the audit committee, or obtain the last bank statement (unopened).

Savings and investment accounts

❏ Are all savings and investment accounts recorded in the financial records? Compare monthly statements to the ledger.

❏ Are earnings or losses from savings and investment accounts recorded in the ledger?

Land, buildings, and equipment records

❏ Are there detailed records of land, buildings, and equipment including date acquired, description, and cost or fair market value at date of acquisition?

❏ Was a physical count of any inventory taken at year-end?

❏ Have the property records been reconciled to the insurance coverages?

Accounts payable

❏ Is there a schedule of unpaid invoices including vendor name, invoice date, and due date?

❏ Are any of the accounts payable items significantly past due?

❏ Are there any disputes with vendors over amounts owed?

Insurance policies

❏ Has a schedule been prepared of insurance coverage in force? Does it reflect effective and expiration dates, kind and classification of coverages, maximum amounts of each coverage, premiums, and terms of payment?

❏ Is workers' compensation insurance being carried as provided by law in most states? Are all employees (and perhaps some independent contractors) covered under the workers' compensation policy?

Amortization of debt

❏ Is there a schedule of debt, such as mortgages and notes?

❏ Have the balances owed to all lenders been confirmed directly in writing?

❏ Have the balances owed to all lenders been compared to the obligations recorded on the balance sheet?

Securities and other negotiable documents

❏ Are any marketable securities or bonds owned? If so, are they kept in a safe-deposit box, and are two signatures required for access?

❏ Have the contents of the safe-deposit box been recently examined and recorded?

Credit cards

☐ Has the organization ensured that its credit card merchant processor and any related systems are secure? A security audit should be available from your processor.

☐ Are there any organization-owned credit cards?

- Is there written documentation for all uses of organization-owned credit cards?

- Has there been an independent review of the organization's use and appropriateness of all organization-owned credit cards?

- Are there any signs of personal use of organization-owned credit cards? This should be avoided. If this does happen, these amounts must be refunded to the organization or added to taxable compensation.

Copyright and licensing issues

☐ Does the organization have a policy prohibiting the unlawful duplication or use of copyrighted works?

☐ Does the organization pay an annual fee to Christian Copyright Licensing, Inc. for the right to reproduce copyrighted music?

☐ Does the organization have a policy which prohibits the showing of rented or purchased videos without authorization of the copyright owner?

☐ Does the organization post a copyright notice at each photocopy machine?

☐ Does the organization comply with all computer software licensing agreements?

General Compliance Matters

☐ Are federal (and state) minimum wage and overtime requirements observed for applicable employees?

☐ Has a documented assessment been performed for all independent contractors noting why they qualify to not be treated as an employee?

☐ If overtime payments are required, has the organization taken steps to avoid paying overtime through compensatory time off?

☐ Is there a record retention policy specifying how long records should be kept?

☐ Are record retention and storage requirements formally considered at year-end?

☐ Does the organization's leader or appropriate personnel know the location of the original deed of all property?

☐ Is the organization in full compliance with restrictions imposed by the deed or mortgage?

☐ Did the organization refrain from participating in (directly or indirectly) a particular candidate's political campaign for public office?

INTEGRITY*Points*

- **Handling incoming funds.** The handling of incoming funds by a church or other nonprofit organization is one of the most critical elements of the financial management process. The potential of embezzlement is often high at the point funds are received.

  Sound policies and procedures should be adopted and followed to ensure no funds are lost at the point of entry. Sound internal controls also protect the staff members or volunteers handling the funds. Pastors and ministry leaders should not be involved in day-to-day financial transactions but should set a strong tone of accountability at the top.

- **Choosing an accounting method.** The choice of an accounting method has many implications. Large organizations generally use the accrual basis of accounting throughout the year and use the same approach for budgeting, while smaller organizations often utilize the cash or modified cash basis of accounting. The basis of accounting used for interim financial statements can be changed at year-end by posting a few journal entries. Reverse the entries on the first day of the subsequent accounting year, and the books are back to the previous accounting method. The following are a few of the accounting methods used:

  ○ Cash basis through the year/accrual basis at year-end

  ○ Modified cash through the year/accrual basis at year-end

  ○ Cash basis through the year/cash basis at year-end

  To ensure comparative financial data, it is important that the same approach (accrual, modified cash, or cash) be used on the accounting records throughout the year as is used for budgeting purposes.

- **Preventing and detecting fraud.** No ministry is beyond the possibility of being a fraud victim. Well planned internal controls and ongoing monitoring by ministry leaders will help to prevent many possible opportunities for fraud.

7 Charitable Gifts

In This Chapter

- Charitable gift options
- Percentage limitations
- Gifts that may not qualify as contributions

- Charitable gift timing
- Acknowledging and reporting charitable gifts
- Quid pro quo disclosure requirements

While most givers care more about the reason for giving than about the potential tax implications, the spirit of giving should never be reduced by unexpected tax results.

A gift is an unconditional transfer of cash or property with no personal benefit to the giver. The mere transfer of funds to a church or charitable nonprofit is not necessarily a gift. For example, when a parent pays the college tuition for a child, there is no gift or charitable deduction despite the tax-exempt educational nature of the organization. Yet, a gift restricted for a specific ministry purpose or for a future time period is an unconditional transfer.

If payments are made to a ministry to receive something in exchange (an "exchange transaction"), the transaction is more in the nature of a purchase. The tax law states that a transfer to a nonprofit is not a contribution when made "with a reasonable expectation of financial return commensurate with the amount of the transfer." When one transfer comprises both a gift and a purchase, only the gift portion is deductible.

The two broad categories of charitable gifts are *outright* gifts and *deferred* gifts. Outright gifts require that the giver immediately transfer possession and use of the gift property to the recipient ministry. In deferred giving, the giver also makes a current gift, but the gift is of a future interest. Accordingly, actual possession and use of the gift property by the recipient ministry is deferred until the future.

Charitable contributions are deductible if given "to and for the use" of a "qualified" tax-exempt organization to be used under its control to accomplish its exempt purposes. ("Qualified" organizations are churches and other domestic 501(c)(3) organizations.)

The following are three types of gifts commonly given to churches and other nonprofit organizations:

➤ **Gifts without giver stipulations.** Contributions received without giver restrictions (e.g., "use where needed most") are generally tax-deductible.

➤ **Personal gifts.** Gifts made through an organization to an individual, where the giver has specified, by name, the identity of the person who is to receive the gift, generally are *not* tax-deductible.

A ministry does not have a sound position to accept personal gifts. However if the ministry accepts personal gifts, charitable gift receipts should not be issued to the giver, and the organization should affirmatively advise givers that these gifts are not tax-deductible.

➤ **Giver-restricted gifts.** Givers often place restrictions on gifts that limit their use to certain purposes or times. These stipulations specify a use for a contributed asset that is more specific than the broad limits relating to the nature of the organization, the environment in which it operates, and the purposes specified in its articles of incorporation or bylaws (or comparable documents for unincorporated entities). A restricted gift generally results whenever a giver selects a giving option on a response device other than "unrestricted" or "where needed most."

Remember

The practice by nonprofits of raising funds with the gifts preferenced for the support of certain employees of the organization is often called deputized or staff-support fundraising. The IRS acknowledges that deputized fundraising is a widespread and legitimate practice, and contributions properly raised by this method are tax-deductible (see Chapter 8).

If gifts are earmarked for a specific individual, no tax deduction is generally allowed unless the organization exercises adequate discretion and control over the funds and they are spent for program activities of the organization (see pages 175–76 for a discussion of preferenced gifts).

Charitable Gift Options

Irrevocable nontrust gifts

The following types of gifts may *not* be revoked by the giver, and they do not involve a trust agreement:

➤ **Cash.** A gift of cash is the simplest method of giving. A cash gift is deductible within the adjusted gross income limitations, depending on the type of the recipient organization. Generally the 60% limit applies (temporarily increased from 50% in tax reform); for gifts to certain types of organizations, the limit is 30%.

➤ **Securities.** The contribution deduction for stocks and bonds held long-term (12 months or more) is the mean between the highest and lowest selling prices on the date of the gift where there is a market for listed securities. The contribution deduction is limited to cost for securities held short-term.

> **Example:** An individual taxpayer plans to make a gift of $50,000 to a college. To provide the capital, the taxpayer planned to sell stock that had cost $20,000 some years earlier, yielding a long-term capital gain of $30,000. The taxpayer decides to donate the stock instead of donating the proceeds of the sale. The taxpayer qualifies for a contribution deduction of $50,000, and the unrealized gain on the stock is not taxable.

➤ **Real estate.** The contribution deduction for a gift of real estate is based on the fair market value on the date of the gift. If there is a mortgage on the property, the value must be reduced by the amount of the debt.

➤ **Life insurance.** The owner of a life insurance policy may choose to give it to a charitable organization. The deduction may equal one of the following: the cash surrender value of the policy, its replacement value, its tax basis, or its "interpolated terminal reserve" value (a value slightly more than cash surrender value). The deduction cannot exceed the giver's tax basis in the policy.

➤ **Bargain sale.** A bargain sale is part donation and part sale. It is a sale of property in which the amount of the sale proceeds is less than the property's fair market value. The excess of the fair market value of the property over the sales price represents a charitable contribution to the organization. Generally, each part of a bargain sale is a reportable event, so the giver reports both a sale and a contribution.

➤ **Remainder interest in a personal residence or life estate.** A charitable contribution of the remainder interest in a personal residence (including a vacation home) or farm creates an income tax deduction equal to the present value of that future interest.

Idea

The American Council on Gift Annuities suggests charitable gift annuity rates for use by charities and their givers. The latest are available at www.acga-web.org.

➤ **Charitable gift annuity.** With a charitable gift annuity, the giver purchases an annuity contract from a charitable organization for more than its fair value. This difference in values between what the giver could have obtained and what the giver actually obtained represents a charitable contribution. The contribution is tax-deductible in the year the giver purchases the annuity.

➤ **Donor-advised funds.** Donor-advised gifts may be made to a donor-advised fund (DAF). A DAF is defined as a fund or account that is separately identified by reference to contributions of a donor or donors, is owned and controlled by a charitable sponsoring organization, and to which a donor (or any person appointed or designated by the donor) has advisory privileges with respect to the distribution or investment of amounts in the fund.

A donor makes an irrevocable contribution of cash and/or securities to the separate fund or account. The donor is eligible for a tax deduction at the time of the contribution to the DAF even though the DAF may distribute the funds to one or more charities in a subsequent tax year. The donor makes recommendations to the trustees for grants to be made out of his or her separate fund with the DAF. The representatives of the DAF then review these recommended grants to verify whether the target organization is a qualified charity.

The right of a donor to make recommendations to the trustees of a DAF generally does not constitute a restricted gift. However, if a gift to a DAF is restricted by the donor as to purpose or time, with the right to make recommendations as to the eventual charitable recipient(s) of the funds, this gift is temporarily or permanently restricted, based on the nature of the restriction.

Irrevocable gifts in trust

The following types of gifts involve a trust agreement, and the gift may not be revoked by the giver:

> **Charitable remainder annuity trust.** With an annuity trust, the giver retains the right to a specified annuity amount for a fixed period or the lifetime of the designated income beneficiary. The giver fixes the amount payable by an annuity trust at the inception of the trust.

> **Charitable remainder unitrust.** The unitrust and annuity trust are very similar with two important differences: (1) the unitrust payout rate is applied to the fair market value of the net trust assets, determined annually, to establish the distributable amount each year, as contrasted to a fixed payment with an annuity trust, and (2) additional contributions may be made to a unitrust compared to one-time gifts allowable to annuity trusts.

> **Charitable lead trust.** The charitable lead trust is the reverse of the charitable remainder trust. The giver transfers property into a trust, creating an income interest in the property in favor of the charitable organization for a period of years or for the life or lives of an individual or individuals. The remainder interest is either returned to the giver or given to a noncharitable beneficiary (usually a family member).

Idea

To set up a charitable remainder trust, a giver places cash or certain assets— such as publicly traded securities or unmortgaged real estate—in a trust that will ultimately benefit a charity. The giver collects payments from the trust and gets an immediate income tax deduction. Before accepting the administration of a charitable remainder trust, a charity should determine if it has the resources to properly administer the trust.

➤ **Pooled income fund.** A pooled income fund consists of separate contributions of property from numerous givers. A pooled income fund's payout to its income beneficiaries is not a fixed percentage. The rate of return that the fund earns each year determines the annual payout.

Revocable gifts

The following are other types of gifts that may be revoked by a giver:

➤ **Trust savings accounts.** A trust savings account may be established at a bank, credit union, or savings and loan institution. The account is placed in the name of the depositor "in trust for" a beneficiary, a person, or organization other than the depositor.

The depositor retains full ownership and control of the account. The beneficiary receives the money in the account when the depositor dies.

➤ **Insurance and retirement plan proceeds.** A nonprofit organization may be named the beneficiary of an insurance policy or retirement plan. The owner of the policy or retirement plan completes a form naming the nonprofit as the beneficiary, and the policy or plan provider accepts the form in writing. The gift may be for part or all of the proceeds.

➤ **Bequests.** By a specific bequest, an individual may direct that, at death, a charity shall receive either a specified dollar amount or specific property. Through a residuary bequest, an individual may give to charity the estate portion remaining after the payment of other bequests, debts, taxes, and expenses.

Percentage Limitations

Charitable deductions for a particular tax year are limited as follows:

➤ Gifts of cash and ordinary income property to public charities and all private operating foundations and certain private foundations are limited to 60% of adjusted gross income (AGI). This limit increased temporarily from 50% to 60% under tax reform and is set to expire after December 31, 2025. Any excess may generally be carried forward up to five years.

➤ Gifts of long-term (held 12 months or more) capital gain property to public charities and private operating foundations are limited to 30% of AGI. The same five-year carry-forward is possible.

➤ Givers of capital gain property to public charities and private operating foundations may use the 50% limitation, instead of the 30% limitation, where the amount of the contribution is reduced by all the unrealized appreciation (nontaxed gain) in the value of the property.

➤ Gifts of cash, short-term (held less than 12 months) capital gain property, and ordinary income property to private foundations and certain other charitable donees (other than public charities and private operating foundations) are generally limited to the item's cost basis and 30% of AGI. The carry-forward rules apply to these gifts.

➤ Gifts of long-term (held 12 months or more) capital gain property to private foundations and other charitable donees (other than public charities and private operating foundations) are generally limited to 20% of AGI. There is no carry-forward for these gifts.

➤ Charitable contribution deductions by corporations in any tax year may not exceed 10% of pre-tax net income (taxable income). Excess contributions may be carried forward up to five years.

Gifts That May Not Qualify as Contributions

Some types of gifts do not result in a tax deduction, and no contribution acknowledgment should be provided by the charity in certain situations:

➤ **Earmarked gifts.** When computing one's tax return, most taxpayers know that they cannot count tuition payments as a charitable deduction, even though the check is made out to a charity. In addition, most taxpayers know that their tuition payments are still not deductible if they are paid to a charity with instructions to forward the funds to a certain educational institution. Unfortunately, far too few givers and charities apply the same logic to other similar circumstances.

Some earmarked gifts may qualify for a charitable gift deduction, e.g., a gift earmarked for the building fund. However, other earmarked gifts generally do not meet the requirements of a charitable gift. Here are some examples:

> "I realize they have no connection with your ministry, but if I give the ministry $500, will you pass it through to them and give me a charitable receipt?"

> "I want to give $10,000 to the ministry so the funds can be passed on to a college to cover the tuition for the pastor's daughter. Will the ministry process this gift and give me a receipt?"

> ### Warning
>
> Gifts restricted for projects by givers qualify for a charitable deduction. Gifts preferenced for support under the deputized fundraising concept (see pages 176–80) may qualify for a charitable deduction. But when a giver places too many restrictions on a gift, especially when he or she wants the gift to personally benefit a certain individual, it often does not qualify for a charitable deduction.

Examples like these are donations "earmarked" for individuals. They are also called "conduit" or "pass-through" transactions. These connotations are negative references when used by the IRS and generally denote amounts that do not qualify for a charitable deduction. To be deductible, the charity must have discretion and control over the contribution without any obligation to benefit a designated individual.

A telltale sign of an earmarked gift is when someone says they want to "run a gift through the ministry," "pass a gift through the ministry," or "process a gift through the ministry." Of course, it is possible the giver will not so clearly signal an earmarked gift and use more general terminology. This is why charities should clearly understand the concept of earmarked gifts in addition to an awareness of telltale terminology.

Though the concept of earmarked gifts in tax law is well-established, it can be hard to apply to specific situations. Several issues may impact the complexities of these gifts:

☐ The giver's motivation may be loving and charitable in a broad sense; he or she really wants to help, and the only problem is the desire for control.

☐ Many organizations are lax in monitoring this area, and the giver may well say, "If your charity won't process this gift for me, I know of another charity that will handle it."

☐ Sometimes the difference between a nondeductible earmarked gift and a deductible restricted gift is not who benefits but only who determines the beneficiary.

It is wise to establish and follow clear policies to prohibit givers from passing money through a ministry simply to gain a tax benefit.

Though many charitable donations are based on a sense of charity, selflessness, and even love, the IRS believes that people may also have other motivations. The law prevents givers from having undue influence over charities and restricts givers from manipulating a charity into serving noncharitable interests and themselves receiving a deduction for it at the same time.

A special category of earmarked gifts is one in which a giver passes a gift through the charity for the giver's personal benefit. Such gifts often raise issues beyond the loss of a charitable deduction. Examples include

☐ Scholarship gifts passed through a charity for the giver's children (instead of paying tuition directly) raise allegations of tax fraud.

☐ A gift to purchase life insurance on the giver benefiting his or her family resulted in a law which can cause substantial penalties for both the giver and organization.

Gifts to a church or nonprofit for the support of missionaries or other workers (often called "deputized fundraising") are subject to a different set of guidelines than those generally associated with earmarked gifts. Gifts made under a properly structured deputized fundraising program are generally tax-deductible to the giver (see Chapter 8).

➤ **Strings attached.** A gift must generally be complete and irrevocable to qualify for a charitable deduction. There is usually no charitable deduction if the giver leaves "strings attached" that can be pulled later to bring the gift back to the giver or remove it from the control of the charity.

Example: An individual makes a "gift" of $10,000 to a ministry. The "gift" is followed or preceded by the sale from the ministry to the giver of an asset valued at $25,000 for $15,000. In this instance, the $10,000 paid to the ministry does not qualify as a charitable contribution. It also raises the issue of private inurement relating to the sale by the ministry.

➤ **Services.** No deduction is allowed for the contribution of services to a charity.

Example: A carpenter donates two months of labor on the construction of a new facility built by a church. The carpenter is not eligible for a charitable deduction for the donation of his time. The carpenter is entitled to a charitable deduction for any donated out-of-pocket expenses including mileage (14 cents per mile for 2018) for driving to and from the project. If the donated out-of-pocket expenses are $250 or more in a calendar year, the carpenter will need an acknowledgment from the church to substantiate the charitable deduction (see page 199 for a sample letter).

> **Warning**
>
> When a person makes a gift of services to a charity, it may be the highest gift that can be made—a gift of one's time and talents. However, the gift of services does not qualify for a charitable deduction, and it should never be receipted by the charity—only express appreciation. Out-of-pocket expenses related to the gift of services qualify as a charitable gift.

➤ **Use of property.** The gift of the right to use property does not yield a tax deduction to the giver.

Example: An individual provides a ministry with the rent-free use of an automobile for a year. No charitable deduction is available for the value of that use. If the individual who provided the car also paid the taxes, insurance, repairs, gas, or oil for the vehicle while it was used by the ministry, these out-of-pocket expenses are deductible as a charitable contribution.

Charitable Gift Timing

A charitable gift is considered made on the date of delivery. This date is important because it determines the tax year in which the gift is deductible, the valuation date, when applicable, and the date for determining whether the gift qualifies for short-term or long-term property, when applicable.

➤ **Checks.** Under the "delivered-when-mailed" rule, if a giver mails a contribution check to a nonprofit organization, the date of the mailing is deemed the date of delivery, if there are no restrictions on the time or manner of payment and the check is honored when presented.

There are two exceptions:

☐ **Postdated checks.** The date of mailing will not make any difference if the check is postdated. A postdated check is not an immediately payable contribution, but it is a promise to pay on the date shown.

☐ **Checks that bounce.** Generally, if a check is dishonored for insufficient funds, the gift will not be deemed to have been made when it was mailed or delivered.

Normally, the date on a U.S. Mail postmark will conclusively establish the date of mailing. A postage meter date may not be sufficient to establish the date of delivery for a gift that is mailed. The "delivered-when-mailed" rule applies to delivery by the U.S. Postal Service, not to private couriers.

Example 1: A giver mails a check with a postmark of December 31, 2018. The ministry does not receive the check until January 7, 2019. The ministry deposits the check in its bank on January 7, and it clears the giver's bank on January 10. The gift is deductible by the giver in 2018.

Example 2: A giver delivers a check to the ministry on December 31, 2018. The giver asks that the check be held for three months. Complying with the giver's request, the ministry deposits the check on March 31, 2019. This gift is deductible by the giver in 2019.

Example 3: A giver delivers a check to the ministry on January 5, 2019. The check is dated December 31, 2018. The gift is deductible by the giver in 2019.

➤ **Credit cards.** A contribution charged to a credit card is deductible by the giver when the charge is made, even though the credit card bill is not paid until the next year.

➤ **Electronic funds tranfers.** Givers may instruct their banks via phone, mobile devices, or the internet to pay contributions to the church or ministry. If a giver uses this method to make a donation, it is deductible at the time payment is made by the bank.

IRS Publication 526 (Charitable Contributions) does not provide specific guidance on electronic funds transfers (EFTs) via the internet or mobile devices. It says "pay-by-phone" arrangements are not deductible at the time the giver directs the payment but rather when the payment is made by the financial institution.

➤ **Pledge.** A pledge is not deductible until payment or other satisfaction of the pledge is made.

➤ **Securities.** A contribution of stock is completed upon the unconditional delivery of a properly endorsed stock certificate to a charity or its agent. If the stock is mailed and is received by the charity or its agent in the ordinary course of the mail, the gift is effective on the date of mailing. If the giver delivers a stock certificate to the issuing corporation or to the giver's broker for transfer to the name of the charity, the contribution is not completed until the stock is actually transferred on the corporation's books.

➤ **Real estate.** A gift of real estate is deductible at the time a properly executed deed is delivered to the charity.

Acknowledging and Reporting Charitable Gifts

Contributors to a church or nonprofit seeking a federal income tax charitable contribution deduction must produce, if asked, a written receipt from the organization for all gifts of cash and other single contributions valued at $250 or more. Strictly speaking, the burden of compliance with the $250 or more rule falls on the giver. In reality, the burden and administrative costs fall on the organization, not the giver.

The IRS can fine a church or nonprofit that deliberately issues a false acknowledgment to a contributor. The fine is up to $1,000 if the giver is an individual and $10,000 if the giver is a corporation.

Idea

Donors are only required to have receipts for single gifts of $250 or more (receipts are required for currency in gifts of any amount). Churches often issue gift acknowledgments on a quarterly, semiannual, or annual basis. However, most parachurch ministries issue receipts for every gift, regardless of the amount.

➤ **Information to be included in the acknowledgment.** All of the following information must be included in the gift receipt:

☐ the giver's name

☐ if cash, the amount of cash contributed

☐ if property, a description, but not the value of the property (if the gift is an auto, boat, or airplane, the ministry must generally provide Form 1098-C to the giver—see pages 156–58 for a more detailed discussion)

☐ a statement explaining whether the ministry provided any goods or services to the giver in exchange for the contribution

• if goods or services were provided to the giver, a description and good-faith estimate of their value and a statement that the giver's charitable deduction is limited to the amount of the payment in excess of that value, and if services were provided consisting solely of intangible religious benefits, a statement to that effect

• if no goods or services were provided to the giver, the acknowledgment must state so

☐ the date the donation was made

☐ the date the acknowledgment was issued (recommended, but not required)

Sample Charitable Gift Acknowledgment

Acknowledgment #1

Received from: Howard K. Auburn

Cash received as an absolute gift:

Date Cash Received	Amount Received
1/2/18	$250.00
1/16/18	50.00
3/13/18	300.00
3/27/18	100.00
6/12/18	500.00
7/10/18	150.00
8/21/18	200.00
10/16/18	400.00
11/20/18	350.00
	$2,300.00

Any goods or services you may have received in connection with this gift were solely intangible religious benefits.

> (*Note:* It is very important for a religious organization to use wording of this nature when no goods or services were given in exchange for the gift.)

This document is necessary for any available federal income tax deduction for your contribution. Please retain it for your records.

Acknowledgment issued on: January 10, 2019

Acknowledgment issued by: Harold Morrison, Treasurer
Castleview Church
1008 High Drive
Dover, DE 19901

1. This sample acknowledgment is based on the following assumptions:
   A. No goods or services were provided in exchange for the gifts other than intangible religious benefits.
   B. The acknowledgment is issued on a periodic or annual basis for all gifts whether over or under $250.
2. All acknowledgments should be numbered consecutively for control and accounting purposes.

Sample Letter to Noncash Givers

**Charitable Gift Acknowledgment for Noncash Gifts
(other than for autos, boats, or airplanes)**

RETAIN FOR INCOME TAX PURPOSES

Noncash Acknowledgment #1

(All acknowledgments should be
numbered consecutively for control
and accounting purposes.)

Giver's name and address

Date Acknowledgment Issued

Thank you for your noncash gift as follows:
    Date of gift:
    Description of gift:
    (Note: No value is shown for the gift. Valuation is the responsibility of the giver.)

To substantiate your gift for IRS purposes, the tax law requires that this acknowledgment state whether you have received any goods or services in exchange for the gift. You have received no such goods or services. (***Note:*** If goods or services were provided to the giver, replace the previous sentence with: In return for your contribution, you have received the following goods or services __(description)__, which we value at __(good-faith estimate)__. The value of the goods and services you received must be deducted from the value of your contribution to determine your charitable deduction.)

If your noncash gifts for the year total more than $500, you must include Form 8283 (a copy of Form 8283 and its instructions are enclosed for your convenience) with your income tax return. Section A is used to report gifts valued at $5,000 or under. You can complete Section A on your own. When the value of the gift is more than $5,000, you will need to have the property appraised. The appraiser's findings are reported in Section B of Form 8283. The rules also apply if you give "similar items of property" with a total value above $5,000—even if you gave the items to different charities. Section B of Form 8283 must be signed by the appraiser. It is essential to attach the form to your tax return.

You might want an appraisal (even if your gift does not require one) in case you have to convince the IRS of the property's worth. You never need an appraisal or an appraisal summary for gifts of publicly traded securities, even if their total value exceeds $5,000. You must report those gifts (when the value is more than $500) by completing Section A of Form 8283 and attaching it to your return.

For gifts of closely held stock, an appraisal is not required if the value of the stock is under $10,000, but part of the appraisal summary form must be completed if the value is over $5,000. If the gift is valued over $10,000, then both an appraisal and an appraisal summary form are required.

If we receive a gift of property subject to the appraisal summary rules, we must report to both the IRS and to you if we dispose of the gift within three years.

Again, we are grateful for your generous contribution. Please let us know if we can give you and your advisors more information about the IRS's reporting requirements.

Your Nonprofit Organization

➤ **When acknowledgments should be issued.** Givers must obtain their receipts no later than the due date, plus any extension, of their federal income tax return or the date the return was filed, whichever date is earlier. If a giver obtains the acknowledgment after this date, the gift does not qualify for a contribution deduction even on an amended return.

If a ministry issues acknowledgments on an annual basis, it is helpful to provide them to givers at least by January 31 each year, and earlier in January if possible. This will assist givers in gathering the necessary data for tax return preparation.

Form 1098-C must be provided within 30 days after the date that a donated vehicle is sold by the ministry or within 30 days of the donation date if the ministry keeps the property.

➤ **Frequency of issuing acknowledgments.** The receipts or acknowledgments can be issued gift-by-gift, monthly, quarterly, annually, or any other frequency. For ease of administration and clear communication with givers, many charities provide an acknowledgment for all gifts, whether more or less than $250.

➤ **Form of acknowledgments.** No specific design of a charitable gift receipt is required, except for Form 1098-C, used for gifts of vehicles (autos, boats, or airplanes). The IRS has not issued any pro forma acknowledgments.

An acknowledgment may be in hard-copy or electronic form. An acknowledgment can be issued as a letter, e-mail, or as an attachment to an e-mail. Additionally, a gift acknowledgment may be downloaded from the ministry's website. There is no requirement for the acknowledgment to be signed. There is also no requirement to include the giver's social security number. Although the IRS has not issued any guidance requiring the ministry's Employer Identification Number (EIN) to be included on gift acknowledgments, there are reported instances of the IRS requiring EINs.

Charitable Contribution Substantiation Requirements

	Not more than $75	Over $75 and under $250	At least $250 and under $500	At least $500 and under $5,000	$5,000 and over
Canceled check acceptable for giver's deduction?	Yes	Yes	No	No	No
Contribution receipt required for deduction?	No*	No*	Yes	Yes	Yes
Charity's statement on giver's receipt of goods or services required?	No	Yes **	Yes**	Yes**	Yes**

*Generally, no if paid by check, credit card, or wire transfer. Yes, if paid by cash.
**May be avoided if the charity meets the low-cost items or *de minimis* benefits exceptions described on page 160.

➤ **Separate gifts of less than $250.** If a giver makes separate gifts by check during a calendar year of less than $250, there is no acknowledgment required since each gift is a separate contribution below the $250 threshold. The canceled check will provide sufficient substantiation. However, many ministries provide a year-end gift summary, including all gifts regardless of whether each gift is under or over $250.

➤ **Donations payable to another charity.** A church member may place a check in the offering plate of $250 or more payable to a missions organization, unrelated to the church, intended to support the work of a particular missionary serving with the mission. No acknowledgment is required by the church. Since the check was payable to the missions agency, that entity will need to issue the acknowledgment to the giver for claiming the gift as a charitable contribution.

➤ **Giver's out-of-pocket expenses.** Volunteers may incur out-of-pocket expenses on behalf of a church or nonprofit. Substantiation from the organization is required if a volunteer claims a deduction for unreimbursed expenses of $250 or more. However, the IRS acknowledges that the church or nonprofit may be unaware of the details of the expenses or the dates on which they were incurred. Therefore, the organization must substantiate only the types of services performed by the volunteer which relate to out-of-pocket expenses.

➤ **Individuals.** Gifts made by a taxpayer to poor or needy individuals or to employees of a ministry, instead of to or for a ministry, generally do not qualify as charitable contributions and are not the basis for a gift acknowledgment.

➤ **Foreign organizations.** It may be inappropriate to accept gifts restricted for a foreign organization even if the charitable purposes of the foreign charity are consistent with the purposes of the U.S. ministry.

> **Example 1:** An individual offers to make a $5,000 donation to a U.S.-based ministry restricted for the Sri Lanka Relief Outreach (a foreign organization) for its relief and development purposes. While the ministry provides funding for various foreign missionary endeavors, it has no connection with the Sri Lanka Relief Outreach and has no practical way to provide due diligence in relation to a gift to this entity. Based on these facts, the gift has the characteristics of a pass-through gift. The funds should generally not be accepted by the ministry.

> **Example 2:** Same fact pattern as in Example 1, except the U.S.-based ministry regularly sponsors short-term mission trips to Sri Lanka and provides funds to the Sri Lanka Relief Outreach, based on the due diligence performed by the ministry's staff and volunteers on mission trips with respect to this particular foreign entity. Based on these facts, the ministry is generally in a sound position to make a gift of $5,000 to the Sri Lanka-based organization as requested by the giver and provide a charitable receipt for the gift.

Since gifts by U.S. taxpayers to a foreign organization do not produce a charitable deduction, givers may try to convince a U.S.-based ministry to accept a gift restricted for a certain foreign organization and pass it through to the entity. When a U.S.-based ministry is no more than an agent of, or trustee for, a particular foreign organization, or has purposes so narrow that its funds can go only to a particular foreign organization, or solicits funds on behalf of a particular foreign organization, the deductibility of gifts may be questioned by the IRS.

There are some acceptable situations in which a U.S.-based ministry may receive gifts for which a deduction is allowed with the money used abroad:

☐ The money may be used by the U.S.-based ministry directly for projects that it selects to carry out its own exempt purposes. In this instance, the domestic organization would generally have operations in one or more foreign countries functioning directly under the U.S.-based ministry. The responsibility of the donee organization ends when the purpose of the gift is fulfilled. A system of narrative and financial reports is necessary to document what was accomplished by the gift.

☐ It may create a subsidiary organization in a foreign country to facilitate its exempt operations there, with certain of its funds transmitted directly to the subsidiary. In this instance, the foreign organization is merely an administrative arm of the U.S.-based organization, with the U.S.-based organization considered the real recipient of the contributions. The responsibility of the U.S.-based organization ends when the purpose of the gift is fulfilled by the foreign subsidiary.

☐ It may make grants to charities in a foreign country in furtherance of its exempt purposes, following review and approval of the uses to which the funds are to be put. The responsibility of the U.S. organization ends when the purpose of the gift is fulfilled by the foreign organization. A narrative and financial report from the foreign organization will usually be necessary to document the fulfillment of the gift.

☐ It may transfer monies to another domestic entity with the second organization fulfilling the purpose of the gift. The responsibility of the first entity usually ends when the funds are transferred to the second organization.

The tax law is clear that money given to an intermediary charity but earmarked for an ultimate recipient is considered as if it has been given directly to the ultimate recipient. It is earmarked if there is an understanding, written or oral, whereby the giver binds the intermediary charity to transfer the funds to the ultimate recipient. The tax law does not allow givers to accomplish indirectly through a conduit (an intermediary charity) what the giver cannot accomplish directly.

➤ **Contingencies.** If a contribution will not be effective until the occurrence of a certain event, an income tax charitable deduction generally is not allowable until the occurrence of the event. Thus, a charitable gift acknowledgment should not be issued until the event has occurred.

Example: A giver makes a donation to a college to fund a new education program that the college does not presently offer and is not contemplating. The donation would not be deductible until the college agrees to the conditions of the gift.

➤ **Charitable remainders in personal residences and farms.** The charitable gift regulations are silent on the substantiation rules for remainder interests in personal residences and farms (a life estate). It should be assumed that the $250 substantiation rules apply to those gifts unless the IRS provides other guidance.

➤ **Charitable trusts.** The $250 substantiation rules do not apply to charitable remainder trusts and charitable lead trusts.

➤ **Gift annuities.** When the gift portion of a gift annuity or a deferred payment gift annuity is $250 or more, a giver must have an acknowledgment from the church or nonprofit stating whether any goods or services—in addition to the annuity—were provided to the giver. If no goods or services were provided, the acknowledgment must so state. The acknowledgment need not include a good-faith estimate of the annuity's value.

➤ **Pooled income funds.** The substantiation rules apply to pooled income funds. To deduct a gift of a remainder interest of $250 or more, a giver must have an acknowledgment from the charity.

In addition to gifts of vehicles (see pages 156–58), certain gifts require IRS reporting, or execution of a form that the giver files with the IRS:

➤ **Noncash gifts in excess of $500.** Noncash gifts in excess of $500 require the completion of certain information on page 1 of Form 8283. For gifts between $500 and $5,000, there is no requirement of an appraisal or signature of the charity.

➤ **Noncash gifts in excess of $5,000.** Additional substantiation requirements apply to contributions of property (other than money and publicly traded securities) if the total claimed or reported value of the property is more than $5,000. For these gifts, the giver must obtain a qualified appraisal and attach an appraisal summary to the return on which the deduction is claimed. There is an exception for nonpublicly traded stock. If the claimed value of the stock does not exceed $10,000, the giver does not have to obtain an appraisal by a qualified appraiser.

The appraisal summary must be on Form 8283, signed and dated by the ministry and the appraiser, and attached to the giver's return. The signature by the ministry does not represent concurrence in the appraised value of the noncash gifts.

If Form 8283 is required, it is the giver's responsibility to file it. The ministry is under no responsibility to see that this form is filed or that it is properly completed. However, advising givers of their obligations and providing them with the form can produce goodwill.

➤ **Charity reporting for contributed property.** If a noncash gift requiring an appraisal summary on Form 8283 is sold, exchanged, or otherwise disposed of by the ministry within three years after the date of the contribution, the ministry must file Form 8282 with the IRS within 125 days of the disposition of the asset.

This form provides detailed information on the gift and the disposal of the property. A copy of the form must be provided to the giver and retained by the

This form must generally be filed by a charity if it disposes of charitable deduction property within three years of the date the original donee received it and the items are valued at $500 or more.

Form **8283**	**Noncash Charitable Contributions**	OMB No. 1545-0908
(Rev. December 2014) Department of the Treasury Internal Revenue Service	► **Attach to your tax return if you claimed a total deduction of over $500 for all contributed property.** ► **Information about Form 8283 and its separate instructions is at** *www.irs.gov/form8283.*	Attachment Sequence No. **155**

Name(s) shown on your income tax return	Identifying number
Mark A. and Joan E. Murphy	392-83-1982

Note. Figure the amount of your contribution deduction before completing this form. See your tax return instructions.

Section A. Donated Property of $5,000 or Less and Publicly Traded Securities—List in this section **only** items (or groups of similar items) for which you claimed a deduction of $5,000 or less. Also list publicly traded securities even if the deduction is more than $5,000 (see instructions).

Part I   **Information on Donated Property**—If you need more space, attach a statement.

1	(a) Name and address of the donee organization	(b) If donated property is a vehicle (see instructions), check the box. Also enter the vehicle identification number (unless Form 1098-C is attached).	(c) Description of donated property (For a vehicle, enter the year, make, model, and mileage. For securities, enter the company name and the number of shares.)
A	Endless Mountain Church 561 Maple, Rochester, NY 14623	☐	Used bedroom furniture
B		☐	
C		☐	
D		☐	
E		☐	

Note. If the amount you claimed as a deduction for an item is $500 or less, you do not have to complete columns (e), (f), and (g).

	(d) Date of the contribution	(e) Date acquired by donor (mo., yr.)	(f) How acquired by donor	(g) Donor's cost or adjusted basis	(h) Fair market value (see instructions)	(i) Method used to determine the fair market value
A	10/1/18	4/10	Purchased	3,400	750	Sales of comparable used furniture
B						
C						
D						
E						

Part II   **Partial Interests and Restricted Use Property**—Complete lines 2a through 2e if you gave less than an entire interest in a property listed in Part I. Complete lines 3a through 3c if conditions were placed on a contribution listed in Part I; also attach the required statement (see instructions).

2a   Enter the letter from Part I that identifies the property for which you gave less than an entire interest ► _____
If Part II applies to more than one property, attach a separate statement.

b   Total amount claimed as a deduction for the property listed in Part I: **(1)**   For this tax year   ► _____
                                             (2)   For any prior tax years   ► _____

c   Name and address of each organization to which any such contribution was made in a prior year (complete only if different from the donee organization above):
Name of charitable organization (donee)
_____

Address (number, street, and room or suite no.)
_____

City or town, state, and ZIP code
_____

d   For tangible property, enter the place where the property is located or kept ► _____
e   Name of any person, other than the donee organization, having actual possession of the property ► _____

		Yes	No
3a	Is there a restriction, either temporary or permanent, on the donee's right to use or dispose of the donated property?		
b	Did you give to anyone (other than the donee organization or another organization participating with the donee organization in cooperative fundraising) the right to the income from the donated property or to the possession of the property, including the right to vote donated securities, to acquire the property by purchase or otherwise, or to designate the person having such income, possession, or right to acquire?		
c	Is there a restriction limiting the donated property for a particular use?		

For Paperwork Reduction Act Notice, see separate instructions.   Cat. No. 62299J   Form **8283** (Rev. 12-2014)

This form must be completed and filed with the giver's income tax return for gifts of property valued at $500 or more. There is no requirement of an appraisal or signature of the donee organization for gifts valued between $500 and $5,000.

Form 8283 (Rev. 12-2014)

Page **2**

Name(s) shown on your income tax return
Mark A. and Joan E. Murphy

Identifying number
392-83-1982

Section B. Donated Property Over $5,000 (Except Publicly Traded Securities)—Complete this section for one item (or one group of similar items) for which you claimed a deduction of more than $5,000 per item or group (except contributions of publicly traded securities reported in Section A). Provide a separate form for each property donated unless it is part of a group of similar items. An appraisal is generally required for property listed in Section B. See instructions.

Part I **Information on Donated Property**—To be completed by the taxpayer and/or the appraiser.

4 Check the box that describes the type of property donated:

- a ☐ Art* (contribution of $20,000 or more)
- b ☐ Qualified Conservation Contribution
- c ☐ Equipment
- d ☐ Art* (contribution of less than $20,000)
- e ☒ Other Real Estate
- f ☐ Securities
- g ☐ Collectibles**
- h ☐ Intellectual Property
- i ☐ Vehicles
- j ☐ Other

*Art includes paintings, sculptures, watercolors, prints, drawings, ceramics, antiques, decorative arts, textiles, carpets, silver, rare manuscripts, historical memorabilia, and other similar objects.

**Collectibles include coins, stamps, books, gems, jewelry, sports memorabilia, dolls, etc., but not art as defined above.

Note. In certain cases, you must attach a qualified appraisal of the property. See instructions.

5	(a) Description of donated property (if you need more space, attach a separate statement)	(b) If tangible property was donated, give a brief summary of the overall physical condition of the property at the time of the gift	(c) Appraised fair market value
A	Residence and two lots:	Good Repair	242,500
B	2080 Long Pond Road		
C	Syracuse, NY		
D			

	(d) Date acquired by donor (mo., yr.)	(e) How acquired by donor	(f) Donor's cost or adjusted basis	(g) For bargain sales, enter amount received	(h) Amount claimed as a deduction	(i) Date of contribution
A	7/20/09	Purchased	236,900		242,500	
B						
C						
D						

Part II **Taxpayer (Donor) Statement**—List each item included in Part I above that the appraisal identifies as having a value of $500 or less. See instructions.

I declare that the following item(s) included in Part I above has to the best of my knowledge and belief an appraised value of not more than $500 (per item). Enter identifying letter from Part I and describe the specific item. See instructions. ▶

Signature of taxpayer (donor) ▶ *Mark A. Murphy*   Date ▶ **11/28/18**

Part III **Declaration of Appraiser**

I declare that I am not the donor, the donee, a party to the transaction in which the donor acquired the property, employed by, or related to any of the foregoing persons, or married to any person who is related to any of the foregoing persons. And, if regularly used by the donor, donee, or party to the transaction, I performed the majority of my appraisals during my tax year for other persons.

Also, I declare that I perform appraisals on a regular basis; and that because of my qualifications as described in the appraisal, I am qualified to make appraisals of the type of property being valued. I certify that the appraisal fees were not based on a percentage of the appraised property value. Furthermore, I understand that a false or fraudulent overstatement of the property value as described in the qualified appraisal or this Form 8283 may subject me to the penalty under section 6701(a) (aiding and abetting the understatement of tax liability). In addition, I understand that I may be subject to a penalty under section 6695A if I know, or reasonably should know, that my appraisal is to be used in connection with a return or claim for refund and a substantial or gross valuation misstatement results from my appraisal. I affirm that I have not been barred from presenting evidence or testimony by the Office of Professional Responsibility.

Sign Here

Signature ▶ *Andrew J. Noble*   Title ▶ **President**   Date ▶ **11/20/18**

Business address (including room or suite no.)
1100 North Adams Street

Identifying number
541-90-9796

City or town, state, and ZIP code
Elmira, NY 14904

Part IV **Donee Acknowledgment**—To be completed by the charitable organization.

This charitable organization acknowledges that it is a qualified organization under section 170(c) and that it received the donated property as described in Section B, Part I, above on the following date ▶ **8/31/18**

Furthermore, this organization affirms that in the event it sells, exchanges, or otherwise disposes of the property described in Section B, Part I (or any portion thereof) within 3 years after the date of receipt, it will file **Form 8282**, Donee Information Return, with the IRS and give the donor a copy of that form. This acknowledgment does not represent agreement with the claimed fair market value.

Does the organization intend to use the property for an unrelated use? . . . . ▶ ☐ Yes ☒ No

Name of charitable organization (donee)
Fairlawn Heights Church

Employer identification number
35-4029876

Address (number, street, and room or suite no.)
PO Box 829

City or town, state, and ZIP code
Oswego, NY 13126

Authorized signature
James A. Black

Title
Executive Pastor

Date
12/15/18

Form **8283** (Rev. 12-2014)

Section B must be completed for gifts of items (or groups of similar items) for which a deduction was claimed of more than $5,000 per item or group.

ministry. A ministry that receives a charitable contribution valued at more than $5,000 from a corporation generally does not have to complete Form 8283.

A letter or other written communication from a ministry acknowledging receipt of the property and showing the name of the giver, the date and location of the contribution, and a detailed description of the property is an acceptable contribution receipt for a gift of property.

There is no requirement to include the value of contributed property on the receipt. A tension often surrounds a significant gift of property because the giver may request the ministry to include an excessively high value on the charitable receipt. It is wise for the ministry to remain impartial in the matter and simply acknowledge the property by description and condition while excluding a dollar amount.

Caution

The IRS places certain reporting requirements on donors and charities with respect to many property gifts. They are suspicious of property valued at one amount on the date of the gift and sold by the charity for much less. Charities should never place a value on a gift of property. This is the responsibility of the donor.

> **Example:** A ministry receives a gift of real estate. The receipt should include the legal description of the real property and a description of the improvements with no indication of the dollar value.

➤ **Acknowledging and reporting gifts of vehicles—autos, boats, and airplanes.** Charities are required to provide contemporaneous written acknowledgments containing specific information to givers of autos, boats, and airplanes (IRS Publication 4302). Taxpayers are required to include a copy of the written acknowledgment (Form 1098-C may be used as the acknowledgment) with their tax returns in order to receive a deduction. The donee organization is also required to provide the information contained in the acknowledgment to the IRS. The information included in such acknowledgments as well as the meaning of "contemporaneous" depends on what the charity does with the donated vehicle.

➤ **Vehicle sold *before* use or improvement.** If the donated auto, boat, or airplane is sold before significant intervening use or material improvement of the auto, boat, or airplane by the organization, the gross proceeds received by the donee organization from the sale of the vehicle will be included on the written acknowledgment. Therefore, for donated property sold before use or improvement, the deductible amount is the gross proceeds received from the sale. A written acknowledgment is considered contemporaneous if the donee organization provides it within 30 days of the sale of the vehicle. The written acknowledgment provided by the charity should include the following information:

- the name and taxpayer identification number of the giver
- the vehicle, boat, or airplane identification number or similar number

- certification that the property was sold in an arm's length transaction between unrelated parties

- the gross proceeds from the sale

- a statement that the deductible amount may not exceed the amount of the gross proceeds

➤ **Vehicle not sold before use or improvement.** Charities may plan to significantly use or materially improve a donated auto, boat, or airplane before or instead of selling the property. In such circumstances, the charity would not include a dollar amount in the written acknowledgment. Instead, the written acknowledgment (prepared within 30 days of the contribution of the vehicle to be considered contemporaneous) should include the following information:

- the name and taxpayer identification number of the giver

- the vehicle, boat, or airplane identification number or similar number

- certification of the intended use or material improvement of the property and the intended duration of such use

- certification that the property will not be transferred in exchange for money, other property, or services before completion of such use or improvement

The deductible amount for contributed vehicles that will be used or improved by the ministry is the fair market value of the property, as determined by the giver, taking into consideration accessories, mileage, and other indicators of the property's general condition.

In certain instances, a vehicle may be sold at a price significantly below fair market value (or gratuitously transferred) to needy individuals in direct furtherance of the donee organization's charitable purpose.

For property that meets this definition, the gift acknowledgment must also contain a certification that the donee organization will sell the property to a needy individual at a price significantly below fair market value (or, if applicable, that the donee organization gratuitously will transfer the property to a needy individual). Additionally, the ministry must certify that the sale or transfer will be in the direct furtherance of the donee organization's charitable purpose of relieving the poor and distressed or the underprivileged who are in need of a means of transportation.

Example: On March 1, 2018, a giver contributes a qualified vehicle to a qualified ministry. The organization's charitable purposes include helping needy individuals who are unemployed develop new job skills, finding job placements for these individuals, and providing transportation for these individuals who need a means of transportation to jobs in areas not served by public transportation. The ministry determines that, in direct furtherance of its charitable purpose, the ministry will sell the qualified vehicle at a price significantly below fair market value to a trainee who needs a means of transportation to a new workplace. On or before March

7878	☐ VOID	☐ CORRECTED		

DONEE'S name, street address, city or town, state or province, country, ZIP or foreign postal code, and telephone no.	1 Date of contribution 1/15/18	OMB No. 1545-1959	**Contributions of Motor Vehicles, Boats, and Airplanes**
Lamont Community Church 101 East Main Street Lamont, KS 66855	2a Odometer mileage 81,980	20**18** Form **1098-C**	

2b Year 2003	2c Make Chevy	2d Model S10 Pickup

DONEE'S TIN 35-0189211	DONOR'S TIN 514-41-8007	3 Vehicle or other identification number 1FAP58923V159753

DONOR'S name Fred Wilbur	4a ☒ Donee certifies that vehicle was sold in arm's length transaction to unrelated party
Street address (including apt. no.) 512 North Main	4b Date of sale 1/25/16
City or town, state or province, country, and ZIP or foreign postal code Lamont, KS 66855	4c Gross proceeds from sale (see instructions) $ 3,000

Copy A

For Internal Revenue Service Center

File with Form 1096.

For Privacy Act and Paperwork Reduction Act Notice, see the **2018 General Instructions for Certain Information Returns.**

5a ☐ Donee certifies that vehicle will not be transferred for money, other property, or services before completion of material improvements or significant intervening use

5b ☐ Donee certifies that vehicle is to be transferred to a needy individual for significantly below fair market value in furtherance of donee's charitable purpose

5c Donee certifies the following detailed description of material improvements or significant intervening use and duration of use

6a Did you provide goods or services in exchange for the vehicle? . . . . ▶ Yes ☐ No ☒

6b Value of goods and services provided in exchange for the vehicle
$

6c Describe the goods and services, if any, that were provided. If this box is checked, donee certifies that the goods and services consisted solely of intangible religious benefits . . . . ▶ ☐

7 Under the law, the donor may not claim a deduction of more than $500 for this vehicle if this box is checked . . . . . ▶ ☐

Form **1098-C** Cat. No. 39732R www.irs.gov/Form1098C Department of the Treasury - Internal Revenue Service

31, 2018, the ministry provides Form 1098-C to the giver containing the giver's name and taxpayer identification number, the vehicle identification number, a statement that the date of the contribution was March 1, 2018, a certification that the ministry will sell the qualified vehicle to a needy individual at a price significantly below fair market value, and a certification that the sale is in direct furtherance of the organization's charitable purpose.

Generally, no deduction is allowed unless givers receive Form 1098-C within 30 days after the date that the vehicle is sold or within 30 days of the donation date if the charity keeps the car. If the vehicle is sold, givers must be informed of the gross selling price.

If the ministry keeps the car, the private-party sale price must be used by givers to figure the charitable tax deduction for donations, not the higher dealer retail price.

Quid Pro Quo Disclosure Requirements

When a giver receives goods or services of value approximate to the amount transferred to a ministry, there is no gift. This is because the person received a "quid pro quo" of an equivalent amount in exchange for the transfer. If the payment to a ministry exceeds the approximate amount of goods or services provided by the ministry to the giver, the difference qualifies as a charitable gift.

The ministry is required to provide an acknowledgment for all transactions where the giver makes a payment of more than $75 to the ministry and receives goods or services (other than intangible religious benefits or items of token value).

Form of the acknowledgment

The charitable gift acknowledgment, in quid pro quo situations, must:

➤ inform the giver that the amount of the contribution that is deductible for federal income tax purposes is limited to the difference of the amount of money and the value of any property contributed by the giver over the value of the goods or services provided by the organization

➤ provide the giver with a good-faith estimate of the value of goods or services that the charity is providing in exchange for the contribution

Only single payments of more than $75 are subject to the quid pro quo rules. Payments are not cumulative. It is not a difference of $75 between the amount given and the value of the object received that triggers the disclosure requirements, but the amount actually paid by the giver.

Calculating the gift portion

It is not a requirement for the donee organization to actually complete the subtraction of the benefit from a cash payment, showing the net charitable deduction. However, providing the net amount available for a charitable deduction is a good approach for clear communication with givers.

When to make the required disclosures

The disclosure of the value of goods or services provided to a giver may be made in the giver solicitation as well as in the subsequent acknowledgment. However, sufficient information will generally not be available to make

> **Warning**
>
> An organization must furnish a disclosure statement in connection with either the solicitation or the receipt of a quid pro quo contribution of over $75. The statement must be in writing and must be made in a manner that is likely to come to the attention of the giver. For example, a disclosure in small print within a larger document might not meet this requirement.

proper disclosure upon solicitation (for example, the value of a dinner may not be known at the time the solicitation is made).

Goods provided to givers

To determine the net charitable contribution, a gift must generally be reduced by the fair market value of any premium, incentive, or other benefit received by the giver in exchange for the gift. Common examples of premiums are books, CDs, DVDs, Bibles, and other resources.

For gifts of more than $75, organizations must advise the giver of the fair market value of the premium or incentive and explain that the value of the premium is not deductible for income tax purposes.

Givers must reduce their charitable deduction by the fair market value of goods or services they receive, even when the goods or services were donated to the ministry for use as premiums or gifts or when they were bought wholesale by the ministry. Therefore, charities cannot pass along to givers the savings realized by receiving products at no cost or buying products at a discount.

In certain circumstances, if givers receive unsolicited free, low-cost articles (free to the giver and low-cost to the distributing ministry) as part of the ministry's stewardship efforts, they are allowed a full tax deduction for the donation:

➤ **Low-cost items.** If an item that has a cost (not retail value) of less than $10.90 (2018 inflation-adjusted amount) and bears the name or logo of your ministry is given in return for a donation of more than $54.50 (2018 inflation-adjusted amount), the giver may claim a charitable deduction for the full amount of the donation. Examples of low-cost items are coffee mugs, key chains, bookmarks, and calendars.

➤ *De minimis* **benefits.** A giver can take a full deduction if the fair market value of the benefits received in connection with a gift does not exceed 2% of the donation or $109 (2018 inflation-adjusted amount), whichever is less.

Examples of the quid pro quo rules

Here are various examples of how the quid pro quo rules may apply:

➤ **Admission to events.** Many organizations sponsor banquets, concerts, or other events to which givers and prospective givers are invited in exchange for a contribution or other payment. Typically, the giver receives a benefit equivalent to the payment and no charitable deduction is available.

But if the amount paid is more than the value received, the amount in excess of the fair market value is deductible if the giver intended to make a contribution.

➤ **Auctions.** The IRS generally takes the position that the fair market value of an item purchased at a charity auction is set by the bidders. The winning bidder, therefore, cannot pay more than the item is worth. That means there is no charitable contribution in the IRS's eyes, no deduction, and no need for the charity to provide any charitable gift substantiation document to the bidder.

However, many tax professionals take the position that when the payment (the purchase price) exceeds the fair market value of the items, the amount that exceeds the fair market value is deductible as a charitable contribution. This position also creates a reporting requirement under the quid pro quo rules.

Remember

Many charities offer products and suggest a donation amount with respect to the products. For example, a charity may offer a book with a suggested donation amount of $30. If the fair market value of the book is $30 and the individual sends $30 to the charity, no charitable donation has been made. However, if the charity receives $50, a $20 charitable deduction is available.

> **Example:** A church youth group auctions goods to raise funds for a missions trip. An individual bought a quilt for $1,000. The church takes the position that the quilt had a fair market value of $50 even though the bidder paid $1,000. Since the payment of $1,000 exceeded the $75 limit, the church is required to provide a written statement indicating that only $950 of the $1,000 payment is eligible for a charitable contribution.

➤ **Bazaars.** Payments for items sold at bazaars and bake sales are not tax-deductible to givers since the purchase price generally equals the fair market value of the item.

➤ **Banquets.** Whether an organization incurs reporting requirements in connection with banquets where funds are raised depends on the specifics of each event.

> **Example 1:** A church sponsors a banquet for missions charging $50 per person. The fair market value of the meal provided is $15 per person. There is no disclosure requirement since the amount charged was less than $75. However, the amount deductible by each giver is still only $35.

> **Example 2:** A church invites individuals to attend a missions banquet without charge. Attendees are invited to make contributions or pledges at the end of the banquet. These payments probably do not require disclosure even if the amount given is $75 or more because there is only an indirect relationship between the meal and the gift.

➤ **Deduction timing.** The same quid pro quo rule applies to goods and services received in a different year. Thus, a giver's deduction for the year of the payment is limited to the amount, if any, by which the payment exceeds the value of the goods and services received in a previous or subsequent year.

Sample Charitable Gift Acknowledgment

Acknowledgment #2

Received from: Charles K. Vandell

Cash received:

Date Cash Received	Gross Amount Received	Value of Goods or Services	Net Charitable Contribution
1/23/18	$80.00	$25.00 [1]	$ 55.00
3/20/18	300.00		300.00
4/24/18	60.00		60.00
6/19/18	500.00	100.00 [2]	400.00
9/04/18	275.00		275.00
10/30/18	200.00		200.00
12/18/18	1,000.00		1,000.00
		Total	$2,290.00

Property received described as follows:

Received on October 22, 2018, 12 brown Samsonite folding chairs.

In return for certain gifts listed above, we only provided you with the following goods or services (our estimate of the fair market value is indicated):
(1) Christian music CDs $25.00
(2) Limited edition art print $100.00

You may have also received intangible religious benefits, but these benefits do not need to be valued for tax purposes.

The deductible portion of your contribution for federal income tax purposes is limited to the excess of your contribution over the value of goods and services we provided to you.

This document is necessary for any available federal income tax deduction for your contribution. Please retain it for your records.

Receipt issued on: January 15, 2019

Receipt issued by: Harold Morrison, Treasurer
Castleview Church
1008 High Drive
Dover, DE 19901

This sample receipt is based on the following assumptions:
A. Goods or services were provided in exchange for the gifts.
B. The receipt is issued on a periodic or annual basis for all gifts whether over or under $250.

All receipts should be numbered consecutively for control and accounting purposes.

➤ **Good-faith estimates.** A giver is not required to use the estimate provided by a donee organization in calculating the deductible amount. When a taxpayer knows or has reason to know that an estimate is inaccurate, the taxpayer may ignore the organization's estimate in determining the fair market value of the goods or services received.

➤ **Rights of refusal.** A giver can claim a full deduction if he or she refuses a benefit from the charity. However, this must be done affirmatively. Simply not taking advantage of a benefit is not enough. For example, a giver who chooses not to make use of tickets made available by the organization must deduct the value of the tickets from his or her contribution before claiming a deduction. However, a giver who rejects the right to a benefit at the time the contribution is made (for example, by checking off a refusal box on a form supplied by the charity) can take a full deduction.

➤ **Sale of products or a service at fair market value.** When an individual purchases products or receives services approximate to the amount paid, no part of the payment is a gift.

> **Example 1:** An individual purchases recordings of a series of Sunday morning worship services for $80. The sale price represents fair market value. Even though the amount paid exceeds the $75 threshold, the church is not required to provide a disclosure statement to the purchaser because the value of the products is approximate to the amount paid to the church.

> **Example 2:** The Brown family uses the fellowship hall of the church for a family reunion. The normal rental fee is $300. The Browns give a check to the church for $300 marked "Contribution." No acknowledgment should be given because no charitable contribution was made. The Browns received a benefit approximate to the amount of their payment.

> **Example 3:** The Smith family uses the church sanctuary and fellowship hall for a wedding and the reception. The church does not have a stated use fee but asks for a donation from those who use the facility. The comparable fee to rent similar facilities is $250. The Smiths give a check to the church for $250 marked "Contribution." No acknowledgment should be given because no charitable contribution was made. The Smiths received a benefit approximate to the amount of their payment. *Note:* It is inappropriate for the church to try to mask a fee by calling it a donation.

> **Example 4:** A church operates a Christian school. The parent of a student at the school writes a check payable to the church for his child's tuition. No acknowledgment should be given because a payment of tuition does not qualify as a charitable contribution.

Receipting a taxpayer other than the giver

Givers or prospective givers sometimes present challenging requests to churches and non-profits. Some requests relate to the receipting of a gift or potential gift. If a giver asks a ministry to issue a gift receipt to a taxpayer other than the one making the gift, what should the organization do?

➤ Should the ministry automatically issue the receipt as requested by the giver?

➤ Should the ministry ask for an explanation?

➤ If the donor provides an explanation that evidences an attempt to understate income or social security taxes, what should the ministry do?

➤ If the ministry provides a receipt to a taxpayer other than the giver, is the ministry aiding tax evasion?

➤ Even if the law does not cover these issues, is there a position of "high ground" for the ministry?

Policy on Issuing Receipts to Someone Other Than the Remitter of the Funds

When the ministry receives requests for receipts to be issued to a taxpayer other than the remitter of the funds, receipts will be issued only to the taxpayer making the gift.

➤ For a cash gift, the person or entity named on the check (or the individual delivering the cash) is the one to whom the receipt is addressed.

➤ The person or entity transferring ownership of noncash assets to a ministry is the giver.

The following exceptions to this policy may be permitted:

➤ If the giver documents the appropriateness of issuing a receipt to a taxpayer other than the giver, an exception may be made to the policy.

➤ To facilitate the processing of modest gifts, an exception may be made for small gifts where the risk of significant fraud is diminished.

Giver privacy

While giver information is treated with the utmost confidentiality by most churches and nonprofit organizations, there is no federal law that mandates giver privacy.

Sample Giver Privacy Policy

Our ministry is committed to respecting the privacy of our givers. We have developed this privacy policy to assure our givers that their information will not be shared with any third party.

Awareness. This policy is shared to make you aware of our privacy policy and to inform you of the way your information is used. We also provide you with the opportunity to remove your name from our mailing list, if you desire to do so.

Information collected. Here are the types of giver information that we collect and maintain:

- contact information: name, organization/church, complete address, phone number, email address

- shipping information: name, organization/church, complete address

- information concerning how you heard about our charity

- information you wish to share: questions, comments, suggestions

- your request to receive periodic updates: e.g., to individuals who request them, we will send periodic mailings related to specific fundraising appeals, prayer concerns, and newsletters

How information is used. Our ministry uses your information to understand your needs and provide you with better service. Specifically, we use your information to help you complete a transaction, communicate back to you, and update you on ministry happenings. Credit card numbers are used only for donation or payment processing and are not retained for other purposes. We use the comments you offer to provide you with information requested, and we take seriously each recommendation as to how we might improve communication.

No sharing of personal information. Our ministry will not sell, rent, or lease your personal information to other organizations. We assure you that the identity of all of our givers will be kept confidential. Use of giver information will be limited to the internal purposes of our ministry and only to further our ministry activities and purposes.

Removing your name from our mailing list. It is our desire to not send unwanted mail to our givers. Please contact us if you wish to be removed from our mailing list.

Contacting us. If you have comments or questions about our giver privacy policy, please send us an email at info@XYZMinistry.org or call us at (800) 555-5555.

Is it acceptable for a church pastor, ministry executive, or fundraising consultant to be given a list of givers, identified either within dollar ranges or with actual contribution amounts? This practice is not prohibited or considered unethical if this information is used within a limited context on a "need to know" basis for a specific function. However, circulating this information outside the charity would be considered unethical.

It is wise and prudent for a ministry to maintain a giver privacy policy to help assure its givers of their privacy in contributing to the organization. Ministries should consider including several components in developing giver privacy policies:

➤ **How the giver information is used.** The giver privacy policy should explain how giver information will be used. Common uses are to process contributions, communicate with givers, and update them about ministry events or programs.

➤ **Who the giver information is shared with.** The privacy policy should specify whether the ministry will share giver information with other organizations. Most ministries have a policy not to share any form of giver information. If, however, a nonprofit does share giver information with other organizations, it is important that it disclose that fact in the giver privacy policy. Doing so allows givers to be aware that any personal information given may be passed on to another organization.

➤ **Removal from the mailing list.** A good giver privacy policy will also include instructions that persons may follow to remove their name from the mailing list.

Ministries may communicate their giver privacy policy in several different places. The policy may be included in fundraising appeals, response vehicles, contribution receipts, annual reports, and on the ministry's website. Ministries can publish their entire giver privacy policy or create a simplified giver privacy statement to be used on documents and websites.

Charitable solicitation registration

Approximately forty states and the District of Columbia currently have laws regulating the solicitation of funds for charitable purposes. These statutes generally require organizations to register with a state agency before soliciting the state's residents for contributions, providing exemptions from registration for certain categories of organizations. In addition, organizations may be required to file periodic financial reports. State laws may impose additional requirements on fundraising activity involving paid solicitors and fundraising counsel. Before soliciting contributions, charitable organizations may wish to contact the appropriate state agency to learn more about the requirements that may apply in their state. In some states, municipal or other local governments may also require organizations soliciting charitable contributions to register and report.

To determine in what state(s) you may be required to register to solicit charitable contributions or hold assets subject to a charitable trust, see the website of the National Association of State Charity Officials: www.nasconet.org.

Gift Acceptance Policy

A ministry should evaluate the following factors in considering potential gifts:

➤ whether the gift is consistent with the ministry's tax-exempt purposes

➤ whether the ministry can exercise sufficient control over the gift

➤ whether the gift has the characteristics of an earmarked transaction

➤ whether it will cost the ministry money to own the asset

➤ whether it will cost the ministry money to sell the asset

➤ staff and volunteer time required to manage or sell the asset

➤ whether owning or selling the asset will expose the ministry to liability

➤ the marketability of the asset and the cash flow it can be expected to generate

Purpose of the Guidelines

1. To protect the interests of the giver, the ministry, or causes named as the beneficiary of a gift

2. To make certain all gifts to the ministry are structured to provide maximum benefits to the giver and the named entity

3. To encourage interested givers to make gifts without encumbering their own or the ministry's financial or other resources

4. To optimize opportunities to secure gifts from individuals to causes without compromising or endangering the reputation of the ministry

General Guidelines

1. No gifts will be accepted that cannot be used or expended consistently with the purpose and mission of the ministry.

2. No irrevocable gift, whether outright or life-income in character, will be accepted if, under any reasonable set of circumstances, the gift would jeopardize the giver's financial security.

3. Any gift presented to the ministry without the approval of a ministry representative shall not be received until after it is determined that the intended gift and the manner in which it is given is in the best interest of the giver.

4. Givers should always be advised of their own need for legal or tax counsel to assist them in the process of making their gift. Ministry staff shall avoid becoming involved in what can be interpreted as unauthorized practice of law.

Any suggestions made to a giver by ministry staff should be accompanied by encouragement to seek advice from the giver's professional counsel and/or financial advisors.

5. Every precaution shall be taken by the ministry staff to protect the privacy and confidentiality of each giver and the giver's family. Permission must be obtained before any public acknowledgment is made of gifts received by the ministry. The right of anonymity must always be respected.

6. The ministry staff shall attempt to have key executives meet with each individual giver prior to, or concurrent with, the execution of a gift agreement. In the case of charitable remainder trusts or other complex arrangements, such a meeting is mandatory. These arrangements must be reviewed by the ministry's legal counsel.

7. In all cases, any professional advisors such as attorneys or CPAs hired by the ministry must recognize that their client is the ministry and that they do not represent the giver. Professional advisors for the ministry will always seek to work with the advisors for the giver.

8. Gifts shall not be accepted where the mental competency of the giver is in question. This does not preclude a person acting in the capacity of attorney-in-fact from making a gift from the estate of the individual granting the power of attorney. In this event every consideration shall be given to the giver's charitable giving habits and financial condition to ensure that the gift is in the best interest of the giver and is carried out in a prudent manner. The giver's power of attorney must specifically grant the power to make charitable gifts.

9. The ministry will provide acknowledgments meeting IRS substantiation requirements for property received by the ministry as a gift. However, except for gifts of cash, no value shall be ascribed to any acknowledgment or other form of substantiation of a gift received by the ministry.

10. Investment considerations and gift considerations are in all cases to be evaluated separately, each on their respective merits. In no event shall the offer of a gift be tied in any way to an investment action or decision by the ministry.

11. The ministry shall in no way compensate—whether through commissions, finders' fees, or other means—any third party for directing a giver to the ministry.

12. All written instruments setting out the description and terms of a gift shall be reviewed by legal and/or tax counsel on behalf of the ministry and a written report made to key staff on its compliance with applicable laws and regulations as well as an explanation of its potential liability to the ministry.

Types of Gifts

1. Both current gifts and deferred gifts shall be actively encouraged. Response to each type of gift should be prompt without regard to the monetary value or timing of the individual gift. The decision to accept or reject any gift, whether current or deferred, shall be weighed on the merits of the individual gift, always regarding the giver's intent and financial condition as well as the benefit to the ministry's causes.

2. Any large gift subject to a restriction shall be accepted only after review by the ministry's legal counsel and/or the governing board. Every effort shall be made to ensure the restrictions on the gift do not negate any potential benefit to the intended cause. Also, the restrictions should not encumber the ministry staff with excessive additional responsibilities that would make the gift inadvisable.

3. The ministry should not be engaged in the execution of notarial wills. The ministry may, however, provide gift clauses for inclusion in wills by givers and/or their personal counsel.

4. Gifts of real estate are acceptable only after the following criteria are met:

   a. A personal inspection is conducted by an appropriate ministry staff member.

   b. Giver has received a copy of "XYZ Ministry Policies Regarding Real Estate."

   c. Determination is made that the property has not been utilized in a manner that would cause embarrassment to the ministry.

   d. An appraisal satisfactory to the IRS gift substantiation requirements has been completed, and the ministry and giver have reached an understanding as to the valuation of the property.

   e. Debt, insurance, homeowners' association fees, property taxes, and other carrying costs have been assessed as to the effect on the advisability of taking the gift.

   f. Appropriate steps have been taken to determine if any other liabilities might attach to the property such as leases, contracts, or servitudes.

   g. All pertinent information regarding the property is supplied by the giver. This would include names of owners and co-owners (and percentage ownership), recent tax statements, address and/or legal description, and description of current use.

   h. Giver must convey all his/her undivided interest in the real estate including any mineral interests. A gift of partial interest is not considered to be a charitable gift by the IRS. This would disqualify such a gift from income-tax and estate-tax deductions.

i. The ministry may recover any costs of managing real estate by charging a fee that is determined by the schedule set by the governing board.

j. The giver must be willing to bear the costs associated with the gift of real estate, such as legal fees, real estate commissions, management fees, and appraisals, or have these costs deducted from the sale of the property.

k. The governing board must approve any exception.

5. Gifts of real estate are ordinarily acceptable only after it has been determined that no reasonable possibility exists that the property could be contaminated by toxic waste. An initial personal inspection shall be made by an appropriate ministry staff member. This inspection shall include both a physical inspection and an investigation of the recent ownership history of the property. If, after inspection, it is determined that there is a substantial likelihood that the property has been environmentally impacted, the property may not be accepted. If, after inspection, it is determined that a reasonable possibility exists that the property has been environmentally impacted, an inspection must be made by a licensed environmental consultant, who must certify, within the context of a Phase 1 Site Assessment, that no contamination exists before the property may be accepted. The inspection should be performed in general conformance with the scope of American Society for Testing and Materials (ASTM) Practice E1527. The expense of inspection must be borne by the giver unless an exception is approved by the governing board.

6. Gift annuity contracts are to be entered into by the ministry upon approval of the Executive Director. In no event shall a gift annuity contract be agreed to which pays an income at a rate in excess of an actuarially prudent rate of return. The ministry will invest the gift in a manner that will attempt to protect the integrity of the principal amount given. Gift annuities will not be funded with real estate or other illiquid assets. Givers must be reminded, in correspondence or conversation with them and their advisors, that a qualified charitable gift annuity is not insurance under the laws of their state.

7. Gifts of life insurance shall be accepted after examination of funding of the policy and the gift substantiation requirements. Ministry staff members shall avoid even the appearance of giving an endorsement, either implied or direct, to any life insurance product, company, or agent.

8. Where a personal residence is the subject of a gift, it will not be accepted without the approval of the governing board if the right to utilize the residence is vested in a person other than the giver. Gifts of personal residences will be subject to the ministry's real estate policies and environmental assessment procedures.

9. Gifts of oil and gas rights may be received absent extenuating circumstances such as extended liabilities or other conditions making receipt of the gift inadvisable. Each potential oil and gas gift shall be examined by a professional advisor with experience in mineral leases to determine if there are extenuating circumstances which would factor against accepting the gift.

10. Donated stocks require special evaluation when the stock relates to closely-held business corporations that are not listed on stock exchanges, partnerships, or limited liability corporations. Marketability can be a challenge since the potential buyers are generally the other owners of the business who may be relatives of the giver. Small business owners often enter into agreements with the other owners that limit their ability to sell their stock.

    Many small businesses, including partnerships, limited liability corporations and "S" corporations (corporations described in sub-chapter S of the Internal Revenue Code) pass taxable income through to the owners.

    For a ministry, income from a pass-through entity may be subject to unrelated business income tax.

Gifts with Restrictions

1. The governing body shall maintain a listing of restricted funds for which the donations will be accepted. Restricted funds shall not be received for restrictions other than these funds without prior board approval.

2. Any giving appeals by the ministry will clearly indicate whether a restricted or unrestricted gift is being sought in the gift appeal.

3. If a gift is received without any giver restrictions (either explicit or implicit restrictions), then such contributions shall be placed in the ministry's unrestricted fund balance. Similarly, if a gift is received with either an explicit or implicit restriction, and it is in conformity with board-approved restrictions, then such contributions shall be placed in the ministry's correlating restricted fund account.

4. Givers shall be informed in gift acknowledgments whether their gift was reflected as an unrestricted gift or a restricted gift. If a gift is a restricted gift, the restriction will also appear on the gift acknowledgment.

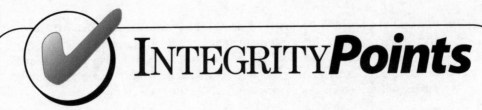

INTEGRITY*Points*

- **Use the proper year for gift acknowledgment reporting.** The timing for which year a charitable gift acknowledgment is a significant integrity issue. Absent clear documentation that a giver is eligible to receive a gift acknowledgment for a prior tax period, an organization should issue the gift acknowledgment for the year in which the gift was received.

- **The importance of proper receipting for noncash gifts.** When noncash gifts are received by an organization, it is important to ensure that the organization provides an appropriate gift acknowledgment. In recent years, a number of major noncash gifts have been disqualified as charitable deductions because the charitable organizations failed to provide an appropriate gift acknowledgment.

- **Transactions which are part gift/part purchase.** These transactions trigger the "quid pro quo" rules and require churches and other nonprofits to demonstrate integrity. Unless the charity fulfills its responsibility to report to the giver the fair market value of the goods or services provided, the giver lacks the necessary information to claim the correct charitable contribution amount.

- **Use of a gift acceptance policy.** Gifts that may seem at first to be a great idea can have unintended consequences, such as a giver offering land that also has environmental liabilities that exceed the fair market value of the property. The use of a gift acceptance policy is an important tool to protect the interests of the church or ministry and outlines how gifts with restrictions should be handled to ensure giver intent is honored.

Special Charitable Gift Issues

Giver-Restricted Gifts

The two fundamental concepts relating to giver-restricted gifts are (1) ministry discretion and control and (2) giver preferences:

> **Ministry discretion and control over giver-restricted gifts.** A common misconception is that the control a ministry board must exercise over any giver-restricted gift is in conflict with, or contradictory to, stipulations by givers. *This is not true.*

Some believe that organizations should not follow giver restrictions, from time to time, to demonstrate their control. *This is inappropriate.*

Board control and giver restrictions are really a "hand in glove" concept. It is not *either/or* but *both/and*! Restricted gifts must be used for a specific exempt purpose, whereas unrestricted gifts may be used for any exempt purpose.

The board must control all contributions to an exempt organization, unrestricted and restricted, to be used exclusively for its exempt purposes. In addition, the board must provide reasonable measures to assure that giver-restricted gifts are used for the intended exempt purpose(s).

Notifying the giver on the gift response that the ministry will exercise discretion and control over the gift does not remove the giver's restriction placed on a gift. Ministries must exercise discretion and control over all charitable gifts, whether unrestricted (may be used for any exempt purpose) or restricted (must be used for a specific purpose).

Giver restrictions arise when an organization accepts contributions that are solicited for or restricted by a giver for a specific area of ministry, such as a program, project, or a type of missionary work (vs. missionary work anywhere in the world); e.g., missionary work in Sri Lanka preferenced for a particular missionary. Unrestricted contributions have no implicit or explicit giver restrictions and are available to be used in any exempt operations of the ministry.

Givers often like to retain some control over their gifts. However, if too much control is retained, the giver's income tax deduction may be endangered.

The preferencing of a gift does not determine whether the gift is unrestricted or restricted for accounting purposes. When a gift is preferenced to support a particular worker, the preferencing may qualify the gift for a charitable tax deduction, but other factors must be reviewed to determine whether the gift is unrestricted or restricted for accounting purposes.

Example 1: Accompanying a gift, a giver communicates: "My preference is that the gift be used for scholarships. However, I give the ministry permission to use the gift for any exempt purpose consistent with the ministry's mission statement." This gift is an unrestricted gift because the ministry has full discretion as to the use of the gift.

Example 2: A prayer letter or appeal letter from a ministry that conducts work in several countries describes the need for religious workers in India. The request is for funds preferenced to enable a particular worker employed by the ministry to carry out certain work in India. A gift in response to this appeal is temporarily restricted for the ministry's program in India (a geographical restriction), and the gift is preferenced to support a particular worker.

A giver's *restriction* on a gift limits the ministry's use of the funds to the purposes specified by the giver; e.g., "This gift is made on the condition that," or "This gift is restricted for XYZ project." This type of gift is generally tax-deductible as a charitable contribution.

It may be inappropriate for a ministry to accept a gift if the restrictions accompanying a gift:

☐ Prevent the ministry from using the donation in the furtherance of its charitable purposes. For example, if a giver restricts a gift for the benefit of a specific individual and the ministry is prevented from exercising discretion and control over the gift (such as a gift restricted for a particular benevolent recipient, an employee of the charity, etc.), the gift is generally not deductible as a charitable contribution.

☐ Are incompatible with the mission of the ministry. Even though a restricted gift is exclusively charitable, it is generally inappropriate for a ministry to accept a gift requiring the expenditure of funds outside the mission of the ministry. For example, if a ministry whose sole purpose is international child sponsorship is offered a gift restricted for inner-city evangelism in the U.S., the gift should generally not be accepted by the ministry because it is inconsistent with the mission of the charity (the overall mission of the ministry is generally described in the organization's governing documents).

☐ **Are at odds with the best interests of the ministry.** A restricted gift could be exclusively charitable and compatible with the mission of the charity and still not be in the best interests of the ministry. A ministry might not have the capacity to comply with gift restrictions. For example, the amount of funds raised for a particular disaster may exceed the ministry's capacity to effectively spend the funds in a reasonable period of time.

Alternatively, the administrative requirements of a restricted gift could consume an inordinate amount of the ministry's resources. For example, the gift of a time share property could be offered to a ministry. However, the ministry may decide the time share is not in the best interest of the ministry because (1) time shares are often unmarketable properties laden with annual costs, and (2) even when sales are made, the low resale market prices can minimize or erase profits.

A giver's *preference* communicates a desire or suggestion which is advisory in nature. A desire or suggestion does not restrict the use of the gift and allows the ministry full discretion to use the gift in relation to the desire or suggestion, or use the funds for any other purpose. Factors that imply a ministry has received a giver preferenced gift and not a restricted gift include:

☐ **Giver intention.** The giver intends only to express a desire or make a suggestion with respect to a gift.

☐ **Charity communication.** Both the solicitation letter and response form (and perhaps the gift acknowledgment) from the ministry clearly communicate to the giver that preferred gifts are sought. Materials include statements such as "We appreciate your desire or suggestion as to the use of the funds. While we will endeavor to use the funds as you desire or suggest, we may use the gift for another purpose." This is very different from the statement "Gifts made to our ministry are under the discretion and control of the ministry." All gifts must be under the discretion and control of the charity, so making that statement does not turn an otherwise giver-restricted gift into an unrestricted gift.

☐ **Giver communication.** The giver communicated in writing or verbally a desire or suggestion as to the use of the funds, but the giver did not restrict the funds for a certain purpose.

If the giver preferences a gift, even when the preference is for the funds to go to a particular individual, the gift may qualify for a charitable tax deduction if the ministry exercises adequate due diligence with respect to the gift. For example, a gift restricted for missions and preferenced for the missionary endeavors involving a certain identified individual or a gift for benevolence preferenced for a particular benevolent recipient may qualify for a charitable tax deduction if the ministry exercises adequate due diligence related to the gift.

Some ministries request that givers not place the name of a preferenced worker on the memo line of the giver's check. This request may send an inappropriate message to givers—i.e., implying that hiding information from the IRS is an acceptable and/or desirable practice. If a giver wants to use the memo line on the check to indicate a preference to support the work of a particular individual ("preferenced for the ministry of Jill Smith"), this should be no more problematic for IRS purposes than checking a box on the response form which contains preferenced wording.

Contributions to Support Missionaries and Other Workers

Donations may be received, payable to a church or nonprofit organization, for the support of a particular missionary (often called deputized fundraising). These gifts generally qualify as a charitable contribution if the ministry exercises sufficient discretion and control over the gift. If so, the ministry should include the amounts in gift acknowledgments issued to givers.

The IRS has acknowledged that deputized support-raising is a widespread and legitimate practice, and the contributions properly raised by this method are tax-deductible.

In its 1999 Technical Instruction Program materials, the IRS outlined two general tests to determine whether a tax-deductible contribution is made to or for the use of a ministry, or whether a gift is a nondeductible pass-through gift to a particular individual who ultimately benefits from the contribution. These two tests, the intended benefit test and the discretion and control test, are explained below.

➤ **Intended benefit test.** The giver's intention must be to benefit the ministry. While the giver's intention is often only in his or her mind, communication provided by the ministry when the gift is solicited and the gift receipt is provided may help clarify giver intent:

☐ **Solicitation.** The best time for the giver to understand that a ministry will have complete discretion and control over a gift is at the point of solicitation—before the gift is ever made—underscoring the principle

Key Issue

There is an extremely fine line between a personal nondeductible gift to a missionary (or other religious worker) and a tax-deductible gift to a charity to provide funding for the ministry of a particular missionary. The key is the intention of the donor to benefit the charity and the ministry's discretion and control over the gift.

of truthfulness in fundraising. And using the suggested wording at the point of solicitation is the best way to communicate the pertinent facts to the prospective giver before the donation is made.

The IRS formally indicated that the following language in solicitations for contributions, with no conflicting language in the solicitations and no conflicting understandings between the parties, will help show that the qualified donee has exercised the necessary control over contributions, that the giver has reason to know that the qualified donee has the necessary discretion and control over contributions, and that the giver intends that the qualified donee is the actual recipient of the contributions:

> "Contributions are solicited with the understanding that [insert name of donee organization] has complete discretion and control over the use of all donated funds."

☐ **Gift receipt.** The IRS has provided the following suggested language for use in gift acknowledgments to help clarify the record of the true intentions of a giver at the time of the contribution:

> "This contribution is made with the understanding that [insert name of donee organization] has complete control and administration over the use of the donated funds."

Thus, use of this language should provide strong evidence of both giver intent and organizational control in the deputized fundraising context.

➤ **Discretion and control test.** The IRS uses the phrase "discretion and control" with respect to a charity's obligation over deputized funds. Informally, the IRS has stated that discretion and control may be evidenced by such factors as adequate selection and supervision of the self-supported worker (a worker who raises part or all of his or her support) and formalizing a budget that establishes the compensation limit and expenses of each deputized individual. Establishing compensation limits and expense reimbursements with reference to considerations other than an amount of money a deputized fundraiser collects is very important. For a complete list of the factors indicating adequate discretion and control, see the box on page 179.

Example 1: When worker A leaves the employment of ministry B, the worker may mistakenly believe that the balance in his or her account should be transferred to ministry C (worker A's new employer), where the worker will be employed. While a transfer to ministry C may be made if it furthers the charitable purpose of ministry B, it is not required.

Example 2: When worker D leaves the employment of ministry E after completing a two-year missionary term, there is a substantial excess of funds raised for the ministry by worker D above what was spent for the ministry of this worker. The worker may mistakenly believe the excess in his or her account should be paid to the worker. While a modest severance payment might be made to the worker in conformity with the ministry's policies, the excess is an asset of the ministry and subject to the ministry's discretion and control.

But how does a ministry know if the "intended benefit" and "control" tests have been met? Unfortunately, the IRS provides little guidance for these tests. Ministries, with advice from their CPAs and attorneys, must design their action plan based on applicable law and informal IRS guidelines. The following is a review of issues that should be considered by ministries using the deputized fundraising approach:

➤ Determine how to put givers on notice that you will exercise discretion and control over the donations. Using the IRS-recommended language in solicitations—written or verbal—*and* on receipts is prudent.

> **Caution**
>
> Prayer or support letters should clearly communicate that gifts are being solicited for the charity. It is permissible to request that the gift be designated for the ministry of John Doe, who is a missionary employed by the charity. But letters should not request gifts "for a certain missionary" because of the implication that it is a nondeductible conduit transaction.

➤ Be sure your organization communicates consistently with your givers. Eliminating written conflicts between solicitation letters (including prayer letters), giver response forms, deputized worker training materials, receipts, and other related documents can be accomplished by a careful review of your current documents. It is also important to establish procedures to ensure that the reviews are ongoing. The more daunting task is the proper training and continuing reinforcement to self-supported workers of the need to clearly and consistently communicate the discretion and control concept to givers.

➤ Use appropriate terminology when communicating with givers. Since the ministry should not infer that contributions will be paid as salary, fringe benefits, and expense reimbursements to a particular person, communication to givers from the ministry or self-supported workers should consistently underscore the ministry's discretion and control over donations. A giver may indicate a preference that a gift to a ministry be used to support the ministry of a certain individual, and the ministry may track the dollars based on the preference. But the ministry and the deputized worker should refrain from any inference that the contributions will be paid as salary or expense reimbursements to the worker. This is a fine line but one that should be observed.

Clear communication with givers about the discretion and control issue not only places givers on notice but also serves to reinforce this concept in the mind of deputized workers. Too often, self-supported workers assume they have an element of personal ownership of funds that they raise for the ministry. For example, when the worker leaves the employment of ministry A, he or she may mistakenly believe that the balance in his account will be transferred to ministry B, where he or she will be employed. While a transfer of funds to ministry B may be appropriate, it is not required.

Factors Demonstrating Discretion and Control Over the Deputized Fundraising Process

According to the IRS, ministries that receive revenues through deputized fundraising—through individual missionaries, staff members, or volunteers conducting grassroots fundraising to support the organization—can demonstrate discretion and control by the following factors:

➤ Control by the governing body of donated funds through a budgetary process

➤ Consistent exercise by the organization's governing body of responsibility for establishing, reviewing, and monitoring the programs and policies of the organization

➤ Staff salaries set by the ministry according to a salary schedule approved by the governing body (Salaries must be set by reference to considerations other than an amount of money a deputized fundraiser collects. There can be no commitments that contributions will be paid as salary or expenses to a particular person.)

➤ Amounts paid as salary, to the extent required by the Internal Revenue Code, reported as compensation on Form W-2 or Form 1099-MISC

➤ Reimbursements of legitimate ministry expenses approved by the organization, pursuant to guidelines approved by the governing body (Reimbursements must be set by considerations other than the amount of money a deputized fundraiser collects.)

➤ Thorough screening of potential workers pursuant to qualifications established by the ministry that are related to its exempt purposes and not principally related to the amount of funds that may be raised by the workers

➤ Meaningful training, development, and supervision of workers

➤ Workers assigned to programs and project locations by the organization based upon its assessment of each worker's skills and training, and the specific needs of the ministry

➤ Regular communication to givers of the ministry's full discretion and control over all its programs and funds through such means as newsletters, solicitation literature, and giver acknowledgments

➤ The financial policies and practices of the ministry annually reviewed by an audit committee, a majority of whose members are not employees of the organization

For more information on this topic, see the *The Guide to Charitable Giving for Churches and Ministries* by Dan Busby, Michael Martin, and John Van Drunen, published by ECFAPress (ECFA.org).

Contributions to Support Short-Term Mission Trips

Many ministries sponsor individuals and/or teams of individuals that serve on short-term mission trips, domestically and internationally. The proper handling of funds raised and expended for short-term mission trips often presents challenging tax, finance, and legal issues for trip participants and sending organizations alike.

The definition of "short-term" varies from one sponsoring organization to another. For church-sponsored trips, a short-term mission trip often means a trip of a week or two in duration. However, for a missions organization, a short-term trip may last as long as two years. Short-term mission trips sometimes only involve adults. Other times, participants are minors supervised by adults, or some combination of adults and minors.

Funding options for short-term mission trips. Short-term mission trips may be funded in a variety of ways. For example, the sponsoring organization may pay part or all of the expenses of the trip from the ministry's general budget. Or a donor may give funds restricted for short-term mission trips without any preference for particular mission trip participants— the donor simply wishes to support the program of sending short-term missionaries. However, most ministries sponsoring short-term mission trips seek gifts that are preferenced for particular trip participants.

➤ **Funding from the sponsoring ministry's general budget.** Expenses relating to short-term mission trips may be funded in full by the sponsoring ministry. This use of funds from the sponsoring ministry's general budget is appropriate if short-term mission trips are consistent with its tax-exempt purposes.

➤ **Funds directly expended by the trip participant with no financial involvement of the sponsoring ministry.** A participant in a short-term mission trip may partially or totally fund trip expenses by making direct payments for airfare, lodging, meals, and other expenses. If a trip is sponsored by a ministry, the trip is consistent with the tax-exempt purposes of the ministry, and there is no significant element of personal pleasure, recreation, or vacation, expenses related to the trip are generally deductible as charitable contributions on the taxpayer's Schedule A, Itemized Deductions. The deduction will not be denied simply because the taxpayer enjoys providing services to the charitable organization. Personal expenses relating to "side-trips" or vacation days unrelated to the mission trip but included during the trip are generally not deductible.

➤ **Funding based on giver-restricted gifts for the trip but with no preference in relation to any trip participant.** Givers may make gifts restricted for a short-term mission trip project. Gifts for the project could be solicited by the charity, or the giver might make an unsolicited gift. These gifts generally qualify as charitable contributions, and it is appropriate for the sponsoring ministry to provide a charitable gift acknowledgment.

If a ministry accepts gifts that are giver-restricted for a short-term mission trip project, the ministry is obligated to spend the funds for the intended purpose.

A giver could change the gift restriction by redirecting the gift to another project. This scenario presumes the donated funds have not already been expended or obligated for the mission trip.

Additionally, an organization can establish, and disclose with gift solicitation information, a board policy regarding the possible redirection of giver-restricted gifts if a mission trip event is canceled or oversubscribed (more funds are received than needed).

➤ **Funding based on gifts preferred for particular trip participants.** Generally, mission trip participants are responsible for soliciting gifts to cover part or all of the expenses necessary for the particular trip (see pages 184–85 for a sample letter from a potential short-term mission trip participant to a potential giver).

When mission trip participants raise part or all of the funds required for a trip, the sponsoring ministry generally identifies the amounts preferred for particular participants to monitor whether sufficient funds have been raised to cover the expenses for each individual's trip.

There is generally no basis for refunding gifts if the preferred individual does not go on the trip. Refunding gifts demonstrates that the sponsoring ministry does not have adequate discretion and control over the gifts and may raise a question of the tax-deductibility of the gifts given in relation to the particular trip.

When a worker or a volunteer (a short-term mission trip participant typically qualifies as a "volunteer") raises some of his or her own support, the IRS has proposed the following two general tests to determine whether a tax-deductible contribution was made to or for the use of a charitable organization, or whether the gift was a nondeductible, pass-through gift to a particular individual who ultimately benefited from the contribution.

1. **The intended benefit test.** The purpose of this test is to determine whether the contributor's intent in making the donation was to benefit the ministry or the individual.

   The IRS has formally indicated that ministries should avoid the use of conflicting language in their solicitations for contributions and conflicts in understandings between the parties. This is to demonstrate that:

   a. the ministry has exercised the necessary control over contributions.

   b. the giver has reason to know that the ministry will have the necessary discretion and control over contributions.

   c. the giver intends for the ministry to be the actual recipient of the contributions.

The authors recommend the following statement be used in solicitations for contributions:

> *Contributions are solicited with the understanding that [insert name of sponsoring organization] has complete discretion and control over the use of all donated funds.*

2. **The discretion and control test.** The IRS uses the phrase "discretion and control" to indicate a ministry's obligation regarding charitable gifts. The IRS has stated that ministries receiving funds for the support of mission endeavors can demonstrate discretion and control with the following factors:

a. Reimbursement of legitimate ministry expenses are approved by the organization, consistent with the governing body's guidelines. Reimbursement should be set by considerations other than the amount of money collected by the individuals who raise funds.

b. Potential trip members are screened according to qualifications established by the ministry.

c. Trip members are given meaningful training, development, and supervision.

d. The ministry assigns trip members to programs and project locations based upon its assessment of each individual's skills and training, and the specific needs of the ministry.

e. Giver acknowledgments communicate the ministry's full discretion and control over its programs and funds.

f. Since the ministry should not commit to restricting the use of contributions to a particular person, potential trip participants should not imply the opposite, verbally or in writing. A giver may indicate a preference that the ministry use a gift to support the trip of a certain individual, and the ministry may track the dollars based on that preference. However, the organization and the potential trip participant should refrain from any inference that the contributions will be paid as expenses to or for a particular worker.

> **Remember**
>
> Gifts preferenced for particular trip participants should generally not be refunded to givers if the preferenced individual does not go on the trip.

Even if the intended benefit and discretion and control tests are met, there may be charitable tax-deductibility issues based on age of trip participants (see Example 2 below), charity authorization, and the pursuit of pleasure or personal gain. Two potentially tax-deductible scenarios follow.

Example 1: Trip participants are adults. The following two scenarios illustrate different funding patterns when trip participants are adults:

a. Participants contribute to the ministry to cover part or all of the trip expenses. The payments by the participants to the ministry are deductible as charitable contributions if the trip involves no significant element of personal pleasure, recreation, or vacation. These trip contributions may be acknowledged by the ministry as charitable contributions.

b. All trip expenses are paid by the ministry, and non-participants make contributions to cover trip expenses. If the ministry has preauthorized the mission trip, the trip furthers the exempt purposes of the ministry, and if the trip involves no significant element of personal pleasure, recreation, or vacation, gifts to cover the trip expenses are generally tax-deductible, even if the givers indicate a preference that gifts be applied to the trip expenses of a particular participant.

Example 2: Trip participants are minors.

If a trip participant is a minor, the minor must actually provide services to carry out the tax-exempt purposes of the trip. The age of the minor and the minor's development may be important factors in determining the minor's capability of providing services to the ministry.

If parents, relatives, and/or friends contribute to the ministry with a preference for a child's trip expenses and the ministry pays the trip expenses, these contributions are generally tax-deductible, assuming the minor significantly contributes to the trip purposes.

➤ **Funding based on gifts *restricted* for particular trip participants.** A giver may express a *preference* for a particular trip recipient, but if a giver expresses a *restriction* for a certain trip recipient, the gift is generally an earmarked gift. Therefore, the gift may not qualify for a charitable deduction and should generally not be accepted (or not acknowledged as a charitable gift if accepted).

Sponsors of short-term mission trips generally should not accept gifts earmarked for individuals because the gifts are not consistent with the ministry's tax-exempt purposes. An earmarked gift is a transfer that is intended to benefit an individual, not the charity ("for Joe Smith's trip costs"). It is a transfer over which the ministry does not have sufficient discretion and control. For example, in the short-term mission trip context, if the ministry accepted a gift restricted for a particular trip participant, the ministry would not have the freedom to use the funds given for another trip participant who fell short of the financial goal for the trip.

> **Caution**
>
> Earmarked gifts (for personal benefit of missionaries) should generally not be accepted by a ministry sponsoring a mission trip.

Sample Short-Term Mission Trip Fundraising Letter

This short-term mission trip fundraising letter demonstrates elements consistent with IRS guidance. The notes in the letter relate to accounting for the gift and qualifying it for a tax deduction.

1232 Main Street

Yakima, WA 98904

509/248-6739

Date

Dear Mr. and Mrs. Giver,

> This paragraph confirms it is a church-sponsored mission trip.

This summer, I have an exciting opportunity to serve the Lord on a mission trip sponsored by our church, Yakima Fellowship, to East Africa. Fifteen members of my church youth group plan to participate in a 10-day trip. We will fly into Nairobi, Kenya on July 21.

Our ministry during this trip is in Nairobi at an orphanage where most of the children have AIDS. Our team will lead a Vacation Bible School, distribute clothes we will take with us, and be available to work with and support the children in the orphanage. Sponsors from our church will accompany our team and provide ministry oversight.

> This paragraph confirms that ministry will be performed on the trip.

One of the ways you can help me is to pray for the trip, the ministry we will perform, and for me personally. Only with prayer support will I be able to bless the children in the orphanage.

> This paragraph confirms that gifts are preferenced for Jodi's trip expenses. (For accounting purposes, gifts are temporarily restricted for the mission trip.)

Yes, there are financial needs. The cost of the trip is $2,100, which each team member is responsible to raise in gifts for our church. Please pray with me that the funds to cover my trip expenses will be provided.

Gifts to the church, with an expression of a preference for my trip expenses, are tax-deductible to the extent allowed by law.

If you will commit to pray, please check the appropriate box on the enclosed card. If you are able to make a gift to the church to assist with my expenses, please check the appropriate box, indicating your interest in helping fund my portion of the trip expenses, and make your check payable to the sponsoring church, Yakima Fellowship. If I am unable to participate in the trip, your gifts will be used to support the short-term missions program of the church.

> This paragraph confirms the church will exercise discretion and control over the funds, implied in: "There are no refunds to givers if I don't go."

May God bless you richly as you consider your involvement in this mission trip!

Sincerely,

Jodi Hunter

Sample Short-Term Mission Trip
Response Form (Trip Expenses Paid by the Ministry)

We want to support the missions outreach of Yakima Fellowship and are sending our gift of $_____.

Our preference is that this gift be used to support the short-term mission trip of Jodi Hunter. We understand that the use of the gift is subject to the discretion and control of Yakima Fellowship.

> These paragraphs make it clear that the giver's intent is to benefit the charity. Their financial support of Jodi Hunter is simply a desire.

Donor(s):

Bill and Karen Smith
2315 Main
Wenatchee, WA 98801

Sample Short-Term Mission Trip
Gift Acknowledgment (Trip Expenses Paid by the Ministry)

Gift Acknowledgment • Please keep this acknowledgment for your tax records

Acknowledgment #2675 Gift Date: 01/02/XX Acknowledgment Date: 01/15/XX Bill and Karen Smith 2315 Main Wenatchee, WA 98801	Preferenced for the mission trip of: Jodi Hunter	**Total Amount** **$100.00**	**Gift Amount** **$100.00**	**Other Amount** 0

Thank you for your contribution which is tax-deductible to the extent allowed by law. While every effort will be made to apply your gift according to an indicated preference, if any, **Yakima Fellowship** has complete discretion and control over the use of the donated funds. We thank God for you and appreciate your support.

Yakima Fellowship
PO Box 4256
Yakima, WA 98904
509/248-5555

No goods or services were provided in exchange for this contribution.

Sample Short-Term Mission Trip
Gift Check (Trip Expenses Paid by the Ministry)

Bill and Karen Smith
2315 Main
Wenatchee, WA 98801

DATE: December 1, 20XX

PAY TO
THE ORDER OF: Yakima Fellowship $ 200.00

Two Hundred and no/100-- DOLLARS

FOR Missions Work   *Bill Smith*

Note: If a giver wishes to identify the preferenced participant on the check, the "preferential" or "to support the trip of" terminology should be used to avoid communicating the gift is earmarked for a particular participant. It is generally preferable for the giver to check an appropriately worded box on the response form indicating a preference to support the ministry of a particular trip participant.

Sample Short-Term Mission Trip
Gift Acknowledgment (Trip Expenses Paid by the Participant)

Gift Acknowledgment • Please keep this acknowledgment for your tax records		
Acknowledgment #4575 Gift Date: 01/02/XX Acknowledgment Date: 01/15/XX Bill and Karen Smith 2315 Main Wenatchee, WA 98801	Description of Services Provided	Built church building in Nairobi, Kenya, on July 21-28, 2018

Thank you for your contribution which is tax-deductible to the extent allowed by law. While every effort will be made to apply your gift according to an indicated preference, if any, **Yakima Fellowship** has complete discretion and control over the use of the donated funds. We thank God for you and appreciate your support.

Yakima Fellowship
PO Box 4256
Yakima, WA 98904
509/248-5555

No goods or services were provided
in exchange for this contribution..

➤ **Accounting issues.** Gifts to a ministry preferenced to support particular short-term trip participants are generally considered to be temporarily restricted contribution revenue under Generally Accepted Accounting Principles (GAAP), because the purpose of the gift is more narrow than the general purposes of the ministry while still meeting the IRS requirements for charitable contributions.

A ministry should have sufficient discretion and control over gifts to permit the organization to redirect the gifts for other short-term trip participants (for example, redirection of funds often occurs when a trip participant raises more or less funds than required for a trip). This redirection does not negate or negatively impact the charitable nature of the gifts. Rather, it is a clear demonstration of a ministry properly exercising discretion and control over gifts.

Ministries may wish to utilize separate accounts for each trip participant. This treatment should not jeopardize the giver's charitable tax deduction as long as the ministry maintains discretion and control over the funds.

Sample Short-Term Mission Trip and Mission Field Assessment Visit Policy

ABC Church occasionally sponsors short-term mission trips. While these trips may provide essential ministry services and encouragement in the field, the visits are primarily intended to introduce trip participants to missions.

Additionally, it is occasionally desirable for church staff and/or volunteers to visit a supported missionary (national or expatriate) in the field, assess a potential field of service for potential future missionary support, or assess a potential field of service for a future short-term mission trip. Visits to missionaries currently supported by the church are to (1) demonstrate the church's commitment to their ministry, (2) provide face-to-face encouragement, and (3) assess the effectiveness of the ministry.

The church desires that God will be honored in every aspect of these trips. Therefore, this policy has been developed and adopted by the church governing board to provide general guidance for these trips.

Trip approval. All short-term mission trips and field assessment visits are recommended by the Missions Committee and approved by the church governing board to be considered under these policies. (*Note:* The trip approval process will vary based on the governance structure of a particular church. In some instances, the governing board may delegate trip approval responsibility to the executive pastor, for example.)

Approval, training, supervision, and assignment of trip participants. Potential non-staff trip members will be screened according to qualifications established by the church, and trip participants are given meaningful training and adequately supervised.

Non-staff trip participants are assigned to programs and project locations based on the assessment of church leaders of each individual's skills and training.

Funding trips. Based on the funding method approved by the church governing board for a particular trip, the following funding approaches may be used:

A. Trip expenses may be fully or partially funded by the church. Funds from the mission or other budget line-items may be identified for this purpose.

B. Trip expenses may be fully or partially funded through resources raised by the trip participants. Funding may be raised to cover direct and indirect trip costs, based on the approval by the governing board of the funding plan. While the church will accept gifts preferenced for the trip of a particular participant, the church will not accept gifts restricted or designated for a particular trip participant. (Reason: Gifts restricted or designated for a particular gift participant do not qualify to receive a charitable gift acknowledgment, and such gifts are not consistent with the tax-exempt status of the church.)

If trip expenses are fully or partially funded by resources raised by the trip participants, all communication to givers—sample text for letters, websites, and blog posting and talking points for the verbal communication about the trip—will be approved by the church.

If resources are raised beyond the goal for a particular trip participant, the excess may be used to provide resources for a trip participant who is under-funded.

If the resources raised by a potential trip participant are less than the financial goal established by the church, the church will determine whether to assign funds sufficient to allow the individual to participate in the trip. The additional funds could come from the church's mission or general funds. Or the additional funds could come from resources raised beyond the goal to fund other potential trip participants.

Issuing charitable gift acknowledgments. At the discretion of the church, charitable gift acknowledgments will be prepared by the church and provided for all gifts that conform with this policy, including gifts from family members and trip participants. However, gifts will not be acknowledged if the trip participant is unable to, or for any reason does not plan to, significantly perform services to carry out the purposes of the trip (for example, a child of age three).

The church will determine the appropriateness of issuing charitable gift acknowledgments when trip participants pay their own expenses for a church-sponsored trip. No charitable gift acknowledgments will be issued for short-term mission trips that have not been approved by the church.

Charitable gift acknowledgments issued by the church will include the following wording:

- An indication that the church has discretion and control over the gifts.
- A statement indicating "no goods or services were provided in exchange for the gifts," if this is true.

In determining whether a gift is preferenced or restricted for a potential trip participant, the church will use the following principles for guidance:

- A preferenced gift merely comes with a preference or a desire that the gift be used to support the trip expenses of a particular trip participant.
- Preferenced gifts generally may be accepted with a gift acknowledgment provided.
- An earmarked gift is a transfer that is intended to benefit an individual, not the church. It is a transfer over which the church does not have sufficient discretion and control. For example, if accepted, the church would not have

the freedom to use the funds for a trip participant who fell short of the financial goal for the trip.

Earmarked gifts generally should not be accepted; therefore, a gift acknowledgment is a moot issue.

Refunding of gifts related to trips. Gifts preferenced for particular gift recipients will not be refunded to givers except in unusual circumstances, such as the cancellation of a trip. Funds preferenced for the trip of a particular participant could be carried forward for a future trip at the discretion of the church.

Discretion and control over gifts. All gifts given to support trips are the property of the church and will be expended under the discretion and control of the church.

Accounting records. The church will separately record revenue and expenses related to each short-term mission trip.

Determining accountable expenses related to trips. Expenses will be reimbursed under the church's accountable expense reimbursement plan. Allowable volunteer expenses include transportation expenses and reasonable expenses for meals and lodging necessarily incurred while away from home. Expenses will not be reimbursed for individuals who have only nominal duties relating to the performance of services for the church or who for significant portions of the trip are not required to render services.

While "a significant element of personal pleasure" is not defined by the tax code or regulations, the current edition of IRS publication 526 provides the following guidance (adapted):

> Generally, trip participants can claim a charitable contribution deduction for travel expenses necessarily incurred while they are away from home performing services for a charitable organization only if there is no significant element of personal pleasure, recreation, or vacation in the travel. This applies whether the participant pays for the expenses directly or indirectly. Expenses are paid indirectly if a payment is made to the ministry and the ministry pays for the travel expenses.

> The deduction for travel expenses will not be denied simply because the participant enjoys providing services to the ministry. Even if he or she enjoys the trip, the participant can take a charitable contribution deduction for travel expenses if he or she is on duty in a genuine and substantial sense throughout the trip. However, if the participant has only nominal duties, or if for significant parts of the trip he or she does not have any duties, travel expenses cannot be deducted.

To prove the extent and duration of services, each trip participant will keep an hour-by-hour itinerary of the entire trip. The itinerary should separate those times when the trip participant is on duty for the church from those times when the participant is free to choose his or her own activities.

Church staff participation in trips. Church staff are encouraged to participate in mission trips by providing them with one week of paid time for one trip per year subject to the approval and staff member's supervisor.

Staff members are responsible to raise the same financial support as other trip participants. (*Note:* The church may determine it is appropriate for a staff member who is leading a team to raise support for the team as a whole, whereby the funding for the leader is paid from the overall trip budget.)

If a staff participant is a non-exempt employee for purposes of the Fair Labor Standards Act and the mission trip responsibilities are not clearly outside the scope of their position description, the church will define the hours on and off duty during the trip to clearly determine any overtime hours. (*Note:* The church may determine staff members participating outside the scope of their position description must use leave time instead of receiving their regular pay.)

Other Special Charitable Contribution Issues

Gifts of inventory

Business owners may contribute some of their business inventory to a ministry and ask for a charitable contribution acknowledgment for the retail value of the merchandise. This is inappropriate because inventory contributions are generally deductible at cost and not at retail value. Acknowledgments issued by a church or other nonprofit organization for inventory contributions should not state the value of the gift—only the date of the gift and a description of the items donated.

Caution

What is the bottom line of inventory contributions? An inventory item can only be deducted once—there is no contribution deduction and also a deduction as a business expense. The tax benefit to the giver is generally equal to the giver's cost of the items, not their retail value.

Example: Bill owns a lumberyard as a C corporation. A ministry is constructing a building, and the lumberyard donates some lumber for the project. The company purchased the lumber during the current business year for $10,000. The retail price of the lumber is $17,000, and it would have generated a $7,000 profit if the company had sold it. What is the tax impact for the company? Generally, the value of the inventory donated ($17,000) must be reduced by the amount of ordinary income that would have been realized had the items been sold ($7,000).

Payments to private schools

Tuition payments to private schools are generally nondeductible since they correspond to value received. The IRS has ruled that payments to private schools are not deductible as charitable contributions if:

➤ a contract exists under which a parent agrees to make a "contribution" and that contract contains provisions ensuring the admission of the child

➤ there is a plan allowing a parent either to pay tuition or to make "contributions" in exchange for schooling

➤ there is the earmarking of a contribution for the direct benefit of a particular individual (student)

➤ there is the otherwise unexplained denial of admission or readmission to a school for children of individuals who are financially able to, but do not contribute

Remember

Tuition payments are personal expenses. However, taxpayers often attempt to construe tuition payments as charitable deductions. The IRS is particularly alert to arrangements that require a certain amount of contributions from a parent in addition to some tuition payments or arrangement in which education is provided "tuition-free."

Some churches operate related private schools on a "tuition-free" basis. These churches typically request that families with children in the school increase their contributions by the amount that they would otherwise have paid as tuition. In reviewing "tuition-free" situations, the IRS often questions the deductibility of gifts to the church if:

➤ contributions of several families increased or decreased markedly as the number of their children enrolled in the school changed

➤ the contributions of parents of students dropped off significantly in the summer months when the school was not in session

➤ the parents were not required to pay tuition

Generally, contributions to a church by parents are not deductible as charitable contributions to the extent that the church pays the parents' tuition liabilities for their children.

Gifts to staff

Ministries often make gifts to employees to show appreciation for their dedicated service. These payments may take several forms and have important implications to the organization, to staff members, and to givers:

➤ **Gifts made by an individual directly to a staff member with no church involvement in the transition.** When the payer of the funds makes the payment directly to a staff member of the church or nonprofit, this is a gift which is not tax-deductible to the giver and is generally not taxable to the recipient. A gift of this nature does not raise any tax issues for the church or nonprofit.

➤ **Gifts made by an individual to the church but earmarked by the giver for a particular staff member and not intended for use by the church or nonprofit.** If contributions are earmarked by the giver and treated as being gifts to the designated individual, they are not tax-deductible as charitable gifts. The earmarking of gifts by givers prevents a church or nonprofit from using the funds to carry out its functions and purposes at its discretion. The use of terminology such as a "love gift for an individual" or a "desire to bless an individual" does not impact the nondeductibility of the gift.

➤ **Gifts to staff members from church or nonprofit funds.** Often gifts are made from organizational funds which are not required by contract or a typical employment plan. The gifts may be given in appreciation near a holiday, a birthday, or an employee anniversary. The gifts may be given in relation to personal, medical, or financial crises.

Gifts to staff members from church or nonprofit funds are taxable and subject to payroll tax treatment and reporting unless they meet one of the following exceptions:

1. *De minimis* **gifts.** These gifts are impracticable of specific valuation and are generally less than $25 in value. IRS rulings have emphasized that the difficulty in valuing a *de minimis* gift is just as important as the small value. Cash, gift cards, or other cash equivalents are not *de minimis* gifts, regardless of how small the value.

2. **Employee achievement awards.** To avoid taxation, achievement awards must meet specific tax law requirements. The law generally requires a written, non-discriminatory achievement award program, which provides awards either upon attaining longevity goals or safety standards and meets other requirements for type of gift and limits on amounts.

3. **Staff member is a church attender.** If the staff member is also a church attender, it is possible for the staff member to receive benevolence assistance in the capacity of a church attender without the assistance being taxable. The benevolence need must be handled and paid through the normal benevolence process. While dual status of being both church attender and employee does not require taxation of assistance provided to the person as church attender, it does require careful documentation to ensure the employee is treated just like nonemployees. Due to the challenge of documenting that the staff member would have received a benevolence payment, and in the same amount if the individual had not been a staff member, many churches adopt policies prohibiting the payment of benevolence funds to employees.

➤ **Gifts to "bless" a particular staff member by raising a "love offering."** In the typical love offering scenario, the funds are received by the church or nonprofit (payments directly to an individual are discussed above). When the giver knows that a gift will go to a specific person, tax law generally treats the gifts as if they were made to the specific person and the gifts are not deductible as charitable contributions. The payment of the love offering is taxable and subject to payroll tax treatment and reporting unless one of the three exceptions is met as noted above.

➤ **Gifts to "bless" multiple staff members by raising a "love offering."** When an occasional love offering is raised for more than one staff person (e.g., when an offering is received for a Christmas gift or for a Pastor's Appreciation gift and the funds will be distributed to more than one staff member), if the church or nonprofit leadership determines the recipients and the allocation of the offering between staff members, then donations to the love offering are generally tax-deductible. The payment of the love offering is taxable as compensation and subject to payroll tax treatment and reporting unless one of the three exceptions is met as noted above.

Gifts to an educational institution to pay tuition for a staff member's dependent. There is no charitable tax deduction for a gift to a church or other nonprofit which is designated for the educational expenses of a staff member's dependent. If the organization uses the funds to pay the tuition of a staff member's dependent, even if the funds are paid directly to the educational institution, the amount is taxable and subject to payroll tax treatment and reporting with respect to the staff member.

Contributions that benefit specific individuals other than staff members and other than the needy

Occasionally individuals give money to a ministry but request that it be sent to a particular recipient who is not on the staff of the ministry, is not a missionary related to the ministry, and does not qualify as a "needy" individual. When told that this "conduit" role is improper, the giver usually responds, "But I can't get a tax deduction otherwise!" The giver is absolutely correct.

In a conduit transaction, the giver is making a gift to the ultimate beneficiary. The IRS will look to the ultimate beneficiary to decide whether the gift qualifies for a charitable contribution deduction.

There are certain limited circumstances in which a ministry may appropriately serve as an intermediary with respect to a gift that will be transferred to another ministry or to a specific individual. In such circumstances, it is essential that the ministry that first receives the monies has the right to control the ultimate destination of the funds.

Giver intent is also a key factor. If the giver intends for a gift to benefit a specific individual instead of supporting the mission of the ministry, the gift is generally not deductible.

Example: Frank Lee makes a gift of $5,000 to Shady Lane Church. Mr. Lee stipulates that the gift must go to a particular music group of which his son is a member. The money will be used to purchase sound equipment. The group will go on tour to present religious music in churches. The group is not an approved ministry of Shady Lane Church. This gift would generally be termed a personal gift to the music group and would not be deductible as a charitable contribution. It is best if the church returns the gift to Mr. Lee. If the church accepts the gift and passes the money on to the music group, the church should advise Mr. Lee that the gift is not deductible and should not provide a charitable acknowledgment.

Contributions to needy individuals and benevolence funds

Gifts made directly by a giver to needy individuals are not deductible. To qualify for a charitable deduction, contributions must be made to a qualified charitable organization. Contributions to benevolence funds may be claimed as charitable deductions if they are not earmarked for particular recipients.

A gift to a ministry involved in helping needy people marked "to aid the unemployed" is generally deductible. Yet if the gift is designated or restricted for the "Brown family" and the organization passes the money on to the Browns, the gift is generally not tax-deductible.

If a giver makes a suggestion about the beneficiary of a benevolent contribution, it may be deductible if the recipient organization exercises proper control over the benevolence fund. The giver's suggestion must be only advisory in nature, and the ministry may accept or reject the suggestion. However, if every "suggestion" is honored by the organization, the earmarking could be challenged by the IRS.

Caution

An area of frequent abuse involves a monetary donation that the donor specifies must go to a particular individual (or family) to assist their financial needs. Before accepting such a gift, a ministry must determine if it can exercise due diligence to ensure the transaction does not actually constitute earmarking of the funds by a donor, which is not deductible as a charitable contribution.

A church or nonprofit organization may want to help a particular individual or family that has unusually high medical bills or other valid personal financial needs. To announce that funds will be received for the individual or family and acknowledge the monies through the church or nonprofit organization makes the gifts personal and not deductible as charitable contributions. One option is for the organization to set up a trust fund at a local bank. Contributions to the trust fund are not deductible for tax purposes, but payments from the trust fund do not represent taxable income to a needy individual or family. This method of helping the needy person or family represents personal gifts from one individual to another.

Granting of scholarships

When scholarship assistance is provided by a church or nonprofit, it requires careful compliance with tax laws and regulations. Three distinct areas of the tax law must be addressed:

> **Protecting the contributor's tax deduction.** The contribution deduction requires the gift be "to or for the use of" a charitable entity, not an individual. To qualify, the gift must be to a church or other qualified nonprofit organization, knowing it will be used for scholarships, but without knowing who will receive the scholarship. A gift designated for a specific individual will not qualify.

Sample Benevolence Fund Policy

Whereas, New Haven Church has a ministry to needy individuals; and

Whereas, The church desires to establish a Benevolence Fund through which funds for the support of needy individuals may be administered; and

Whereas, The church desires to operate the Benevolence Fund according to the highest standards of integrity;

Resolved, That New Haven Church establish a Benevolence Fund to help individuals in financial need and will develop written procedures to document the need, establish reasonable limitations of support per person during a specified time period, and obtain external verification of the need; and

Resolved, That the church will accept only contributions to the Benevolence Fund that are "to or for the use" of the church, and their use must be subject to the control and discretion of the church board. Givers may make suggestions but not designations or restrictions concerning the identity of the needy individuals; and

Resolved, That the church will provide a charitable contribution receipt for gifts that meet the test outlined in the previous resolution. The church reserves the right to return any gifts that do not meet the test.

Five guidelines for protecting the contribution deduction are as follows:

1. The ministry determines all scholarship recipients through the use of a scholarship committee.

2. The ministry has a well-published policy stating that it determines the recipients according to its own policies and that it expressly rejects any effort to honor a giver's recommendation(s).

3. All scholarship policies contain the following statement: "Scholarships are awarded without regard to sex, race, nationality, or national origin."

4. Recipients of scholarships and the amount they are to receive will be based on funds already received.

5. The criteria for scholarship qualification are in writing.

➤ **Protecting the status of the payments to the scholarship recipient.** Only a candidate for a degree can exclude amounts received as a scholarship. A qualified scholarship is any payment to or for the student if it is for "tuition and fees" or for enrollment or "fees, books, supplies, and equipment" required for specific courses. It is not necessary for an organization granting a scholarship to confirm that it will be used only for qualified uses. The person receiving the scholarship must report excess amounts as taxable income.

➤ **Employee dependent scholarship programs.**
Generally, scholarships for an employee's dependents will be considered taxable compensation to the employee unless they meet the following precise guidelines. A few of the requirements include the following:

1. The existence of the program must not be presented as a benefit of employment by the organization.

2. Selection of beneficiaries must be made by an independent committee.

3. Selection must be based solely upon substantial objective standards that are completely unrelated to the employment of the recipients or their parents and to the employer's line of business.

4. Generally, not more than 25% of eligible dependents may be recipients of scholarships.

Key Issue

Too often, well-meaning people want to help a relative or a friend pay their school bills, plus they want a tax deduction for the assistance. So instead of making a personal nondeductible gift to the intended beneficiary, they make a "gift" to a ministry with a request to provide a scholarship for a designated individual. This transfer of funds is not a charitable contribution, and the funds should not be accepted by the ministry.

Donated travel and out-of-pocket expenses

Unreimbursed out-of-pocket expenses of a volunteer performing services for a church or nonprofit are generally deductible. (Volunteer reimbursements using the per diem method triggers taxable income to the volunteers for the reimbursements in excess of actual expenses.) The expenses must be directly connected with and solely attributable to the providing of the volunteer services.

The type of expenses that are deductible include transportation; travel (mileage at 14 cents per mile for 2018), meals, and lodging while away from home if there is no significant element of personal pleasure, recreation, or vacation associated with the travel, postage, phone calls, printing and photocopying, expenses in entertaining prospective givers, and required uniforms without general utility.

It is generally inappropriate to provide a volunteer with a standard charitable receipt, because the ministry is usually unable to confirm the actual amount of a volunteer's expenses. But a letter of appreciation may be sent to the volunteer thanking the individual for the specific services provided. The burden is on the volunteer to prove the amount of the expenses.

Volunteers who incur $250 or more in out-of-pocket expenses in connection with a charitable activity are subject to the acknowledgment rules. The acknowledgment should identify the type of services or expenses provided by the volunteer and state that no goods or services were provided by the charity to the giver in consideration of the volunteer efforts (see page 199 for a sample letter to volunteers).

Sample Letter to Volunteers

Date _____

Dear Volunteer:

We appreciate the time, energy, and out-of-pocket costs you devote to our cause as follows:

<u>Description of Services/Expenses Provided/Date Provided</u>

_____

_____

_____

No goods or services were provided to you by our church, except intangible religious benefits, in consideration of your volunteer efforts.

You may deduct unreimbursed expenses that you incur incidental to your volunteer work. Transportation costs (travel from home to our church or other places where you render services), phone calls, postage stamps, stationery, and similar out-of-pocket costs are deductible.

You can deduct the IRS approved charitable mileage rate (14 cents per mile for 2018) in computing the costs of operating your car while doing volunteer work as well as unreimbursed parking and toll costs. Instead of using the cents-per-mile method, you can deduct your actual auto expenses, provided you keep proper records. However, insurance and depreciation on your car are not deductible.

If you travel as a volunteer and must be away from home overnight, reasonable payments for meals and lodging as well as your travel costs are deductible. Your out-of-pocket costs at a convention connected with your volunteer work are deductible if you were duly chosen as a representative of our church.

You cannot deduct travel expenses as charitable gifts if there is a significant element of personal pleasure, recreation, or vacation in the travel.

You cannot deduct the value of your services themselves. For example, if you devote 100 hours during the year to typing for us and the prevailing rate for these services is $8.00 per hour, you can't deduct the $800 value of your services. Although deductions are allowed for property gifts, the IRS doesn't consider your services "property." Nor is the use of your home for meetings a "property contribution."

Finally, you may be required to substantiate your deduction to the IRS. Be prepared to prove your costs with canceled checks, receipted bills, and diary entries. If your expenses total $250 or more for the calendar year, you must have this acknowledgment in hand before you file your income tax return.

Again, thank you for furthering our cause with that most precious commodity: your time.

Castleview Church

When a giver requests a refund or transfer of gift funds

Occasionally, givers request a refund of a charitable gift they have made. Since contributions must be irrevocable to qualify for a charitable deduction, there generally is no basis to return a charitable gift to a giver. In the rare instances where a refund is justified, legal and tax advice should be sought (at least for refunds of significant amounts).

In some instances, after a giver makes a restricted gift to a ministry, the giver requests that the funds be transferred to a second ministry. This sometimes occurs when a deputized worker moves from one ministry to a second ministry, and a giver who has given funds to ministry A asks that the money be transferred to ministry B. It is within the discretion of ministry A to determine whether the funds are retained by ministry A or a gift/grant is made to ministry B. A gift/grant by ministry A to ministry B is appropriate only if ministry B is qualified to carry out the giver's restrictions and is consistent with ministry A's exempt purposes.

A few preventive steps may be helpful in this area:

➤ **Adopt a proactive policy.** Start from a position of generally providing no refunds of charitable gifts. Include guidance relating to how the ministry will communicate with givers relating to situations where a restricted project may be overfunded, underfunded, or cancelled. Provide guidance on how the ministry will communicate with givers concerning gift preferences.

> **Warning**
>
> Ministries should have policies and procedures in place to address requests for the return of charitable donations. Significant gifts should be returned only after consulting with legal and tax counsel and after approval by the governing board.

➤ **Clearly communicate with givers.**
Particularly when accepting gifts with giver preferences (see page 174), clearly communicate that the ministry has discretion and control over the gift. This does not suggest that giver preferences will be ignored. It simply means that the ministry has the right to expend the funds for similar purposes if the preferences are not honored.

When raising or accepting gifts with giver restrictions, it is often wise to communicate to givers that if gift restrictions cannot be met by the ministry, the ministry will use the funds for another project or make a grant to another ministry that is able to fulfill the giver's restrictions.

Avoid duplicity in communicating with givers. *Example:* A church offering envelope provides an opportunity to check a box for a gift for the building fund, the missions fund, or to use where needed most. The following sentence is added: "The church may use this money for any purpose at the discretion of the board." Wording of this nature is very confusing to givers. It suggests to them that a gift they may wish to restrict for missions might be used to pay the pastor's salary.

➤ **Make wise administrative decisions.** When gifts with giver restrictions cannot be spent for the intended purpose, make a decision within a reasonable period regarding how the funds will be expended. While there are no hard and fast rules on how quickly restricted gifts must be used, the longer the time it takes the ministry to expend the funds, the greater the risk of creating a public relations issue with givers.

Child adoption gifts

It is not surprising that ministries and givers often seek ways to provide financial support to couples involved in the adoption process. The cost to adopt a child often exceeds the financial resources of the adopting couple.

While there are a few ways ministries can legitimately assist adoptive parents, these options are very limited. A ministry should carefully scrutinize any gifts that are designated for a particular adoptive family. The IRS may consider such gifts as conduit or pass-through transactions which do not qualify for a charitable receipt by a ministry or a charitable deduction by a giver and could endanger the tax status of a ministry.

The following are some considerations for providing support for adoptive parents:

➤ **Personal gifts to the adoptive parents.** An individual may make a personal gift to adoptive parents to assist with adoption expenses. Personal gifts are not deductible as charitable gifts but are not taxable to the adoptive parents.

➤ **Gifts for adoptive parents by a ministry whose purpose and nature are not consistent with such gifts.** If gifts by a ministry to adoptive families are not consistent with the broad limits imposed by the ministry's purpose and nature, the gifts are generally not a proper use of tax-exempt funds.

➤ **Gifts for adoptive parents from the operating fund of a ministry.** If adoption assistance is consistent with the ministry's purpose and nature, a ministry generally has a sound basis to provide assistance for adoptive parents from the ministry's general funds (budgeted or unbudgeted); e.g., the ministry has available funds that were not designated by a giver for a particular adoptive family. Payments for adoptive families are often made on the basis of financial need and paid directly to the adoption agency to assure that the funds are properly used. These payments are tax-free to the adoptive parents.

➤ **Gifts to a ministry's adoption fund not preferenced for a particular adoptive family and gifts for an adoptive family from the fund.** If adoption assistance is consistent with the ministry's purpose and nature, a ministry generally has a sound basis to establish a restricted fund (either temporarily restricted or permanently restricted) to accept gifts that are not designated by a giver for a particular adoptive family. Gifts to such a fund will generally qualify as charitable gifts. Payments for adoptive families are often made on the basis of financial need. Payments should typically be made directly to the adoption agency or reimbursed to the adoptive parents based on adequate documentation to assure that the funds are properly used.

➤ **Gifts to a ministry preferenced for a particular adoptive family and gifts for the adoptive family from the fund.** Even if adoption assistance is consistent with the ministry's governing documents, gifts that are preferenced by a giver for a particular adoptive family may raise conduit or pass-through transaction issues. To be deductible, the ministry must generally have discretion and control over the contribution without any obligation to benefit a preferenced individual, obtain adequate information about the potential recipient of the funds (including financial resources), avoid refunding gifts to givers if a particular adoption is not completed, and avoid conflicts of interest between those approving and receiving a loan or a grant. Before considering accepting gifts of this nature and making related gifts to adoptive parents, a ministry should seek qualified legal counsel.

Providing Assistance to or for Adoptive Parents Implications for Charitable Deduction Purposes	
Type of Gift	**Qualifies as a Charitable Deduction**
Gift from a ministry to/for an adoptive family based on need [1, 2]—not based on gifts designated by the giver(s), e.g., from the ministry's general fund.	Yes
Gift from a ministry to/for an adoptive family based on gifts restricted for the ministry's adoption fund but not restricted or preferenced for a particular adoptive family.	Yes
Personal gifts from one individual to/for another individual to assist in an adoption.	No
Gift from a ministry to/for an adoptive family based on gifts preferenced for a particular adoptive family and the giver's intent is to benefit the adoptive family, not the ministry.	No
Gift from a ministry to/for an adoptive family based on gifts restricted for a particular adoptive family. *The ministry is unable to provide adequate discretion and control over the payment because of the giver(s) restriction.*	No
Gift from a ministry to/for an adoptive family based on gifts restricted for a particular adoptive family—the adoptive family and the giver are the same taxpayer.	Generally, no (may be tax fraud because of the circular nature of the transaction)
Gift from a ministry to/for an adoptive family based on gifts preferenced for a particular adoptive family. *The ministry exercises adequate discretion and control over the gift.*	Based on facts and circumstances

[1] As a best practice, the payments should either be made directly to the adoption agency or reimbursed to the adoptive parents based on adequate documentation to assure that the funds are properly used.

[2] Personal gifts from an individual to another individual may have estate tax implications if the gifts to an individual exceed the annual gift tax limitation.

INTEGRITY*Points*

- **Crossing the line from a restricted to an earmarked gift.** Givers may restrict gifts either as to purpose or to time. When the restriction only relates to a project (such as a capital campaign, the mission budget of a church, or the benevolence fund), the issue of earmarked gifts does not arise. When gifts are preferenced for the support of a particular missionary or a benevolent recipient and the preferencing is only an expression of a desire, not a restriction, the gift is restricted for accounting purposes and the earmarking line generally has not been crossed.

  However, when the gift is not preferenced, but restricted for an individual, the earmarked issue arises. Charitable gift deductions are generally not available for earmarked gifts. Integrity requires carefully monitoring the restricted, preferenced, and earmarked gift issues.

- **Raising money for a mission trip.** The deputized fundraising concept applies to raising money for career and short-term missionaries. When an organization accepts gifts under this concept, it assumes the responsibility for the discretion and control of the gifts. Additionally, the ministry must be precise in its proper communication with the supported missionary and the givers. It is very easy to cross the line from a gift restricted for missions, perhaps even in a particular region of the world or a specific country, to a gift earmarked for a particular missionary.

  Sponsors of short-term mission trips most often cross the restricted to earmarked line when refunds are provided in relation to individuals who planned to go on a mission trip but were unable to make the trip. These refunds should be avoided.

- **Gifts to assist others.** Gifts to assist others, such as benevolence and scholarships, are a wonderful way to provide for those with needs. A ministry must make it clear that such gifts cannot be for a specific person, but rather are made to an organizational fund which then is under the discretion and control of the ministry in alignment with giver intent; e.g. a gift for benevolence will be used by the organization to assist a person in need in alignment with the ministry's benevolence policy.

Sample Policy on Suspected Misconduct, Dishonesty, Fraud, and Whistleblower Protection

If any person knows of, or has a suspicion about, misconduct, dishonesty, or fraud, the executive director should be contacted. If the alleged wrongdoing concerns the executive director, then the president or other officer or director of the ministry should be notified instead.

If the executive director, president, or other officer of the ministry receives information about misconduct, dishonesty, or fraud, he or she shall inform the board (or, alternatively, the executive committee, if such a committee exists), which shall determine the procedure for investigating all credible allegations.

At all times, the privacy and reputation of individuals involved will be respected. There will be no punishment or other retaliation for the reporting of conduct under this policy made in good faith. If the person providing the information requests anonymity, this request will be respected to the extent that doing so does not impede any investigation.

Honoraria Policy Guidelines

When board or staff members speak on behalf of a ministry, they often receive contributions, honoraria, or expense reimbursements. It is generally helpful for ministries to adopt policies regarding the ownership, control, and handling of such funds. The most significant part of an honoraria policy is the determination of whether the ministry or the ministry representative benefits from honoraria payments.

If the honoraria policy states that all honoraria payments are to be forwarded to the ministry, the potential for conflict of interest does not exist. However, if the honoraria policy allows ministry representatives to keep honoraria payments, a potential for conflict of interest exists.

A conflict of interest related to honoraria payments may occur when the individual requested to speak (and thereby receives honoraria payments) makes scheduling decisions. If the individual is motivated by the honoraria payments they receive, they may schedule themselves for venues that have the highest honoraria potential, rather than the venues most appropriate for the ministry to be represented.

Ministries can prevent such situations from occurring by either not allowing individuals to keep honoraria payments, or by establishing oversight by the board or senior ministry leaders over the scheduling of ministry representative speaking engagements.

If the organization determines that individuals may keep honoraria payments from speaking engagements, the amounts received should be included in taxable income for the individual.

If, during a speaking engagement, an individual receives payment in the form of cash or a check written to the individual, and it is ministry policy for honoraria to benefit the ministry, the individual should make arrangements to promptly remit the amount to the organization, usually by check.

Sample Board Ethics Policy

The board commits itself and its members to biblical, ethical, business-like, and lawful conduct, including proper use of authority and appropriate decorum when acting as board members.

1. Members must have loyalty to the ministry as a whole, not conflicted by loyalties to staff, other organizations, and any personal interest as a beneficiary.

2. Members must avoid conflicts of interest with respect to their fiduciary responsibilities.

   a. There will be no self-dealing or business by a board member with the organization. Board members will annually disclose their involvements with other organizations, with vendors, or any associations that might be or might reasonably be seen as being a conflict.

   b. When the board is to decide upon an issue about which a member has an unavoidable conflict of interest, that member shall recuse himself or herself without comment from not only the vote, but also from the deliberation.

   c. Board members will not use their board position to obtain employment or financial support in the organization for themselves, family members, or close associates. Should a board member apply for employment or financial support, he or she must first resign from the board.

3. Board members may not attempt to exercise individual authority over the organization.

   a. Board members' interaction with the chief executive officer/executive director/president (or person holding a similar position) or with staff must recognize the lack of authority vested in individual board members except when explicitly board authorized.

   b. Board members' interaction with public, press, or other outside entities must recognize the same limitation and the inability of any board member to speak for the board except to repeat explicitly stated board decisions.

   c. Except for participation in board deliberation, board members will not express individual judgments of performance of employees of the chief executive officer/executive director/president (or person holding a similar position).

4. Board members will respect the confidentiality appropriate to issues of a sensitive nature.

5. Board members will be properly prepared for board deliberation.

6. Board members will financially contribute to the organization during the year and introduce friends who may be interested in contributing to the ministry.

7. Board members commit themselves corporately and individually to holding the biblical convictions contained in the organization's Statement of Faith.

8. Board members are expected to conduct themselves in both public and private life in such a way that honors God and favorably reflects on the ministry.

Sample Staff and Volunteer Ethics Policy

All employees and volunteers will uphold the highest standards of ethical, professional behavior, above reproach in the sight of God and man. To that end, all employees and volunteers shall dedicate themselves to carrying out the mission of this ministry with honesty, loyalty, trustworthiness, fairness, integrity, and respect for others.

They shall commit to the following:

1. Taking into account biblical mandates, obey the laws of both the United States and, when the ministry has international involvement, the laws of the respective countries.

2. Hold paramount the safety, health, and welfare of the public in the performance of professional duties.

3. Act in such a manner as to uphold and enhance personal honor, integrity, and dignity.

4. Treat with respect and consideration all persons, regardless of race, religion, gender, maternity, marital or family status, disability, age, or national origin.

5. Collaborate with and support other staff and volunteers in carrying out the ministry's mission.

6. Build reputations on the merit of services and refrain from competing unfairly with others.

7. Recognize that the chief function of the ministry at all times is to serve God and the best interests of its constituency.

8. Accept as a personal duty the responsibility to keep up-to-date on emerging issues and to conduct themselves with competence, fairness, impartiality, efficiency, and effectiveness.

9. Respect the structure and responsibilities of the ministry's governing board, provide them with facts and advice as a basis for policy decisions, and uphold and implement policies adopted by the governing board.

10. Conduct ministerial and operational duties with positive leadership exemplified by open communication, creativity, dedication, and compassion.

11. Exercise whatever discretionary authority they have under the law to carry out the mission of the ministry.

12. Serve with respect, concern, courtesy, and responsiveness in carrying out the ministry's mission.

13. Demonstrate the highest standards of personal integrity, truthfulness, honesty, and fortitude in all activities in order to inspire confidence and trust in such activities.

14. Avoid any interest or activity that is in conflict with the conduct of their official duties.

15. Respect and protect privileged information to which they have access in the course of their official duties.

16. Strive for personal and professional excellence and encourage the professional developments of others.

Projected 2019 Employer Tax Filing Dates

January

15 Monthly deposit of Social Security, Medicare, and withheld income tax

31 Distribute Form 1099 to recipients and file with the IRS

31 Distribute Form W-2 to recipients and file with the IRS

31 Mail or electronically file Copy A of Form(s) W-2 and W-3 with the SSA

31 Form 940 for unemployment tax

31 Form 941 due for Social Security, Medicare, and withheld income tax

February

15 Monthly deposit of Social Security, Medicare, and withheld income tax

15 Federal tax withholding deductions reset for anyone who has not given their employer an updated Form W-4

March

15 Monthly deposit of Social Security, Medicare, and withheld income tax

April

15 Monthly deposit of Social Security, Medicare, and withheld income tax

30 Quarterly Form 941 due

May

15 Form 990 and 990-T due for calendar year-end organizations (other year-ends, 15th day of the 5th month after your year-end)

15 Monthly deposit of Social Security, Medicare, and withheld income tax

June

17 Monthly deposit of Social Security, Medicare, and withheld income tax

July

15 Monthly deposit of Social Security, Medicare, and withheld income tax

31 Quarterly Form 941 due

August

15 Monthly deposit of Social Security, Medicare, and withheld income tax

September

16 Monthly deposit of Social Security, Medicare, and withheld income tax

October

15 Monthly deposit of Social Security, Medicare, and withheld income tax

31 Quarterly Form 941 due

November

15 Monthly deposit of Social Security, Medicare, and withheld income tax

December

16 Monthly deposit of Social Security, Medicare, and withheld income tax

Citations

Chapter 1, Faithful Administration

- **Expenses of spouses of board members**

  INFO 2000-0236

- **Per diem expense payments to board members**

  Rev. Rul. 67-30

Chapter 2, Tax Exemption

- **Criteria for qualifying as a church**

  Spiritual Outreach Society v. Commissioner, T.C.M. 41 (1990)

  Joseph Edward Hardy v. Commissioner, T.C.M. 557 (1990)

- **Exemption from filing Form 990 for certain missions organizations**

  Treas. Reg. 1.6033-2(g)(1)(iv)

- **General**

  501(c)(3) organization established for religious purposes
  Treas. Reg. 1.511-2(a)(3)(ii)

- **Local sales taxes**

  Thayer v. South Carolina Tax Commission, 413 S.E. 2d 810 (S.C. 1992)

  Quill Corp. v. North Dakota, S. Ct. No. 91-194

  Jimmy Swaggart Ministries v. Board of Equalization of California, 110 S. Ct. 688 (1990)

- **Private benefit/private inurement**

  Treas. Reg. 1.501(a)-1(c)

  G.C.M. 37789

- **Property taxes**

  Trinity Episcopal Church v. County of Sherburne, 1991 WL 95745 (Minn. Tax 1991)

- **Public Disclosure of Information Returns**

  P.L. 100-203

- **Tax-exempt status revoked for excessive UBI**

  United Missionary Aviation, Inc. v. Commissioner, T.C.M. 566 (1990)

  Frazee v. Illinois Department of Employment, 57 U.S.L.W. 4397, 108 S. Ct. 1514 (1989)

  Hernandez v. Commissioner, 819 F.2d 1212, 109 S. Ct. 2136 (1989)

- **Unrelated business income: general**

  Code Sec. 511-13

- **Unrelated business income: affinity credit card programs**

  T.C.M. 34 (1996)

  T.C.M. 63 (1996)

- **Unrelated business income: jeopardy to exempt status**

  Ltr. Rul. 7849003

- **Unrelated business income: organization's tour programs**

  Ltr. Rul. 9027003

- **Unrelated business income: affinity card programs**

  Ltr. Rul. 9029047

  G.C.M. 39827, July 27, 1990

- **Unrelated business income: mailing list profits**

  Disabled American Veterans v. U.S., 94 TC No. 6 (1990)

  American Bar Endowment v. U.S., 477 U.S. 105 (1986)

- **Unrelated business income: rental income**

  Ltr. Rul. 200222030

- **Unrelated business income: other**

  Hope School v. U.S., 612 F.2d 298 (7th Cir. 1980)

  Rev. Rul. 64-182

Chapter 3, Compensating Employees

- **Accountable expense reimbursement plans**

  Treas. Reg. 1.62-2

  Treas. Reg. 1.274-5(e)

  Ltr. Rul. 9317003

- **Deferred compensation**

  Code Sec. 409A

  IRS Notice 2005-1

- **Documenting employee expenses**

  T.A.M. 200435018-22

- **Fair Labor Standards Act**

  DeArment v. Harvey, No. 90-2346 (8th Cir. 1991)

  U.S. Department of Labor v. Shenandoah Baptist Church, 899 F.2d 1389 (4th Cir.) cert. denied, 111 S. Ct. 131 (1990)

  Shaliehsabou v. Hebrew Home of Greater Washington, 363 F.3d 299 (4th Cir. 2004)

- **Flexible spending accounts**

  Rev. Rul. 2003-102

  Code Sec. 125

- **Health reimbursement arrangements**

  Code Sec. 105

  Rev. Rul. 2002-41

  Notice 2002-45

  IRP 80,600

- **Health Savings Accounts**

  Code Sec. 233

  IRS Notice 2004-2

  Rev. Proc. 2004-22

  IRS Notice 2004-23

  Rev. Rul. 2004-38

  Rev. Rul. 2004-45

  IRS Notice 2004-50

- **Health care flexible spending accounts**

  Code Sec. 105(b), (e)

  IRS Notice 2004-42

- **Ministerial exception**

  Hosanna Tabor v. EEOC, 132 S. Ct. 694 (2012)

- **Tax-sheltered annuities**

  Code Sec. 403(b)

  Code Sec. 1402(a)

  Code Sec. 3121(a)(5)(D)

  Rev. Rul. 78-6

  Rev. Rul. 68-395

  Azad v. Commissioner, 388 F. 2d74(8th Cir.1968)

  Rev. Rul. 66-274

Chapter 4, Employer Reporting

- **Classification of workers**

  Rev. Proc. 85-18

  Sec. 530 of the Revenue Act of 1978

- **Employee v. self-employed for income tax purposes**

  Rev. Rul. 87-41

- **Moving expenses**

  Code Sec. 82

  Code Sec. 3401(a)(15)

- **Noncash remuneration**

  Code Sec. 3401(a)

- **Payment of payroll taxes**

  Triplett 115 B.R. 955 (N.D. Ill. 1990)

  Carter v. U.S., 717 F. Supp. 188 (S.D. N.Y. 1989)

- **Per diem allowances**

  IRS Publication 1542

  T.D. 9064

- **Personal use of employer-provided auto**

  Temp. Reg. Sec. 1.61-2T

  IRS Notice 91-41

- **Rabbi trusts**

  Rev. Proc. 92-64

- **Reasonable compensation**

  Truth Tabernacle, Inc. v. Commissioner of Internal Revenue, T.C.M. 451 (1989)

  Heritage Village Church and Missionary Fellowship, Inc., 92 B.R. 1000 (D.S.C. 1988)

- **Taxability of benefits paid under cafeteria plans**

  Ltr. Rul. 8839072

  Ltr. Rul. 8839085

- **Temporary travel**

  Rev. Rul. 93-86

  Comprehensive National Energy Policy Act of 1992

- **Unemployment taxes**

  Code Sec. 3309(b)

  St. Martin Evangelical Lutheran Church v. South Dakota, 451 U.S. 772 (1981)

  Employment Division v. Rogue Valley Youth for Christ, 770 F.2d 588 (Ore. 1989)

- **Voluntary withholding for ministers**

  Rev. Rul. 68-507

Chapter 5, Information Reporting

- **Backup withholding**

  Code Sec. 3406

- **Cash reporting rules for charities**

  T.D. 8373

  G.C.M. 39840

- **Issuing Forms 1099-MISC**

  Rev. Rul. 84-151

  Rev. Rul. 81-232

- **Moving expense reporting**

  IRS Announcement 94-2

- **Nonresident alien payments**

  Code Sec. 1441

  Code Sec. 7701(b)

- **Volunteer fringe benefits**

  Prop. Reg. 1.132-5(r)

- **Withholding of tax on non-resident aliens**

  Pub. 515

Chapter 7, Charitable Gifts

- **Charitable remainder unitrusts**

  IRS Notice 94-78

- **Contribution earmarked for a specific individual**

  Ltr. Rul. 9405003

  IRS Announcement 92-128

  Ltr. Rul. 8752031

  Rev. Rul. 79-81

- **Contribution of autos**

  IRS Publication 4302

  American Jobs Creation Act of 2004

- **Contribution of church bonds**

  Rev. Rul. 58-262

- **Contribution of promissory note**

  Allen v. Commissioner, U.S. Court of Appeals, 89-70252 (9th Cir. 1991)

- **Contribution of services**

  Rev. Rul. 67-236

  Grant v. Commissioner, 84 T.C.M. 809 (1986)

- **Contribution of unreimbursed travel expenses**

  Tafralian v. Commissioner, T.C.M. 33 (1991)

  Rev. Rul. 84-61

  Rev. Rul. 76-89

- **Contribution that refers to giver's name**

  IR-92-4

- **Deductibility of gifts to domestic organizations for foreign use**

  Ltr. Rul. 9211002

  Ltr. Rul. 9131052

  Ltr. Rul. 9129040

  Rev. Rul. 75-65

  Rev. Rul. 63-252

- **Deductibility of membership fees as contributions**

  Rev. Rul. 70-47

  Rev. Rul. 68-432

- **Deductibility of payments relating to fundraising events**

  Pub. 1391

  Rev. Rul. 74-348

- **Determining the value of donated property**

  IRS Pub. 561

  Rochin v. Commissioner, T.C.M. 262 (1992)

- **Gift of life insurance**

  Ltr. Rul. 9147040

  Ltr. Rul. 9110016

- **Incentives and premiums**

  IRS. Pub. 1391

  Rev. Proc. 96-59

  Rev. Proc. 92-102

  Rev. Proc. 92-49

  Rev. Proc. 90-12

- **IRA rollovers**

  Pension Protection Act of 2006

- **Payments in connection with use of ministry services**

  Rev. Rul. 76-232

- **Payments to a retirement home**

  T.A.M. 9423001

  U.S. v. American Bar Endowment, 477 U.S.105 (S. Ct. 1986)

- **Substantiation rules**

  Omnibus Budget Reconciliation Act of 1993

  T.D. 8690

- **Travel tours**

  Ltr. Rul. 9027003

Chapter 8, Special Charitable Gift Issues

- **Church school gifts**

  Rev. Rul. 83-104

- **Contribution denied/indirectly related school**

  Ltr. Rul. 9004030

- **Contribution designated for specific missionaries**

  Hubert v. Commissioner, T.C.M. 482 (1993)

- **Contribution sent to children who are missionaries**

  Davis v. U.S., 110 S. Ct. 2014 (1990)

- **Contribution to needy individuals**

  Stjernholm v. Commissioner, T.C.M. 563 (1989)

  Ltr. Rul. 8752031

  Rev. Rul. 62-113

- **Contributions of inventory**

  Code Sec. 170(e)

  Reg. 1.161-1

  Reg. 1.170A-1(c)(2), (3), (4)

  Reg. 1.170A-4A(c)(3)

  Rev. Rul. 85-8

- **Criteria used to determine deductibility of payments to private schools**

  Rev. Rul. 83-104

  Rev. Rul. 79-99

- **Deduction of out-of-pocket transportation expenses**

  Treas. Reg. 1.170A-1(g)

  Rev. Rul. 76-89

- **Scholarship gifts**

  Ltr. Rul. 9338014

  Rev. Rul. 83-104

  Rev. Rul. 62-113

Federal Tax Regulation (Reg.)

Treasury Decision (T.D.)

Private Letter Ruling (Ltr. Rul.)

Field Service Advice (F.S.A.)

Revenue Ruling (Rev. Rul.)

Revenue Procedure (Rev. Proc.)

Tax Court Memorandum (T.C.M.)

Technical Advice Memorandum (T.A.M.)

Index

10 Biggest *T*ax and *F*inancial *M*istakes *M*ade by *C*hurches and *N*onprofits

1. Not setting up and adequately monitoring an accountable expense reimbursement plan for employees. (Chapter 3)

2. Failure to comply with the Fair Labor Standards Act for churches and other nonprofits. (Chapter 3)

3. Not reporting taxable fringe benefits and social security reimbursements as additional compensation to employees. (Chapter 3)

4. Deducting FICA tax from the salary of qualified ministers, whether employed by a church or other nonprofit. (Chapter 4)

5. Failing to file Form 1099-MISC for independent contractors. (Chapter 5)

6. Weak controls over revenue, including failing to have offerings and other cash and checks controlled by two individuals until the funds are counted. (Chapter 6)

7. Inadequate controls over disbursements, leaving the ministry at risk for embezzlement. (Chapter 6)

8. Failure to issue a proper receipt (including the fair market value of the goods or services provided) when a donor makes a payment of more than $75 and receives goods or services. (Chapter 7)

9. Providing receipts for the donation of services and the rent-free use of property. Receipting contributions designated for individuals without proper discretion and control exercised by the donee organization. Placing values on noncash gifts. (Chapter 7)

10. Accepting earmarked gifts with the charity exercising inadequate control when the gift is disbursed to another charity or benevolent recipient. (Chapter 8)

10 Tax and Finance Questions Most Frequently Asked by Churches and Nonprofits

1. **Tax exempt status.** Should our church or nonprofit file for tax exemption with the Internal Revenue Service? Are we required to annually file Form 990? (Chapter 2)

2. **Unrelated business income exposure.** Do we have any filing requirements for unrelated business income? If we have some unrelated business income, will we lose our tax-exempt status? (Chapter 2)

3. **Public disclosure.** Is our organization required to disclose any documents to the public based on appropriate requests for them? If so, which documents? (Chapter 2)

4. **Political activities.** Are the activities of our organization consistent with the political activity law? (Chapter 2)

5. **Housing allowance.** How do we determine whether a minister qualifies for a housing allowance designation? Are the rules for qualifying for the housing allowance identical for churches and other nonprofits? (Chapter 3)

6. **Reporting compensation.** Which payments to employees are taxable and must be reported on the annual Form W-2? (Chapter 5)

7. **Handling gifts.** What steps can we take to ensure the highest integrity in processing gifts, especially cash offerings, and providing acknowledgments to givers? (Chapter 6)

8. **Internal and external auditing.** Should we have an audit, review, or compilation by an independent CPA? If not, how can we perform a valid internal audit of our financially related processes? (Chapter 6)

9. **Noncash gifts.** How do we handle noncash gifts? What type of receipt should we provide? Should we ever place a value on a noncash gift, including gifts of services? (Chapter 7)

10. **Giver-restricted gifts.** When a giver restricts a gift, how do we determine whether we should accept the gift and whether it qualifies as a charitable contribution? (Chapter 8)